KT-104-327

Standards and Criteria

Standards and Criteria in Higher Education

Edited by GRAEME C. MOODIE

The Society for Research into
Higher Education & NFER-NELSON

Published by SRHE & NFER-NELSON
At the University, Guildford, Surrey GU2 5XH

First published 1986
© The Society for Research into Higher Education

ISBN 1 85059 015 X
Code 8953 02 1
Library of Congress Cataloguing in Publication data

Standards and criteria in higher education.
  Bibliography: p.
  1. Education, Higher–Aims and objectives.
2. Education, Higher–Standards. 3. Education,
Higher–Great Britain–Aims and objectives.
I. Moodie, Graeme C. II. Society for Research into
Higher Education.
LB2325.S77 1986   378'.01   86-19975
ISBN 1-85059-015-X

All rights reserved, including translation.
No part of this publication may be reproduced
or transmitted in any form or by any means,
electronic or mechanical, including photocopying,
recording or duplication in any information
storage and retrieval system, without permission
in writing from the publishers.

Typeset by First Page Ltd., Watford.
Printed in Great Britain by A. Wheaton & Co. Ltd, Exeter

Contents

The Contributors

DAVID BILLING is Pro-Rector, Polytechnic of Central London, and Vice-Chairman, Society for Research into Higher Education. Formerly he was on the staff of the Council for National Academic Awards and Associate Director of the West London Institute of Higher Education.

TOM CANNON is professor of Business Studies at the University of Stirling and Director of the Scottish Enterprise Foundation. He has previously held academic appointments at Durham and Warwick as well as working in industry.

ALAN GIBSON is a staff inspector at the Department of Education and Science.

GRAEME C. MOODIE is professor of Politics at the University of York and chairman of the SRHE working group on questions of quality. He is a former chairman and founding member of the Society for Research into Higher Education. He is the author (with Rowland Eustace) of *Power and Authority in British Universities* (1974).

GUY NEAVE is professor of Comparative Education at the University of London. For ten years he was Maître de Recherche at the European Institute of Education and Social Policy, Paris. He is joint editor of the *European Journal of Education*. Among his publications is *The EEC and Education* (1984).

JOHN NISBET is professor of Education at the University of Aberdeen. He has held visiting appointments in California, Australia, New Zealand and Illinois. He has been chairman of the Educational Research Board in London and the Scottish Council for Research in Education in Edinburgh. His books include *Educational Research Methods* and *Learning Strategies*.

PATRICK NUTTGENS was Director of Leeds Polytechnic, 1969-1985. Before that he had held chairs in York and Leeds, a lectureship in Edinburgh and for six years was Director of the Institute for Advanced Architectural Studies, University of York. He is a regular contributor to the *Times Higher Educational Supplement* and other journals, and his books include *The Story of Architecture* (1983).

S.G. OWEN, CBE, FRCP, was Second Secretary Medical Research Council, 1968-1982. Previously he had held clinical, research, and teaching appointments at the schools of medicine of Newcastle-upon-Tyne and Pennsylvania and at the National Heart Hospital, London.

PAUL RAMSDEN holds a research position at the Centre for the Study of Higher Education, University of Melbourne. Previously he had held appointments in the Educational Development Services, Newcastle-upon-Tyne Polytechnic and the Centre for Research and Development in Post-Compulsory Education, University of Lancaster.

MICHAEL SHATTOCK is Registrar of the University of Warwick. He was Specialist Adviser to the House of Commons Select Committee on Education, Science and Arts, 1980-83. He is a former chairman of the Society for Research into Higher Education. He edited *The Structure and Governance of Higher Education* (1983) and, with Gwynneth Rigby, *Resource Allocation in British Universities* (1983).

HAROLD and PAMELA SILVER have worked together, as authors and researchers, on many projects. He was until 1986 Principal of Bulmershe College of Higher Education and is a member of Council of the CNAA. Among his publications are *Education and the Social Condition* (1980) and *Education as History* (1983), not to mention a regular column in the *THES*.

GARETH WILLIAMS is professor of Educational Administration at the University of London. Previously he had been professor and the Director of the Centre for Research and Development in Post-Compulsory Education at the University of Lancaster; he has also held a research appointment in the London School of Economics. He has written extensively on, in particular, the economics of education. He is present Chairman of the Society for Research into Higher Education.

1

Fit for What?

Graeme C. Moodie

The extent and nature of recently-voiced anxieties about quality and standards have come as something of a surprise to many in higher education, and more particularly to those in the universities. The Robbins Report (1963), in its one extended reference to 'the maintenance of standards' (as Paragraph 40 was sub-titled), emphasized 'achievement and quality' and 'high excellence', and went on to say, but without supporting argument, that universities could be expected to continue to 'set the tone and the pace for other institutions'. In the university sector we (or many of us) have been glad to accept this view as a matter of course, unreflectingly and even complacently. In doing so we have undoubtedly struck others as arrogant, but have also been guilty of collective amnesia. We forget that as recently as last century the English and Welsh institutions of higher education, including Oxford and Cambridge colleges, prepared their students for examinations that were conducted (initially at least) by institutions external to them – by the universities of Oxford, Cambridge, Victoria and London – and that many of the newer foundations did not acquire the authority to confer their own degree until after the Second World War. True (as Michael Shattock points out in Chapter 4 of this book), the validators were other components of the university system (and not a 'quango' like the Council for National Academic Awards in today's public sector); their existence is nevertheless a clear indication of past concern for standards.

Underlying the feeling of injustice and bewilderment among so many academics (on all sides of the binary line) in the face of public doubt about their standards are not only complacency and forgetfulness but also the sheer unexpectedness of it all. The fact is that the Robbins Committee had not been alone in feeling that the undoubted quality of British higher education required no supporting argument. One must therefore ask why the situation changed and why the question of standards in higher education has become so prominent in public debate?

I will not pretend to any certain and complete explanation, but part of the answer must surely lie in the simple fact that higher education has become very costly. It is a conspicuous target for any government anxious to control public expenditure, and especially for one which seems to regard every form of public expenditure as suspect until proved innocent (ie clearly more beneficial than any alternative). When to the quest for economy is added a conscience, it is not unnatural to seek to discriminate between institutions and activities on the basis of their relative merit or degrees of excellence. There need be no intellectual discomfort in pursuing both of Sir Keith Joseph's (1984) principal objectives, quality and value for money, within a wider framework of fiscal puritanism; not, of course, that this is to settle the practical and moral questions raised in later contributions to this book.

The expansion of higher education must itself bear some responsibility for the questions about its quality, even apart from the issue of cost. For one thing, even within the university system, the larger numbers of subjects (especially in the social sciences), of departments within subjects, and of staff within departments, have made the old 'grape-vine' monitoring of standards less reliable. Few individuals can now have as confident an assessment of institutions as once most did, and the informal social pressures for good performance may well appear to be weakened. The increase in the numbers of students and institutions – new public sector institutions and new universities – has also been too great for the old 'external degree' system to cope with. Greater responsibility has therefore fallen on the members of other institutions who are involved in university examining and on the new validating body, the Council for National Academic Awards. And since each appears to be the only check on degree standards in its own area of operation (and is certainly the most visible), each is not unsurprisingly exposed to scrutiny – though the urgency with which they have been exposed to Reynolds (1984-6) and Lindop (1985) cannot be explained merely in these terms.

A final explanatory factor is a change in mood, a suspiciousness about the entire enterprise of higher education, which seems to have affected many in high places (but not only there). This has varied roots, ranging from certain economic and technological failures that higher education has not prevented happening to the philistinism endemic in so much of English society. Its manifestations are also varied, but are perhaps most evident in a 'backlash' against the social sciences, seen, for example, in the seriousness with which many received the picture of academic life portrayed in the televised version of Malcolm Bradbury's *The History Man*, or in the enforced change in name of the one-time Social Science Research Council. (They also include the cuts in the total research budget to which Dr Owen refers in Chapter 9.) The outside world has, however, always regarded the academic world with mixed feelings, and suspicion has often been one of them. Sadly, there has been no reliable and generally accepted response to the current hostility. In the area of standards, as elsewhere, there has been relatively little research on higher education (before the Society for Research into Higher Education was founded, one might have referred to the almost total lack of it) and a failure to realize how difficult it is to explain to outsiders, let alone justify to them, the ways of academics. The public and governments will properly continue to evaluate higher education; what matters is that their judgements should be well-informed.

The primary purposes of this book are therefore to disseminate knowledge and, above all, to ventilate some of the problems and arguments central to any serious consideration of standards in higher education. In the space available, no complete survey could be attempted, but I hope readers will find that no major problem about standards in higher education has been completely ignored. In what follows, however, it should be borne in mind that the aim has been to raise questions more than to propound solutions, questions that policy makers (those who are forced to act as if there were solutions) should not ignore.

At times, public lamentation about declining standards or the need to improve quality is difficult to follow. When, for example, it is suggested that 'more means worse', it is not always clear whether the 'extra' students are of a lower standard than previous generations (and how, it may be asked, does the critic distinguish the 'extras' from those who would have been admitted in previous ages?), or that the additional numbers put such a strain on facilities and resources that they learn less (and how is that measured?). To say, as others do, that the standards of degrees have fallen is similarly ambiguous; it could mean either that a larger number of those examined do not obtain a 'good' degree (however defined) or that a larger number of mediocre performances are being rewarded with a 'good' degree. In the remainder of this introductory chapter I will therefore suggest certain guidelines to the more precise use of such words as standards, criteria, quality, and excellence, words that are central to the debate but are used sometimes interchangeably, often loosely, and only on occasion with clear and distinct meanings.

To call attention to ambiguity or even confusion is not necessarily to imply that the critics are sloppy thinkers; the fact is that these terms have overlapping usages which only sometimes lead one into difficulty. Thus definitions in the Shorter Oxford English Dictionary (3rd ed., 1964) of 'standards' and 'criteria' merge: a standard is defined as, among other things, 'a criterion', and the latter is defined as, among other things, 'a standard by which anything is judged'. A standard is also defined, however, as 'an example of measure or weight', a yardstick as it might be; and a criterion as deriving from a Greek word meaning 'a means for judging'. In these alternatives can be detected a way of distinguishing the concepts: a standard is a literal or metaphorical yardstick, an exemplar of some means of measuring a dimension. (In areas like morals, aesthetics, and politics, however, where precise measurement is impossible, a standard would be a position on some spectrum or an index of a particular attribute, as it might be good/bad, beautiful/ugly, or right/left. Education is probably a similar area.) One may still, however, have to exercise a judgement about whether or not something meets, falls short of, or surpasses a particular standard or yardstick – the bases for such judgements are criteria. Where a precise measure is available – of spatial length, for example – the usage I am suggesting may be a distinction without a difference, but in other circumstances the difference is real and the distinction necessary. Thus the standards expected of a senior lecturer are undoubtedly higher than those expected of a newly-appointed lecturer; but in most institutions it is felt necessary to list the criteria (publications, teaching skills, experience, promise and so on) by which candidates for promotion will be judged, not to mention additional criteria (the senior/junior staff ratio, or the availability of finances, for example) which have no bearing whatsoever on the standard reached by candidates.

Another common source of ambiguity is that 'standards' are sometimes used to refer to some ideal or high level (as in calls to 'defend standards') and at other times, more neutrally, to refer simply to the idea of having any defined or agreed 'yardstick'. On the whole it seems desirable to adopt the second usage as the normal one (and otherwise to talk explicitly of 'high' or 'ideal' standards, usually when referring to behaviour, for there is no 'high' yard or metre, even if some do regard the 'metric' as the more desirable unit of measurement). Not only does this usage help remind us that there are standards relevant to pass degrees as well as to 'firsts', it also makes it easier to think about what standards *ought* to apply to different levels and spheres of activity in education (at what age ought which kinds of children to know about conic sections? and by what stage, if any, ought students in higher education to be able to write their own computer programme or an essay in a foreign language?), without presuppositions about 'higher' and 'lower'. It also makes it easier to contemplate 'lateral' shifts of standards, ie changes from one kind rather than one level of performance to another (as is advocated for university teaching by Paul Ramsden in Chapter 7).

Discussions of higher education would undoubtedly benefit if both defenders and critics of standards were more explicit in what they say. In the absence of such clarity, however, one sometimes has the impression that many academics defend themselves against what is really a charge of applying the wrong standards (literary or 'anti-business' rather than practical, for example) by claiming that it is more difficult than it used to be to gain admission to higher education and no easier to graduate from it – but that both parties think they are debating the same thing, namely, doubts about standards. (Tom Cannon's chapter (10) provides interesting examples of variations in the kind of standard, rather than level, endorsed within education and within business.) The gulf between participants is widened when arguments about standards are confused with arguments about criteria or evidence: when, for example, student scores in 'A' level examinations are said to *define* entry standards rather than merely provide imperfect evidence or one possible criterion for selection which, like a price in the market, can serve only as a surrogate for measures of inherent worth.

In other practical contexts, it is not the distinction between standards and criteria that is immediately important, it is, rather, the related question of quality and how it should be judged. The distinction is nevertheless relevant, if only as a means of emphasizing that quality is not the same thing as 'meeting high standards'. Indeed, conventional or accepted standards, in changing circumstances, may become the enemy of high quality (as established rules of composition and harmony are sometimes said to inhibit musical creativity). To put it another way, it must not be forgotten that the criteria for deciding whether a standard is met may well diverge from those appropriate to judgements of quality. Dr Owen's discussion of research funding in Chapter 9 contains an excellent illustration of these points. He argues that the overriding criteria for discriminating between different applications for funds are 'timeliness and promise'. These are not standards, however, even if they indicate a route to the highest quality of research. Furthermore, they are not the only appropriate criteria for a research council to apply (he lists many others). They might, of course, entail meeting certain standards – for example, of equipment or methodology. Equally, of course, if I may extend the argument, the likelihood of achieving high quality research could be impeded by other standards – for example, those relating to the 'racial purity' or skin-colour of scientists, to some arbitrary ratios about categories of staff, or to a rigid time-limit for results.

None of this, however, brings one any nearer to answering the question of how quality, in research or any other aspect of higher education, is to be defined or even recognized (most people being happier to claim the ability to recognize quality than to define it). In either case, the crux is to state the criteria of quality, and the real problem is that the relevant aspects of higher education, as each of the following chapters makes abundantly clear, are complex phenomena. As such, and unlike relatively simple events such as races, or other forms of athletic contest (as Gareth Williams points out in Chapter 3), they do not lend themselves to evaluation by reference to such relatively simple and impersonal criteria as speed, or height, or distance, or goals and points scored. To detect quality in education is more akin to judging the winner in a classical music-playing competition. It is therefore often said to be arbitrary and subjective. If by that is meant no more than that judgements of quality are liable to be controversial and in some degree contingent, one must agree; but this is not to say that they are purely personal or *mere* matters of individual preference and taste. It is still sensible, even necessary, to ask of any judgement of quality: 'In virtue of what characteristics in the object is the judgement made?'. It is also possible to offer intelligible (if not necessarily fully persuasive) answers. The fact remains that judgement is required only in the absence of certainty; and, in the absence of certainty, disagreement is endemic and who judges becomes a matter of moment. Yet there is still no need to retreat into complete subjectivism.

To say that there are many dimensions to the quality of complex phenomena does not mean that there are no criteria on which there is general agreement, and no consensus as to which are more and which are less important. Moreover, it must be granted that the exercise of judgement in any complex area requires a recognizable degree of competence, knowledge, and integrity; and that some people have track records which establish their reputations as sound judges. Richard Wollheim (1980), in discussing aesthetic evaluation, has persuasively argued that 'only the experiences of those who appropriately understand the work should be counted' (p.234). If this be so in aesthetics, in other disciplines it may be even more the case that the shared views of the informed, especially if publicly stated and defended, provide a reasonably reliable index of quality in a world where infallibility is unattainable. It is in any event indubitable that no more reliable index exists than such 'peer review' – and that harm comes only if its reliability is treated as though it were infallibility or discarded as though it were capricious. This is not to say that there is no room for improvement in the manner in which peer review is carried out, or that it is a strong enough reed to carry all the burdens that might be thrust upon it by the UGC and others – about these things no one can speak with great authority in the absence of more systematic study. It is only to say that peer review is tried and tested and is the best means we have of evaluating quality in higher education.

It has become fashionable, however, to define quality at least partly in terms of 'fitness for purpose' (Ball 1985). Sir Keith Joseph (1984), addressing the House of Commons, prefaced a list of elements in quality with the view that 'there is no single ideal [institution]....Quality is about whether institutions are fitted to their purpose and are achieving excellence at least in some areas....' Now it is undeniable that no informed judgement about quality can be made in ignorance of the nature and identity of what is being judged, and that purpose might be one of the characteristics by which nature and identity are specified; but that is by no means the same as defining quality by reference to purpose, or making it depend upon fitness for some known and agreed purpose. As Lewis Elton has pointed out (1986), the purpose of an institution or activity may be uncertain, controversial, or multiple; there may be no way of determining how far a purpose is in fact being furthered; and to impose or nominate a purpose from outside might have adverse effects upon the institution or activity. An additional, and more straightforward, objection is that the agreed purpose of any institution of learning tends either to be so vague as to provide no guide to action and policy, or so specific as to be no longer agreed and non-trivial (this point is amply illustrated by David Billing in Chapter 5). It may be that Elton was too harsh when he went on to suggest, as a metaphor, that 'true novelists are governed by a duty to themselves [to pursue quality]; it is those who satisfy performance criteria who write best sellers'; but he has á point.

To use the distinctions introduced earlier, it is not quality that depends (in any important respect) on purpose, but standards whose specification must vary, both in level and in kind, according to the context and/or purpose of the relevant course, project, or institution. In scientific and scholarly discourse, if not always elsewhere, what makes a piece of work or a lecture first-rate or of high quality is not affected by, say, the discipline or institution in which it is carried out, or the standing of its author, but is a matter of such generally applicable factors as originality, depth of understanding, clarity, elegance, organization of material, vigorous use of evidence and argument and so on. In this sense, quality is not a relative concept. Paradoxically, however, that other key term, 'excellence', is relative, despite its often being used as a synonym for the highest quality. Thus there is no obvious contradiction in statements like '(s)he did an excellent job with the materials available, but they were too shoddy to permit her/him to make a high-quality product'. The point is that to excel (Shorter Oxford English Dictionary) means 'to be superior ... to surpass', and excellence 'the fact ... of surpassing merit', and that both definitions imply the notion of relative performance – of a person doing *better* than others, or an achievement that is *better* than others. And 'excellence' is indeed often used in such a relative sense, as when we talk of people excelling themselves on some occasion or at some particular activity, but although we usually imply that this is a desirable state of affairs, there is no necessary implication that it is of inherently high quality. A five-year old can, for its age, read 'excellently' without reading particularly well. At the other end of the scale, 'excellence' may well be used to mean surpassing all previous performances – as when the first 4-minute mile was run. In that case excellence set new standards as well as being superior to all competitors. Similarly, that much-used concept, the pursuit of excellence, is perhaps best thought of as a striving to improve quality and raise standards, but not as a measure of quality or, perhaps for lack of resources, as a guarantee of its attainment. (To talk of a 'centre of excellence' is, however, to imply that the pursuit of it is both unremitting and at least partly successful.)

There appears to be a real gulf between the academic and governmental approaches to quality – one which the University Grants Committee seems to be trying to bridge and the National Advisory Body to narrow. One suspects that most academics (and others close to higher education) would accept, as a statement about both public and private sectors, what the UGC said about universities in 1925, that they 'first, and above all, stand for quality; they aim at providing the highest type of education available' (quoted by Shattock in Chapter 4). (On this view, incidentally, according to which the purpose of the institutions is educational quality, it would not be helpful to *define* quality as fitness for purpose.) By contrast, the government's purpose seems to be what Peter Brooke, when Under-Secretary of State, declared it to be with respect to access, namely, to achieve 'a proper balance between quality, opportunity and cost' (House of Commons, 26.10.84). The academic bias, this is to say, but not the government's, is to see quality in non-instrumental terms, as residing in certain values intrinsic in academic work but not relative to extrinsic ends. Individual academics and institutions have, of course, a mixture of goals (as well as motives), but the distinctive feature of 'the highest type of education available' is its tendency to transcend immediate purposes, to shift the terms of argument, and to judge itself ultimately with reference only to understanding and knowledge – much of which may in fact turn out (as Owen reminds us in Chapter 9) to be extremely useful.

Inevitably, and throughout history, there have therefore been tensions between academics and their external financiers or controllers, whether churchmen, local 'worthies' and industrialists, or potentates and politicians. Society and those who act in its name, not to mention sponsors and the employers of graduates, are bound to have their own legitimate concerns which will often differ from those inside higher education and which, on occasion, may conflict with an overriding commitment to academic quality. Inevitably, and in my view quite properly, these 'outsiders' will want to know what academics are about and to ask of higher education: Fit for what purpose? It is also proper for academics to ask the purpose behind the question. My argument is that it should not be asked in order to determine the quality of the academic enterprise (nor even to provide the proper framework for such evaluation). The purpose behind the question should be to elicit clear decisions about how much room to leave for the highest quality and about how far extraneous and instrumental criteria, or goals and standards designed for other kinds of activity and institutions, should circumscribe (and how far facilitate) the academics' pursuit of their own kind of excellence.

The question 'Fit for what?' is currently raised most urgently by civil servants and politicians. Any answer will be a matter for political debate and, ultimately, for political decision, a fact which many academics find distressing. It is only the possible outcomes that should provoke anxiety, however. It must be accepted that any matter of such moment to society as the future form and content of higher education, and one on which disagreement and uncertainty are characteristic, is a matter that is fit for politics (Moodie 1984) – though not necessarily for a purely party political resolution. That being so, it may be permissible to end with gratuitous and dogmatic advice to academic colleagues, to the following effect.

In present circumstances we, the professionals in higher education, must be more prepared to accept that our's are not the only criteria with which to evaluate the relative costs and benefits of higher education and by which, therefore, to decide on the level and direction of funding (a view for which Shattock seems to have some sympathy in his conclusion to Chapter 4). Thereafter we must be prepared to do two other things: to argue our case in the political arena (though not necessarily as partisans or in the same manner as the political professionals) and, through research and publication, to seek out and distribute the information and understanding without which governmental and other decision makers may not be fit for their own purpose of determining the future of higher education. I see this collection of essays as a contribution to such a process of education.

References

Ball, Christopher (1985) What the hell is quality? In his *Fitness for Purpose* SRHE & NFER-NELSON

Elton, Lewis (1986) Quality in higher education: Nature and purpose *Studies in Higher Education* 11(1) 83-84

Joseph, Sir Keith (1984) Speech to the House of Commons, 26 October *Parliamentary Debates* 65 (210) 470

Lindop, Sir Norman (1985) *Academic Validation in Public Sector Higher Education* Cmnd 9501. London: HMSO

Moodie, Graeme C. (1984) Politics is about government. In Adrian Leftwich (Ed.) *What is Politics?* Oxford: Basil Blackwell

Reynolds, Phillip (1984-6) Reports and Notes of the Academic Standards Group of the Committee of Vice-Chancellors and Principals

Robbins, Lionel (later Lord) (1963) *Report of the Committee on Higher Education* Cmnd 2154. London:HMSO

Wollheim, Richard (1980) Art and evaluation. In his *Art and its Objects* 2nd edn. Cambridge University Press

2

The Escaping Answer

Harold and Pamela Silver

The question of what precisely quality is, and how it should be assessed (let alone measured) has ... persistently escaped answer; and this is possibly inevitable. (NAB 1984)

The Chase

During the First World War the University College of Southampton attempted to define what it meant by the standard of a university degree. It was

> a guarantee that the holder has attained to a standard of education which justifies his employment in any one of many professions or occupations. It is at the same time evidence of diligence in study, power of concentrating attention, and intelligence in interpreting the bearings of facts. (Southampton 1915-16. p.24)

These benchmarks, with the possible exception of 'interpreting', would have been unthinkable in the commentaries of the main nineteenth-century spokesmen for university education. During the Second World War Southampton's Principal reflected on the College's history and future. Progress was difficult, 'in view of the pressure of public opinion with regard to "results" on the one side, and on the other the fact that the College has to deal with an external examination.' It was essential to avoid becoming 'a factory for procuring degrees for those who may or may not deserve them.' The pressures and aims were different from those of a quarter of a century earlier. The concern now was for 'educated men and women who can think and reason with pliable and lively minds ... who can become leaders in the generation that is to follow.' They needed, of course, 'knowledge, accuracy, and understanding', but 'above all capacity for handling problems and gathering round them willing co-operators in the work of developing a new society' (Vickers 1942. p.20). The grounds for judging achievement shift as the world changes; the heights to be scaled do not remain the same.

The transitions of the 1862 Hartley Institution through the Hartley University College to the University College of Southampton and, in 1952, to the University of Southampton, and from London external degrees to autonomy, from the intimacies of a small institution to the modern scale, from standards as internally debated and negotiated with the University Grants Committee to the external scrutinies of the late twentieth century – these would be one detailed case study through which to approach the elusive concern – or lack of concern – with standards and quality. Any other university institution would serve the same purpose. The emergence in the twentieth century of a public sector of 'higher education', the changing vocabularies of 'sponsorship', 'advisory committee', 'validation' and 'accreditation', are all entry points to considerations of standards. So are nineteenth- and twentieth-century comparisons with other debates about standards in higher education – and the American comparison is by far the most revealing. Some of these threads in the history of the pursuit of standards are our concern here.

The Nineteenth-Century Hunt

The main nineteenth-century debates concerning higher – that is, university – education were about provision and curriculum – about a liberal education, about the social-class and religious exclusiveness of Oxford and Cambridge, about the range of studies in new and aspiring institutions. The creation of London University and later the provincial colleges raised explicit questions about their purposes rather than about standards – though there were concerns that the new metropolitan university, for instance, might result in an 'indiscriminate and unlimited issue of degrees' (Anon 1836, p.4). The notion of standards was more implicit in the discussion of institutional hierarchies, the association of different institutions with different social and occupational clienteles, and the acquisition of access by religious and social groups previously debarred in England and dependent on Scotland and Europe for post-school opportunities.

Within the ancient universities the slow processes of reform related not only to the modernization of curricula and wider access, but also to the control and encouragement of student learning and attainment. At the end of the eighteenth century Cambridge introduced not only its mathematics tripos but also, in 1792, a system of 'marks' for mathematics papers, beginning a process of proxy representation of attainment which spread during the nineteenth century, replacing oral methods of examining – 'the major single step towards a mathematized model of reality' (Hoskin 1979, p.144). Other examination structures were set in place. The tripos was extended to classics in 1824 and offered a model that was to be irresistible in nineteenth-century conditions. It

> stressed method – technique, precision, logic and rigour – and method was transferable.... The tripos was held to be scientific in ideals, content, and in its method of determining ability. Unlike Oxford, Cambridge ranked its honours men on a strict order of merit.... This intensified the competition for honours and made many believe that the tripos system of marking was a scrupulously objective method of selection. (Rothblatt 1968, p.182)

In this and other ways university and school education for the privileged and for widening circles of children of the middle and professional classes was being subjected to scrutiny. The new institutions needed to present their staff, students, courses and graduates as of a suitable standard to meet the expectations of those under whose gaze they were created and sustained. Their qualifying examinations put pressure on the schools to raise the standard of entrants. After its foundation, Owens College, Manchester, found that 'the school education of Manchester was so bad...that the students were insufficiently prepared to receive the benefits of true collegiate training.' The College, struggling to adhere to high standards, 'literally pulled up the schools to a much more thorough training both as to discipline and teaching' (Thompson 1886, pp.141-2). As professional studies penetrated the universities and colleges later in the century, the institutions were affected by the competition and by the expectations of the growingly status-conscious professions concerned. Ben-David describes this process as one of improvement in the quality of education based not 'on a general conception but on ad hoc judgements' (by which requirements of, for example, the Society of Apothecaries were compared with those of the Royal College of Physicians, or the teaching of a subject at University College, London, with that at Oxford). There were no basic criteria of professional or academic quality (Ben-David 1977, p.55).

Long before mid-century, therefore, Oxford and Cambridge were responding to the new nineteenth-century context with a structure of examinations, but the increasing commitment to examinations was not without controversy and opposition. The accuracy of Cambridge's tripos ranking was challenged, as was the effect of examinations in 'vulgarizing the student's mind' (Sir John Seeley in Sanderson 1975, pp.112-13). The confidence in examinations, however, was strengthened by their introduction as selection mechanisms for the Indian and home civil service, by their matriculation function, and by the professionalization of academic life. Departmental structures, reflecting the professional frontiers of subjects, sought credibility by demonstrating that the symbols of quality were comparable with those elsewhere. By 1903 Manchester's Senate had realized that the 'choice of a professor was perhaps the most important factor in the University's endeavour to establish and maintain the highest standards of scholarship' (Charlton 1951, p.35). The machinery of judgement of subjects, professors, departments and universities included their ability to admit the 'right' students to share that scholarship, and to produce graduates who had demonstrably shared in it.

Colleges and universities were under increasing pressure in the late nineteenth century to meet various public, if nebulous, criteria of quality. This became particularly true when in 1889 Parliament first agreed a grant for university education, and appointed commissioners to advise on the institutions applying for a share. The Commissioners reported the following year that the Hartley Institution did not have 'a professional staff adequate for the complete teaching of University subjects' (and also that there was no 'proper representative Governing body'). A new principal, other new appointments, funding from the County Borough Council of Southampton, and an increase in advanced work convinced the Commissioners in 1902 of progress and 'highly creditable' results, and an annual grant of £1000 was agreed by Parliament (Southampton 1905-6, pp.16-17). The elements of public accountability as interpreted by institutions and their various outside constituencies were beginning to assume a configuration to be familiar in the twentieth century. There are other elements that could be given greater prominence – including the élite social status of Oxford and Cambridge, the movements for their reform, and the forms of their responses, but the most important thread for any approach to standards, their definitions and guardianship in this period is the variety of roles of the University of London.

The most important of these roles in the nineteenth century was the system of external degrees enshrined in its 1858 Charter. London had by that date, in the twenty-two years since its first Charter, 'affiliated' a scatter of institutions, inside and outside London. With the affiliation of Owens College, London decided to throw open access to its degrees without requiring students to have any institutional membership. Before 1858 the University 'possessed no visitorial authority and no right to inquire into the methods of teaching, or to effect improvements.' The sole means by which Senate could test the efficiency of the colleges, their courses and teaching, was the examination of their students. The 1858 Charter practically abolished the 'exclusive connexion' of the University with the affiliated colleges (London 1912, pp.11-12). It opened the degrees of the University to all students (except in medicine) 'irrespective of the place or manner of their education' (Committee of Enquiry 1972, p.5). The colleges were left to concentrate in their own ways on preparing students for the London-controlled examination, and students could sit for them (both to matriculate for entry, and to graduate) at the colleges or other local centres – and the regulations governing the latter had to do entirely with costs and practical arrangements. The Charter enshrined the written examination as the ultimate test of the quality of the student and of the education received, and made it possible for colleges to develop under the auspices of its national currency. It was 'the most momentous innovation in higher education until the C.N.A.A. and the Open University' (Lawson 1975, p.8), 'the most momentous step ever taken in the history of the English universities' (Simmons 1959, p.21).

The external degree soon, and throughout its history, raised questions about the appropriateness and justice of examinations divorced from teaching. While that separation looked attractive – including to American onlookers – as a guarantee of objectivity, students faced examinations whose standards were based on criteria often unrelated to or in conflict with those of the teaching situation. Owens College protested in 1872 at the 'unsuitable selection' sometimes made of topics for examination in the faculty of arts. Questions were not only severe, but often bore no relation to what had been studied, with examiners trotting out 'their hobbies irrespective of teachers or taught' (Thompson 1886, p.517). The currency of London's degrees, however, was to become international as well as national, and the fact that external students were subject to the same examiners as internal students was central to the acceptance of the degree standard. Under new statutes in 1898 London increased its involvement in those institutions admitted as Schools of the University – including the right of visitation to monitor efficiency, and the approval of Appointed Teachers of the University. In other institutions the University could 'recognize' teachers, and where appropriate such institutions could enter students in certain fields and under certain conditions for internal degrees (London 1912, pp.83,87).

The criteria of judgement were widening and incorporating new vocabularies. When the federal Victoria University was created in 1880, it was to admit colleges in towns such as Liverpool and Leeds if 'of adequate efficiency and stability' (Lawson 1975, p.8).

The Persistent Chase

The most important twentieth-century context for the discussion of standards was eventually to be the pressure for expansion following the Second World War. In the intervening half-century the elements of a 'higher education system' can be seen emerging. Other professional demands were being made, new universities and colleges were being created, with London continuing to define the standard of their external degrees until they achieved independence. Existing university colleges murmured from time to time about such independence, looking at the new universities which emerged from the break-up of Victoria University. The universities adjusted to new demands on their scholarship and resources from pressures for research, and the arrival in Britain of the PhD – with Oxford the first to accept it in 1917, and London last two years later (Simpson 1983). The UGC came into existence in its present form in 1919. The external examiner system became increasingly crystallized. The period ends after the Second World War with the establishment of the University College of North Staffs at Keele, the transition of some colleges to university status, and mounting pressures of demography, demand and higher technology. All of these have some bearing on issues of standards, but it is possible to emphasize a few.

The first half-century produced a concern about the components of standards, as a result of diversification and growth. 'More means worse' was to be a slogan of the 1960s, but was part of the consciousness of earlier decades. Hull University College, for example, took its first students in 1928. In the same year a book on *The New Universities* took Hull as its illustration of what Britain did not need. Although a good case could be made out for it, Hull would herald 'a spate of new universities', which would either 'lower the standard of education in the universities that are already in being... or else they will form a new and surely necessary type, perhaps most like the American small town college.... If English education and English standards of research are to be kept at their present level we do not want these small town colleges' (Herklots 1928, p.88). A more complex hierarchy of institutions was being created – and interestingly from this example of opposition, research had become accepted as a hallmark of quality. Owens' elevation to university status had been helped considerable by its commitment to research on the European model (Charlton 1951, p.55) and increasingly in the early decades of the twentieth century research was becoming an element in the judgement of university-level institutions. The inspectors appointed to supervise and report on the institutions receiving Treasury grants (prior to the establishment of the UGC) commented on research performance. Southampton's record was praised in 1909 as contributing to the intellectual life of the district, and in 1907 the inspectors commended Leeds for the contribution its technology, science teaching and research were making to Yorkshire industries (Patterson 1962, p.126; Shimmin 1954, pp.73-4).

Quantity, quality and responsiveness to national and local needs were becoming issues. Hull provides a clear case. In a leaflet entitled *Why a University at Hull?* the College staked out its claim to be 'the centre of the intellectual and cultural life of the community which it serves', but at the same time the trustees had insisted that the area 'must have nothing less than the best'. The policy of quality before quantity would 'surely arouse the enthusiasm of every man and woman of vision in this proud corner of England' (Hull 1929, pp.1-3). The following year the Principal described the College's awareness of the 'critical gaze of the existing University institutions' and its responsibilities 'in appealing for admission to the academic comity of the country' (Hull 1930, pp.1-2). Justifying such an appeal in terms of standards was not easy. The new institutions had to contend with often poorly qualified and ill motivated students, some of whom had passed the Higher School Certificate and were exempt from the London Intermediate course and examination, but others of whom were not. Hull had to take steps to cater for the latter, providing extra work in preparation for Final examinations, or advising students to 'choose a subject not taken for the Higher School Certificate'. More importantly, the College set up a 'Committee on Standards of Study' which, with the Principal in the chair, considered suggestions 'for raising the standard of work and for correcting the demeanour of the students.' Under the heading of 'Methods of Study', the committee set out some of the points to which the Principal was asked to draw students' attention at the beginning of each session, including: 'application to work generally', 'difference between College and School life', 'responsibility to their parents, to the people responsible for the payment of their fees, for proper use of scholarship funds', and 'organisation of their work generally – attendance at lectures, compulsory attendance at examinations....' Heads of department would doubtless 'acquaint their students from time to time with the technique of examinations' (Hull, 1931).

While the standard of students was in various respects problematic, so also was the quality of staff. Staff appointments have been called 'the moment of truth for Universities' (Christopherson 1967, p.107), and for the new institutions struggling to establish reputations, the question of staffing was often paramount. Hull in its early years was publicly apologetic that some of its departments would be headed by lecturers and not by professors. Under the London external degree system staff gained experience of teaching, but often not of examining, at degree level – and in the case of colleges like Exeter acquiring independence after the Second World War this was to prove a serious problem (Clapp 1982, p.123). Victoria University and the universities which emerged from it provided a new base for fuller staff participation. In the Schools of London University, as the University's 'inspectors' found on their visitations in the 1920s and 1930s, the staff was mostly one of 'distinction', as measured by 'the selection of publications, and tables of examination results' (in the case of Bedford College), and 'highly qualified and their record of research is good' (in the case of Westfield College) (London 1936, p.2). Such reports and the conditions they reflected have to be contrasted, however, with the problems of, for instance, Southampton, with students of uncertain quality and an overworked staff whose low salary scale 'meant that able young lecturers and assistant lecturers, as well as rising professors, frequently left for better-paid posts elsewhere which offered them greater facilities for individual work than the College yet possessed' (Patterson 1962, p.185).

University institutions were now all being subjected, however discreetly, to forms of regular scrutiny. London's visitation procedures under the 1898 Statutes meant that not only were its own Schools being regularly inspected (the term 'inspectors' was still being used for its visiting teams until the late 1930s), but also the institutions with 'recognized teachers'. The visitors to Woolwich Polytechnic in 1938, for example, reported that an Academic Board had been set up (as recommended on the previous visitation in 1932). The seven recognized teachers covered a reasonable proportion of the final and higher degree work, and were either personally or through supervision responsible for 'a creditable amount of published research work' (though the library was inadequate). The visitors were impressed by the progress made in the previous five years, by 'the general standard of efficiency', and the 'satisfactory provision for the instruction of Internal Students and for the instruction of students pursuing courses of advanced study or research' (London 1938, pp.1-2). The UGC, with its quinquennial visits, was at the same time promoting other processes of scrutiny and self-scrutiny. The universities reviewed their work in advance of a visit and considered priorities for the next five years. The UGC then made its judgements and estimated the institutions' ability to carry out its proposals – and gave the Treasury strategic advice. This process was scarcely concerned with standards in later understandings of the term. It was concerned more with subject range and balance, effective use of resources, and the avoidance (rarely successful) of competition. Within the universities

> the typical attitude of the majority of academics to the five year planning cycle was that it seemed a necessary chore in order to achieve a satisfactory submission to the U.G.C. to enable the University to get its fair share (or more) of the allocation. (West 1981, pp.18-20)

Other considerations arose. The quality of campus life surfaced occasionally – as it had done ever since the creation of London in the early nineteenth century had provoked anxieties about the temptations of the metropolis. Effective management and deployment of resources, and effective academic structures for the maintenance of teaching, scholarship and research, had indeed become part of the agenda. The ground rules for scrutiny and self-scrutiny were, however, never made clear, and the standards of judgement remained uncertain.

Examinations remained central. In its worries about student learning and behaviour in the 1930s Hull, like other institutions, was conscious of the judgements ultimately to be made of the College through its examination results – hence its anxieties about admission standards (including advice to students not to enter before they were eighteen) and examination technique.

Crucial for the development of the examination system, however, was the adoption of the 'external examiner' system, in order to guarantee equivalent, or at least comparable, standards. For institutions whose students sat for London's external degree, the 'external examiner' had always simply been one who taught and examined students in London's own Schools. From the beginning there were pressures from Owens College to have 'external and internal' examiners (Thompson 1886, p.158), but these were aimed at enabling Owens' teachers to be involved in examining their own students. In the 1860s, amidst controversy about the desirability of new universities, the question of comparability with existing degrees was constantly raised, and in Owens' 1880 Charter, therefore, examinations loomed large. Students were to attend, would be taught, and would be examined by their teachers, but, 'as a concession to those who thought there were moral or intellectual dangers in this combination, owing to favouritism or competition, external examiners were to be added' (Fiddes 1937, p.80). Bedford College, under the conditions of its Trust, employed men of 'high standing' in the university world to certify, as outside examiners, to the soundness of the education. This system of 'special examination from outside did much towards ensuring a sound standard of teaching within' (Tuke 1939, pp.122-3). The system continued until the girls took London University and other examinations in the 1880s. In the first half of the twentieth century, however, the external examiner became as crucial to the concept of examination standards as London University's seal of quality through the external degree had been in the previous century.

The Great Escape

All such attempts to establish and guarantee standards were put under strain, intensified and extended in the four decades which followed the Second World War. In the increasingly pervasive industrial culture and the international economic competition and uncertainties of much of this period, in Britain as elsewhere, higher education had to adapt to rapidly changing conditions of scale, structure, function and expectation. For higher education, old and new, in the 1960s especially, the paramount concern was 'incontrovertibly, to define and to clarify its function', within an industrial culture: 'how, then, to exemplify "concepts of excellence" within such a culture? No more important task faces the universities' (Betsky 1969, p.7). Anxieties about the standards that would prevail in a higher education expanding to incorporate larger numbers of students, in newly created and promoted institutions with different nomenclatures and awards, and in curricula broadening to meet new demands, were made more and more explicit.

Throughout the 1950s and 1960s the UGC constantly faced such issues. Courses were becoming overloaded (UGC 1953, pp.45-6; 1958, pp.37-9). In conditions of expansion the quality of students and awards both needed to be watched. In 1953 the UGC welcomed increased numbers on condition that they 'should not involve a decline in the standard reached by students when they obtain their first degree.' In 1958, following up this concern, it announced that work was in progress to assess numbers obtaining first-class degrees, numbers dropping out, and related information. In 1964, when the colleges of advanced technology (CATS) were being proposed for university status, the UGC reported that its proposal had been accepted that each one should be given an academic advisory committee (AACs) 'for keeping under review the standard of the education provided in the university and of the degrees awarded' (UGC 1953, p.22; 1958, pp.20-1; 1964, p.106).

Expansion brought opportunities, including those of *higher* standards in some people's view, since greater attention was being paid to many neglected aspects of education, but it brought defensive positions also. The Robbins committee on higher education believed, in 1963, that numbers and quality could go together. Hoggart, two years later, agreed cautiously: 'I am in favour of expansion. I *think* it need not lower standards' (Hoggart 1965, p.3). Expansion placed everything under a microscope – admissions, staff appointments, research, courses (including for new awards such as the Diploma in Technology), examinations, resources, conditions for learning and living. At the heart of almost all debate was student demand, an issue which had captured academic discussion a decade before Robbins. Sir John Wolfenden, addressing Reading University's Court in 1956, considered the by now familiar question, 'And what about standards?':

> I cannot get away from the elementary view that in fact at the present moment university standards... throughout the universities as a whole, are dictated by the simple numerical fact of the number of university places there are. I suspect that there are very few university places left vacant on the ground that candidates of sufficient merit have not presented themselves....

He believed, though it is doubtful whether his was the prevailing view in the upper echelons of the universities, that 'to talk of "university standards" as if they represented something absolute, or even relatively permanent, is a misconception' (Holt 1977, p.327). The terms of the debate were very different from those of the earlier years of the century.

The terms changed markedly in relation to institutional status. The university colleges aspired to independent status against a background not only of current anxieties, but of historical attempts to define what constituted a university. At the end of the war Lord Eustace Percy had offered a definition: it must be 'a fully self-governing community of teachers and students, working together in one place, with substantial endowments of its own, mature enough to set its own standards of teaching and strong enough to resist outside pressures, public or private, political or economic' (Simmons 1959, p.162). These and related criteria were a context in which Exeter or Leicester or Southampton sought independence. What they had to demonstrate was that escape from the London external degree would not result in a decline in standards. Southampton proposed a solution for the transition which proved acceptable both internally and to London University. London had established 'special relationships' as a temporary measure in the establishment of some overseas colleges, and Southampton proposed adopting a similiar strategy. In 1948 the Principal, aware that 'there is bound to be a period of some anxiety for the college when we pass from the London External Degree, with its established reputation, to a Southampton Degree that has to justify itself to both the academic and the outer world', proposed a transitional arrangement. The college was to propose a date until which it would continue to prepare students for the external degree, and a period to follow during which, under the special relationship, 'students will pursue courses on syllabuses drawn up by the College and will take examinations conducted by the College supervised and assessed by London University.'

These students would receive a London degree, but at the end of the period independent status under a Royal Charter would be sought. Southampton's Senate agreed this procedure in 1948, as did a joint committee of Senate and Council (Southampton, 1948). The Senate of London University agreed the scheme, subject to Southampton's recognition by the UGC, and sufficient progress 'within a few years of obtaining a Charter for separate establishment as a University' (London 1949, pp.87-8). The details were agreed, and the special relationship ended, in fact, only three years later, when Southampton became an independent university. Using the same procedure, London agreed such an arrangement for Hull in 1952 (London 1952, p.153).

Standards were from this point to be protected by a variety of such transitional and sponsorship arrangements. The postwar development of a university college in North Staffordshire was built on the notion of sponsorship, and when established at Keele the college was empowered to award its own degrees, but under the sponsorship of the Universities of Oxford, Birmingham and Manchester – each of which, under the 1949 Charter, had two representatives on its Academic Council (Mountford 1972, pp.68-81). Similarly, in order to avoid institutional sponsorship, the UGC agreed with groups planning new universities at the end of the 1950s and early 1960s that they should have academic advisory committees, to appoint the first principal and professors, and to advise on range of courses and standards. When, in the 1960s, the colleges of advanced technology achieved university status, the academic advisory committees proposed by the UGC fulfilled similar transitional roles. Although there were variations in their interpretation of their roles, they were all concerned with such problems affecting the standards of the new institutions as their academic structure and the transfer of staff to university-grade posts (Venables 1978, pp.57-61). They were also concerned with 'appropriate' curricula. The chairmen of the AACs met in 1964 to discuss a coherent approach, and agreed that the former CATs should retain a technological bias and their 'distinctive character' – for example, integrating course work and industrial training – and that they should resist the 'new university' model in the national interest (Chelsea 1965, p.1). The chairman of the Chelsea College AAC, at the meeting at which this was reported, also commented on the debate taking place in the college about permanent or rotating heads of departments, and supported the Governing Body preference for permanent heads partly on the grounds that 'it would not be possible to find good candidates prepared to accept posts under a situation of rotating Chairmanships and government by committee' (Chelsea 1965, p.2).

In such conditions the notion of standards was arousing controversy across a widening spectrum of issues. In the 1960s especially, new meanings were being sought for concepts of standards or quality or excellence, which had once seemed absolute and measurable. The diverse elements of judgement were being itemized. London University's admission of an institution was dependent on questions of 'government, quality and conditions of the staff, equipment, standard of instruction, and the number of students likely to proceed to degrees' (London 1950, p.53). The UGC had emphasized that the maintenance of standards depended among other things on the quality of life and education – as well as of the students (UGC 1948, p.35). Senior university people were in the 1960s establishing their positions. The maintenance of standards meant guaranteeing, for example, that students on completion of their courses had 'some familiarity with the basic ideas in a particular field of study', some experience of 'living and working with other people of similiar ability in other fields of study', and were 'at least equal to others who have done the same course in earlier years' (Christopherson 1967, p.106). The maintenance of standards meant the ability and the wish to change (Butterworth in *Universities Quarterly* 1969, p.259). The central implication, to be a dominant theme of the 1980s, was the means of evaluating or measuring the various components of such definitions. In Britain (and also in the United States) there were to be attempts to distinguish between the quality of the educational process and the quality of graduates (eg Crombag 1978; Adelman 1983). The Lindop inquiry into validation was to emphasize the quality of the academic community (Committee of Enquiry 1985), and an analysis of 'higher education in a harsh climate' in 1983 was to look at 'the quality of teaching', 'the quality of student assessment' and 'the quality of teachers' (Williams and Blackstone 1983). All such itemization had roots in the shift to the wider questions raised by the changes of context and scale.

Although considerations of standards have so far focused on university processes and understandings, the major change heralded by the postwar developments was the direct and continuing concern of the newly designated public sector institutions of higher education, and the processes of validation and review which they promoted. The National Council for Technological Awards and its successor in 1964 – the Council for National Academic Awards (CNAA) – were urgently confronted with the need to establish that the Dip Tech and then the CNAA's degrees were, in the words of the CNAA's Statutes, 'comparable in standards to awards granted and conferred by Universities' (CNAA 1983, p.11), though this made the questionable assumption that 'the latter comprise a single, indivisible entity' (Taylor 1979, p.27). The polytechnics designated at the end of the 1960s needed to attain, redefine and demonstrate standards in very different institutional contexts. They were orientated, in the view of one college principal, 'to a quite different concept of excellence to the academic one' (Brosan in *Universities Quarterly* 1969, p.263).

The relationship between the polytechnics and the CNAA was the pivot of the new approach, largely through the operation of peer evaluation and review. The press was continually to report on CNAA judgements about standards raised, or adverse reports which put courses or institutions at risk. Summing up the position after a decade, Eric Robinson wrote: 'recalling experiences of degree courses in technical colleges in the fifties, I marvel at the advances in standards and status that have been made.' Weaknesses in the polytechnics were weaknesses of 'the whole of academia at the present time' (Robinson 1979, pp.13-14). As evaluation processes took shape – including for the colleges and institutes of higher education from the mid-1970s – comparisons between the accountability measures of the 'public' sector and the invisible or inexplicit ones of the universities became more frequent. Comparing the CNAA system with university standards was questionable, 'since who evaluates and establishes the standards of universities with which these comparisons are to be made?' Testing one half of the binary system in this way was 'irrational and unscholarly' (Davey 1971, p.17).

The universities which engaged in validation from the 1970s could not make their evaluation processes and standards as explicit as those of the CNAA, and many, for various reasons, abandoned the field to the CNAA during the first decade of validation of the colleges of higher education. The CNAA, on the other hand, had constantly to reassert its commitment to acceptable, publicly validated standards, however difficult – as in the case of the Diploma of Higher Education, for example – it was to do so with any precision. Its guidance to institutions on the Diploma contained a section on 'Standards' which indicated:

> ... it has been necessary to establish a standard for the validation of the Diploma and this has been set for DipHEs validated by the CNAA at a level comparable to two years of a full-time course.... Validating parties may therefore be expected to evaluate proposals against this standard. The criteria will include content and process as well as the personal and intellectual challenge which the course makes upon the student... this does not represent an absolute standard since it must be read in a context of different honours degree course patterns (CNAA nd, p.4).

The Lindop inquiry into public sector validation reported – whatever the pros and cons of CNAA validation procedures – that 'the standards being achieved on degree courses are generally satisfactory and in many cases excellent.' Welcoming this judgement, the National Advisory Body for Public Sector Higher Education (NAB) paid tribute to 'the CNAA's contribution to this achievement', seeing in it confirmation of the NAB's previously expressed view:

> Its insistence on rigorous documentation, specification of objectives and course structures, and compliance with standard regulations, together with its pressures for adequate (sic) resourcing research and staff development, and institutional self-evaluation have been instrumental in the fulfilment of its statute that the Council's degrees should be comparable in standard to those awarded by universities. (NAB 1985, p.14)

The CNAA had become involved in course evaluation at a time when curricula were under strain. The new universities had often broadened and remodelled a traditional curriculum which had been criticized as haphazard, excellent in detail but the product of inertia and the pressures of subject imperialism (Livingstone 1948, p.12), criticisms to be frequently echoed in US debates about standards in the 1980s. Problems of course structure included the implications of breadth and joint degrees – as a Nuffield inquiry discovered in the mid-1970s (Nuffield 1974, 1975) – and a growing rejection of the separation of honours and general degrees. Southampton, for instance, reported to the UGC that its faculties of arts and science were strongly opposed to general and honours tracks, and intended to abolish them (Southampton 1960, pp.5,13). At Leeds, before the war, Sadler had tried to persuade staff that '"ordinary" and "honours" were different in kind but *not* in standard' (Shimmin 1954, pp.72-3), but the belief had become increasingly untenable everywhere.

The 'container revolution' that the Nuffield inquiry described in higher education applied particularly to 'modular' and 'unit' courses. The attempt to restructure in some polytechnics along these lines was intended to provide wider choice and avoid the problems of 'finals'. The Nuffield inquiry found that the new structures produced little in the way of examination novelty – merely more frequent traditional examinations (Mansell 1976, pp.30-1). Modular courses were criticized as conforming to a model being rejected in favour of more effective ones in the United States (Church nd, pp.4-11). The need for 'continuous assessment' to be built in was asserted – though not always with much clarity about the nature of such assessment (Quinn 1978). Institutions were aware, however, that modular courses had to conform to the CNAA's conception of standards. Oxford Polytechnic, for example, adopted complex processes to monitor the programme, the teaching, assessment standards within and across modules, student performance and other features. It evolved a termly and annual review, occasional analysis in detail across a number of years, the appointment of a Modular Course Evaluation Officer, and a variety of other measures. By 1985 it was analysing in depth such aspects as the relationship between larger course enrolments (as a result of economy measures) and average marks, disparities in marking accross subjects, and average marks per module across time (Oxford Polytechnic, 1984-5; 1983; Lindsay and Paton 1985). The Polytechnic was seeking to provide 'the maximum amount of choice compatible with the maintenance of academic standards', and incorporating a 'progressive mode of assessment (based on periodic hurdles rather than a final high jump)' (Watson 1985). No approach to standards prior to the 1960s had involved so many explicit elements.

The quality of staff and of teaching was also receiving attention, more tentatively, and with fewer criteria to apply. In 1985 the Committee of Vice-Chancellors and Principals (CVCP) underlined that there had been little attempt by the universities to appraise staff regularly, and recommended an annual review (CVCP 1985, pp.28-9). One of the traditions of British universities had, in general, been a studied avoidance of confronting the quality of their teaching. Oxford and Cambridge were described in the 1960s as being, paradoxically, 'not really interested in education', indifferent to teaching methods, with 'a complete absence of curiosity about the effects of examinations', and a 'purely anecdotal attitude to the psychology of the learning process' (Rose and Ziman 1964, pp.228-9). Points of change were becoming visible. The Hale report on university teaching methods did not produce major change in practice or consciousness, but it did signal a move towards a more public process of evaluation and staff development. In a discussion of the report Lionel Elvin mentioned that five years previously, in a discussion of the same subject, 'a distinguished professor told us that we were not teachers; we were scholars willing to share our scholarship with the more promising of the young.... After five years the mood has changed' (Home Universities Conference 1964, p.32). By 1982 a Times Higher Education Supplement leader could proclaim that 'We are all Teachers Now' (THES, 7 May 1982, p.32). The criteria in use operationally were changing rapidly as new requirements had to be met. In 'vocational' higher education industrial or other experience was part of the measure of staff effectiveness (Locke 1970, p.126); in teacher training and other appointments some combination of the professional and the academic was increasingly required. While it was possible to analyse teacher characteristics, the question still remained – 'Is it Possible to Assess Teaching?' (Elton 1975).

What had emerged, therefore, was an increasingly complex concern with quality control. Examinations, for so long the pillars of the standards edifice, were being viewed with suspicion from some directions. Robbins evaded the issue of the reliability and merits of examinations ('we are aware that there is a good deal of current discussion of these matters') by recommending research and exchange of experience – with a particularly clear role reserved for the future CNAA (Committee on Higher Education 1963, p.189). The reliability of examinations and marks had been challenged in the 1930s, with Hartog and Rhodes demonstrating the fragility of the standards applied in written examinations. Various techniques proposed to improve marking reliability had not silenced anxieties about differences amongst subjects, and within subjects from year to year (Cox 1967). Dale in 1959 castigated staff for their ignorance of the pitfalls of examining, and their belief that they carried in their heads an absolute standard of 40 per cent. He pointed particularly to the wide disparities of first class honours awards in different subjects, ranging from 1/4 in applied science to 1/70 in arts (Dale 1959; Phillips 1959 for a reply). Williams pointed to a decade of uninvestigated, substantial disparities in marking at the University of Leeds (Williams 1979, p.168). What was being discovered was 'The Complexity of the Assessment Task' (Miller and Parlett 1973, ch.3). By the 1980s the same reservations were appearing with regard to the role of the external examiner, whose presence did not appear to guard against arbitrary differences, and whose experience of 'comparability' was questionable, since course variations were too great and 'strictly speaking, no one group of students ever has an exactly identical performance requirement for all its members. The variations between different groups... are naturally even greater' (Oxford Polytechnic, Summer 1985, pp.12-15; Bee and Dolton, 1985; Becher and Kogan 1980, p.157). In the late 1950s and 1960s there was support for the introduction of 'objective tests' as in the United States (Dale 1959; Cooper and Fry 1967; Oppenheim 1967) but resistance was greater.

Alternatives were sought – including in some cases a call for the abandonment of examinations. Discussion frequently focused on continuous assessment, its justice and dangers. In 1960 Wrigley argued against the belief that continuous assessment might cause standards to fall, being represented as a '"soft option", demanding less work from students. In fact the opposite might happen' (Wrigley 1960, p.311). Radical opinion went further. Failure rate fluctuations meant that examinations were 'a random process of selection'. The issue was how to make education a process of discourse 'between staff and students... conducted between equals in terms of power.... The aim must be to overthrow the university 'management' and replace it by a democratic power' (Fawthrop 1969, pp.99-102). An Anarchist group at University College, London, pointed to examinations as unreliable, a cause of suicides, serving social not academic purposes. Continuous assessment was no better: employers should conduct their own entrance examinations and leave universities free to teach what they wished (Butterworth nd).

By the 1970s the examination 'revolution' of the previous century had become part of a broad search for appropriate forms of evaluation. Styles of evaluation were under constant discussion (Becher and Kogan 1980, pp.149-51), and even proponents of new forms of evaluation – including the 'illuminative' – were anxious that they should not become an excuse for lax standards (Stenhouse 1979). Measures, their targets and what they reflected were more widely examined (Crombag 1978). Size of unit became a factor – in the planning of the polytechnics, for example: 'many departments and colleges are too small to sustain high academic standards' (DES 1966, p.5). Sheila Browne when offering advice on quality to the NAB, underlined that just as quality was 'neither absolute nor static, so its components will vary according to the area of study and the purpose of the qualification sought' (Browne 1984, p.45). The NAB itself in 1984, in compiling a table of quality indices that might be applied to programmes and institutions, emphasized 'the essentially subjective nature of a quality judgement' (NAB 1984, p.5).

While the range of approaches was applied to the internal and external procedures of validation, it only rarely was so in the case of the universities themselves, whose course control mechanisms remained enormously varied, difficult to ascertain or unexplored (Church 1983, pp.61-4). Only rarely also have universities submitted themselves to external review. They have reluctantly admitted Her Majesty's Inspectors to scrutinize their teacher education (without public report as in the public sector), and have accepted 'accreditation' (not validation, the CVCP has made clear) by professional bodies, with the universities protecting their responsibility 'as autonomous bodies... for the academic standards of their own degree courses.' Accreditation has been confined to 'the training element of a course', to give students exemption from the examinations of the professional bodies (CVCP 1984, p.6). Outside review has been at times of crisis. Stirling University commissioned an independent report on the policies and running of the University following disturbances in October 1972 (Young 1973). Chelsea College invited extensive peer review (by Fellows of the Royal Society) following damaging criticism of the college by the Swinnerton-Dyer committee on the rationalization of London University (*THES*, 11 December 1981, p.4).

Alongside these processes have gone attempts to establish performance indicators of many kinds, not without controversy and difficulty (Bevan 1984; Billing 1980; Lindsay 1981; Sizer 1981). Sustained attempts have been made to correlate student performance in school and university examinations. Judgements about the quality of students' experience of and performance in higher education have remained elusive since, as Sheila Browne points out, real evidence about that quality 'lies in the subsequent performance of the student' (Browne 1984, p.45). In all of these cases the answers have indeed proved difficult to catch. Absolute or comparable standards have been elusive particularly as the system, whatever its expansions and contractions, has remained hierarchical – although with interlocking and complex hierarchies. The traditional social and intellectual hierarchies have remained intact, whilst adapting to hierarchies established by new universities, new styles of academic life and community, new sectors, new statuses of subjects and graduate employment. The roles of government, paymasters and moderators of standards have changed; new bodies and roles have emerged. When *The Times Higher Education Supplement* produced a series of articles on quality control in October-December 1982, it looked at the CNAA, polytechnics, Her Majesty's Inspectors, Regional Advisory Councils, external examiners, course approval mechanisms in universities, students' and heads of departments' views, the Open University, American ranking of institutions, the Business and Technician Education Council, and evaluation in professional scientific institutions.

Accusations of élitism have doubtless been confirmed by the ways in which quality questions have been addressed – given the problem of reconciling standards and quality with wider constituencies of students. This was an issue, in different forms, and with different target groups, when London University was created, when the university colleges were created, and when the system expanded after the Second World War. The main controversies around the notion of standards have related essentially to expanded student access, and recent tensions around questions of quality and equality in Britain and elsewhere have simply revived old themes. One of the most telling comments on this tension is contained in the diaries of R.H. Tawney, an extract from which was added by *Universities Quarterly* to its 1969 report of a conference on 'Concepts of Excellence':

> ... the business of the university is twofold: to uphold an intellectual standard and to uphold a moral standard. The intellectual standard it upholds by maintaining a severe intellectual discipline; the moral standard it upholds by making that discipline accessible to all who will submit to it – by relaxing it for none merely because they are well-to-do or socially influential, by depriving none of it merely because they are poor or uncouth or socially incompetent. (*Universities Quarterly* 1969, p.319)

Identifying, defining and relating all the elements in such an analysis, or in an updated version in changed and changing circumstances, has never ceased to be difficult, 'and this is possibly inevitable'.

Acknowledgements

We are grateful to the Nuffield Foundation for funding the research of which this paper is one of the outcomes. We would also like to thank Clem Adelman, Keith Hoskin and David Watson for their help, Sam Crook for access to material relating to London University's external degrees, and the archivists of Southampton and Hull Universities for their assistance.

References

Adelman, C. (1983) The major seventh: Standards as a leading tone in higher education. In J.R. Warren (Ed.) *Meeting the New Demand for Standards* San Francisco: Jossey-Bass
Adelman, C. and Alexander, R.J. (1982) *The Self-Evaluating Institution* London: Methuen

Anon (1836) *Metropolitan University. Remarks on the Ministerial Plan of a Central University Examining Board* London:Effingham Wilson

Becher, T. and Kogan, M. (1980) *Process and Structure in Higher Education* London:Heinemann

Bee, M. and Dolton, P. (1985) Degree class and pass rates: An inter-university comparison *Higher Education Review* 7 (2)

Ben-David, J. (1977) *Centres of Learning: Britain, France, Germany, United States* New York: McGraw-Hill

Betsky, S. (1969) Concepts of excellence. Universities in an industrial culture *Universities Quarterly* 24 (1)

Bevan, J.S. (1984) *The Inter-Relationship and Impact of Performance Criteria for Higher Education* London:mimeo

Billing, D. (Ed.) (1980) *Indicators of Performance* Guildford: Society for Research into Higher Education

Broady, M. (1978-9) Down with academic standards *New Universities Quarterly* 33 (1)

Browne, S. (1984) NAB and 'Quality' *Higher Education Review* 17 (1)

Butterworth, B. and Powell, A. (nd) *Marked for Life: A Criticism of Assessment at Universities* London: University College London Union Anarchist Group

Charlton, H.B. (1951) *Portrait of a University 1851-1951* Manchester: Manchester University Press

Chelsea College of Science and Technology (1965) Report of the Seventh Meeting of the Academic Advisory Committee held at the College on the 28th January, mimeo

Christopherson, D.G. (1967) Standards – The concept of excellence *The British Universities Annual 1967* London: Association of University Teachers

Church, C.H. (1983) Course control in the university sector. In C.H. Church (Ed.) *Practice and Perspective in Validation* Guildford: Society for Research into Higher Education

Church, C.H. (nd) *Modular Courses in British Higher Education: A Critical Assessment* Lancaster:mimeo

Church, C.H. and Murray, R. (1983) Of definitions, debates and dimensions. In C.H.Church (Ed.) *Practice and Perspective in Validation* Guildford: Society for Research into Higher Education

Clapp. B.W. (1982) *The University of Exeter: A History* Exeter: The University of Exeter

Committee of Enquiry into the Academic Validation of Degree Courses in Public Sector Higher Education (Lindop) (1985) *Academic Validation in Public Sector Higher Education* London:HMSO

Committee of Enquiry into the Governance of the University of London (1972) *Final Report* London: University of London

Committee of Vice-Chancellors and Principals (1984) *The External Examiner System for First Degree and Taught Master's Courses* London: CVCP

Committee of Vice-Chancellors and Principals (1984) *External Involvement in Maintenance and Monitoring of Academic Standards* London: CVCP

Committee of Vice-Chancellors and Principals (1985) *Report of the Steering Committee for Efficiency Studies in Universities* London: CVCP

Committee on Higher Education (Robbins) (1963) *Higher Education. Report* London:HMSO

Cooper, B. and Foy, J.M. (1967) Examinations in higher education – A review *Journal of Biological Education* 1 (2)

Council for National Academic Awards (nd) *Diploma of Higher Education* London: CNAA

Council for National Academic Awards (1983) *Handbook of CNAA's Policy and Regulations* London: CNAA

Cox, R. (1967) Examinations and higher education: A survey of the literature *Universities Quarterly* 21 (3)

Crombag, H.F.M. (1978) On defining quality of education *Higher Education* 7 (4)

Currie, H.M. (1982) Is the idea of 'Honours' out of date? *Times Higher Education Supplement* 18 June

Dale, R.R. (1959) University standards *Universities Quarterly* 13 (2)

Davey, W. (1971) Distrust of polytechnic standards 'Irrational and Unscholarly' *Times Higher Education Supplement* 15 October

Department of Education and Science (1966) *A Plan for Polytechnics and Other Colleges* London: HMSO

Elton, L.R.B. (1975) Is it possible to assess teaching?. In University Teaching Methods Unit *Evaluating Teaching in Higher Education* London: UTMU

Entwistle, N., Percy, K.A. and Nisbet, J.B. (1971) *Educational Objectives and Academic Performance in Higher Education* Lancaster: University of Lancaster

Fawthrop, T. (1969) Education or Examination?. In A. Cockburn and R. Blackburn (Eds) *Student Power. Problems, Diagnosis, Action* Harmondsworth: Penguin

Fiddes, E. (1937) *Chapters in the History of Owens College and of Manchester University 1851-1914* Manchester: Manchester University Press

Fletcher, R. (1975) *What's Wrong with Higher Education?* London: Methuen

Fulton, J. (1964) *Experiment in Higher Education* London:Tavistock

Green, V.H.H. (1969) *The Universities* Harmondsworth: Penguin

Halsey, A.H. (1962) British universities *European Journal of Sociology* 3 (1)

Herklots, H.G.G. (1928) *The New Universities: An External Examination* London:Benn

Hoggart, R. (1965) *Higher Education and Cultural Change: A Teacher's View* Newcastle: University of Newcastle upon Tyne

Holt, J.C. (1977) *The University of Reading: The First Fifty Years* Reading: Reading University Press

Home Universities Conference (1965) *Report of Proceedings 1964* London: Association of Commonwealth Universities

Hoskin, K. (1979) The examination, disciplinary power and rational schooling *History of Education* 8 (2)

Hoskin, K.W. and Macve, R.H. (1986) Accounting and the examination: A genealogy of disciplinary power *Accounting, Organization and Society* 11 (2)

Hull (chronological order, archive references)

University College of Hull (1928) *Prospectus. Session 1928-9* (ULD 331 cl)

Hull University College (1929) *Why a University at Hull?* Hull: Hull University College (ULD 335 H9 Rev E6747)

Hull University College (1930) *The University of Hull: What it is and what it does* Hull: Hull University College (ULD 335 H9 Rev E6749)

University College of Hull, Committee on Standards of Study (1931) Minutes of first meeting held at the college... 21st May, mimeo (V.C. 34)

Morgan, A.E. (1930) *The Project of a University College at Hull* (reproduced from *The University Bulletin*) (ULD 335 M8 [1] Rev F335)

Jones, F. (1982) Top marks for polys after visit *Times Higher Education Supplement* 23 July

Latham, H. (1877) *On the Action of Examinations Considered as a Means of Selection* Cambridge: Deighton, Bell

Lawson, J. (1975) Higher education before Robbins *Aspects of Education* 18

Lindsay, A. (1981) Assessing institutional performance in higher education: A managerial perspective *Higher Education* 10 (6)

Livingstone, R. (1948) *Some Thoughts on University Education* London: Cambridge University Press

Locke, M. (1970) *Traditions and Controls in the Making of a Polytechnic: Woolwich Polytechnic 1890-1970* London: Thames Polytechnic

London (chronological order)
(see also Committee of Enquiry, University of London, Wilson)

University of London (1907) *Regulations for External Students*

University of London (1932) *Regulations for External Students*

University of London (1936) *Visitation under Statute 114. Bedford College. Report of Inspectors* (with Senate Minutes, A.C.6)

University of London (1936) *Visitation under Statute 14. Westfield College. Report of Inspectors* (with Senate Minutes A.C.7)

University of London (1938) *Inspection under Statute 125. The Woolwich Polytechnic. – Report of Inspectors* (with Senate Minutes A.C.3)

University of London (1949) *Minutes of Senate* 24 June (item 31: University College, Southampton – Special Application)

University of London (1952) *Minutes of Senate* 23 July (item 49: University College, Hull – Special Application)

Mansell, T. et al. (1976) *The Container Revolution: A Study of Unit and Modular Courses* London: Nuffield Foundation

Miller, C. and Parlett, M. (1973) *Up to the Mark: A Research Report on Assessment* Edinburgh:University of Edinburgh (also an edited version, 1974, SRHE)

Mountford, J. (1972) *Keele. An Historical Critique* London:Routledge & Kegan Paul

National Advisory Body for Local Authority Higher Education (1984) *Quality* London: NAB, mimeo

National Advisory Body for Public Sector Higher Education (1985) Response to the Lindop Report, 1985 *NAB Bulletin* Summer

Nuffield Foundation Group for Research and Innovation in Higher Education (1974) Broader education *Newsletter* No.4

Nuffield Foundation (1975) *The Drift of Change: An Interim Report of the Group for Research and Innovation in Higher Education* London: Nuffield Foundation

Oppenheim, A.N., Jahoda, M. and James, R.L. (1967) Assumptions underlying the use of university examinations *Universities Quarterly* 21 (3)

Oxford Polytechnic (chronological order)
(See also Watson)

Oxford Polytechnic (1983) *Application to the Council for National Academic Awards for Renewal and Approval of the Modular Course. Central Volume*

Oxford Polytechnic (1983) Modular Course Annual Review for 1983-84 mimeo
Oxford Polytechnic *Modular Course: Summary of Results of Module Examinations for Academic Year 1984-85 All Terms* mimeo
Turner, D.J. (1985) An analysis of differences in marks obtained by students in different modules. In *Teaching* (Oxford Polytechnic) 11
External Examiners under Fire (1985). In *Teaching* (Oxford Polytechnic) 12
Lindsay, R.O. and Paton, R. (1985) *Effects of Changes in Higher Education on the Modular Course – 1981-2 – 1984-5* mimeo
Patterson, A.T. (1962) *The University of Southampton: A Centenary History* Southampton: University of Southampton
Percy, K.A. and Salter, F.W. (1976) Student and staff perceptions and 'The Pursuit of Excellence' in British higher education *Higher Education* 5
Phillips, E.G. (1959) University standards *Universities Quarterly* 13 (3)
Quinn, T.F.J. (1978) A critical appraisal of modular courses and their relevance to the British system of higher education *British Journal of Educational Technology* 9 (1)
Richmond, A. (1971) Academic standards broadened by merging traditions and disciplines *The Times* 15 January
Robinson, E (1979) The 'People's Universities': A progress report *Times Higher Education Supplement* 14 December
Rose, J. and Ziman, J. (1964) *Camford Observed* London:Gollancz
Rothblatt, S. (1968) *The Revolution of the Dons: Cambridge and Society in Victorian England* London: Faber & Faber (Cambridge University Press edn., 1981)
Sanderson, M (Ed.) (1975) *The Universities in the Nineteenth Century* London: Routledge & Kegan Paul
Sandford, C.T. (1963) CAT to university: Problems of transition *The British Universities Annual 1963* London: Association of University Teachers
Santinelli, P. (1983) Academic standards 'being put at risk' *Times Higher Education Supplement* 7 October
Shimmin, A.N. (1954) *The University of Leeds: The First Half Century* London: Cambridge University Press
Simmons, J. (1959) *New University* Leicester: Leicester University Press
Simpson, R. (1983) *How the PhD Came to Britain: A Century of Struggle for Postgraduate Education* Guildford:Society for Research into Higher Education
Sizer, J. (1981) Indicators of institutional performance. In Manchester Polytechnic Staff Development Unit *Measuring Up to the Future: Institutional Evaluation and Renewal* Manchester: Manchester Polytechnic
Southampton (chronological order, archive references)
   (see also Patterson)
Bond, F.T. (1863) *Report on the Organization and Management of the Hartley Institution* Southampton: Town Council of Southampton (LF 781.4 Univ. Coll.)
Hartley University College, Southampton *Calender for the Session 1904-5* (LF 782.2 Univ. Coll.)
The University College of Southampton *Handbook for the Session 1915-16* (LF 783. 2 Univ. Coll.)
(Vickers, K.H.) (1942) *Looking Back and Looking Forward* (report by the Principal) (LF 780 UNI)

University College of Southampton (1948), 3 mimeo documents:
R.S.W., Memorandum to Standing Committee of Senate, September
R.S.W., Memorandum to Senate, November
R.S.W., Approach to University Status, November
(LF 780 UNI, Joint Development Committee, Minutes and Papers, 1948)

University of Southampton *Calendar 1953-54*

University of Southampton (1960) *Visit of the University Grants Committee, December 1960* (draft documentation for Senate, 29 June 1960) (UGC Visit, 1960. Correspondence and Papers)

University of Southampton (1960) *Academic Developments in the Quinquennium 1962-67* (draft documentation for Senate, 10 May) (UGC Visit, 1960. Correspondance and Papers)

Stenhouse, L. (1983) The concept of standards in the theory of education. In *Authority, Education and Emancipation* London: Heinemann

Stenhouse, L. (1979) The problem of standards in illuminative research *Scottish Educational Review* 11 (1)

Tawney, R.H. (see *Universities Quarterly*)

Taylor, W. (1979) Degrees of excellence *Times Higher Education Supplement* 23 November

Thole, J (1964) Academic standards in liberal studies *Liberal Education* 6

Thompson, J. (1886) *The Owens College: Its Foundation and Growth; and its Connection with the Victoria University, Manchester* Manchester: Cornish

Times Higher Education Supplement (1981) Chelsea Ranks with the Best, say Academics, 11 December

Times Higher Education Supplement (1982) Rewards for 'Excellence', 30 July

Times Higher Education Supplement (1982) We are All Teachers Now, 7 May

Times Higher Education Supplement (1982) Series of 15 articles on Quality Control, 29 October – 3 December

Tuke, M.J. (1939) *A History of Bedford College for Women 1849-1937* London: Oxford University Press

Universities Quarterly (1969) Concepts of Excellence: 1969-1989, reports of a conference, January 1969 *UQ* 23 (3) (including contributions by Butterworth and Brosan, and extract from Tawney diaries)

University Grants Committee (1964) *Report of the Committee on University Teaching Methods* (Hale) London: HMSO

University Grants Committee (1948) *University Development from 1935 to 1947* London: HMSO

University Grants Committee (1953) *University Development: Report on the Years 1947 to 1952* London:HMSO

University Grants Committee (1958) *University Development 1952-1957* London: HMSO

University Grants Committee (1964) *University Development 1957-1962* London: HMSO

University of Birmingham (1972) *Report of the Review Body appointed by the Council of the University of Birmingham* Birmingham: University of Birmingham

University of London (1970) *The Future of the External System: First Report* London: University of London

University of London (1912) *The Historical Record (1836-1912)* London: University of London Press

Venables, Peter (1978) *Higher Education Developments: The Technological Universities 1956-1976* London: Faber & Faber

Warren, W.C. (1963) The right kind of higher education *The British Universities Annual 1963* London: Association of University Teachers

Watson, David (1985) The Oxford Polytechnic Modular Course 1973-83: A case study *Journal of Further and Higher Education* 9 (1)

West, J.C. (1981) The potential of periodic review for institutional renewal – The universities' view. In Manchester Polytechnic Staff Development Unit *Measuring Up to the Future: Institutional Evaluation and Renewal* Manchester: Manchester Polytechnic

Williams, G. (1971) Are more dons worse dons? *New Society* 29 April

Williams, G. and Blackstone, T. (1983) *Response to Adversity: Higher Education in a Harsh Climate* Guildford: Society for Research into Higher Education

Williams, W.F. (1979) The role of the external examiner in first degrees *Studies in Higher Education* 4 (2)

Wilson, S.G. (1923) *The University of London and its Colleges* London: University Tutorial Press

Wrigley, J. (1965) Measuring the Mind. In P. Gordon (Ed.) *The Study of Education: A Collection of Inaugural Lectures* London: Woburn Press (1980)

Young, R. (1973) *Report on the Policies and Running of Stirling University from 1966-1973* Stirling: mimeo

3

The Missing Bottom Line

Gareth Williams

This paper explores the idea of standards in higher education from the standpoint of economics. It makes six main points.

1 Discussions of 'standards' and discussions of 'quality' are often confused. There is a strong case for post-school education with a great variety of standards, especially in the area of continuing education.

2 Peer review and expert judgement are inevitably the main procedures for assessing most aspects of performance in higher education. They have the advantage of relevance, flexibility and internalization of the standards being evaluated. There are, however, dangers: they encourage conventionality and discourage innovation. Furthermore it may be difficult to avoid self-interest when allocation of resources is influenced by the judgements made.

3 Market response and expert judgement are the least arbitrary ways of allocating resources in higher education and they should be used in conjunction with one another. Experts establish criteria and markets allocate resources on the basis of these criteria.

4 The procedures by which experts themselves are selected and evaluated are critical. Staff appraisal at all levels as part of supportive staff development programmes should be a regular feature of higher education.

5 There are dangers that the definition of performance indicators and their narrow interpretation will distort the activities of higher education institutions.

6 While any serious shortage of resources almost inevitably results in low standards, for example through its effect on the quality and morale of staff, the quality of the output of higher education is a function not only of the *amount* of resources available but the way they are used. Higher education institutions can often make better use of the resources they do have: and funding mechanisms can provide incentives for them to do so. In particular there could be greater use of team teaching, with part-time staff, joint appointments, graduate students and research assistants contributing to well organized course teams.

Definition and Analogies

Simplified models and analogy have a place in the analysis of economic and social issues. Of course there are dangers when theorists attempt to apply simplistic economic models to the real world. But the opposite failing is more common – at least in Britain. Common sense and pragmatic empiricism have their dangers too. Only when the essential mechanisms responsible for the functioning of a system are properly understood can we begin to try to apply social theories with any hope of successfully avoiding the unintended consequences which are the outcome of most policy decisions. This essay starts with definitions, moves on to analogy, continues with models and then finally considers at a more practical level some of the central economic questions of the relationship between inputs and performance in higher education.

There is often ambiguity in discussions of educational standards between the idea of 'standards' and the idea of 'excellence'. Those who wish to promote or defend 'standards' are usually concerned with what they perceive to be high standards. However the concept of a standard is normatively neutral. As a noun it has six separate definitions in the Shorter Oxford Dictionary but they all include the idea of a fixed scale of reference against which other phenomena of a similiar type can be assessed. Clearly a standard has much in common with the Socratic *ideal* with which objects in the real world can be compared. In the pre-scientific past such standards were essentially arbitrary and depended on the conventions of the times. The standard yard and a standard foot have a physical existence which may originally have derived from the average stride and the average length of foot of some bygone race of giants. Since many of the various standards of length, area, volume and mass were determined independently there is a variety of forgettable conversion factors which many British school children still have to spend long hours committing to memory – 1760 yards to a mile and 112 pounds to a hundredweight, 5½ yards to a rod, pole or perch for example. As modern science developed it became necessary to adopt some coherent system of standard measures for the scientific study of the natural world. The metric system is ultimately based on the arbitrary measure that a metre is .0000001 of the distance from the pole to the equator but all other standards are derived from this, applying multiples based on the decimal system of counting – 1000 metres is one kilometre, 10,000 square metres is one hectare, 1000 cubic centimetres is one litre and so on. The system also gives rise to elegant relationships easy to remember but more difficult to comprehend – for example that a pendulum one metre long swings once every second, however strong the original impetus it is given.

Other standards are less universally accepted: the ideal is subjective in that there exists no concrete expression of the standard against which other material manifestations of the phenomena can be compared. Beauty is one such, intelligence may be another.[1] Most people imagine they can identify beautiful objects or intelligent people when they come across them, and indeed people often agree with each other about their judgements, but perceptions vary between people and they change over time. 'I know what I like' really is the last word I can say in art or literary criticism unless attempts to persuade other people to share my tastes prove to be successful, or unless they can persuade me to share theirs.

Another effect of scientific advance is that many standards which previously depended on qualitative judgement are replaced or supplemented by the development of objective measures. Colour and sound are both examples of phenomena where previous subjective judgements can now be supplemented by measures of wavelength and frequency, which permit the sharper definition of, for example, 'green' or 'middle C' that is necessary for the scientific investigation of colour blindness or tone deafness.

More obviously analogous to education are ideas of standards of conduct – 'no gentleman would behave in such a way' – and financial and monetary standards. The analogy between the gold standard and the honours degree that dominates British higher education has often been drawn. It is worth pointing out, however, that the gold standard did nothing to prevent violent fluctuations in average price levels and other major indicators of economic performance. These were determined by random factors such as the discovery of new goldfields rather than by conscious attempts at collective decision-making. A second point is that when it was subjected to severe strains in an expanded world economy the gold standard simply collapsed.

The world of sport offers several examples of different types of standard as well as several lessons for higher education, if only because sport is a popular activity and the economic health of British higher education during the next decade depends largely on its regaining some of its popular appeal.

In some sports the aim is to cover a specific distance in the shortest possible time. Apart from a few measurement problems there is no doubt about the standard of performance of any individual, and it is possible to compare the performance of today's athletes with those of the past. We can state quite confidently that the standards of achievement both of star athletes and of most ordinary joggers have risen considerably during the past quarter of a century.

Other sports are intrinsically combative and norm referenced. The only way, ultimately, of knowing whether one football team is better than another is to know if it finishes the season in a higher position in the league. There is no way of knowing whether the Liverpool of the early 1980s really was better than the great Arsenal teams of the 1930s.

In a third category of sport, that includes gymnastics or ice dancing, and such quasi-sporting events as the Eurovision Song Contest and the Leeds music festival, the standard deemed to have been reached by the performers depends ultimately on the opinion of expert judges whose assessment is based on knowledge and experience. Peer review sets the standards and decides the extent to which they have been reached. We may hypothesize that the judgments made by those who have themselves internalized all the norms of the sport or a discipline are likely to be convential. It is rare for an unconventional performer to take the prizes in any activity where decisions about what constitutes high standards depend on peer review. This raises interesting reflections about judgement of performance in applied science and technology compared with more academic subjects. In the former case the bottom line is 'Does it work?'. In the latter case final judgements are made by other specialists.

Another reflection relevant to higher education which is inspired by the use of peer review to judge sporting performance is that it is rare for the judges to be selected from amongst the protagonists. There are some observers who claim that the early dominance of the Council for National Academic Awards by university academics, inevitable as it was, had a distorting effect on academic criteria in the public sector. There are others who believe that a University Grants Committee consisting of individuals from a small number of universities is quite incapable of making objective decisions about the allocation of resources between all of them. It is also interesting to reflect that in widely popular activities such as ice skating and popular music contests, the marks of individual judges are normally made public so that the extent of agreement or disagreement can be seen. In areas of high culture such as classical music festivals and literary prizes the decision of the judges is announced collectively and only the prying of journalists enables competitors or outsiders to know the extent of the correlation of the recommendations of the individual judges. Are there echoes here of the secrecy with which the UGC has conventionally judged universities compared with the much greater openness of the National Advisory Body?

Of course most people take part in sport because they enjoy it. Athletes who need eight hours to complete the London Marathon usually feel that they have done something worthwhile even though by the highest standards of marathon running their performance is not very good. Most sport is like this: people do it because they enjoy it. They are not going for gold. However, a professional sportsperson who expects to earn a living from performing or teaching the sport must reach certain objective or competitive standards if he or she is to retain the interest of the public. The parallels with post-compulsory education are surely obvious. If students believe they obtain benefit from studying, it should not matter what standards they bring with them or ultimately what they achieve. Facilities ought to be available for them just as it is now considered desirable to provide a range of sporting activities within the reach of every individual who wants to use them. However, the paid staff of educational and sporting institutions ought to be able to demonstrate continuing high levels of competence.

On the whole the simpler is an activity the more readily applicable are objective criteria or standards: the more complex the activity the more standards depend on judgement. Running a hundred metres is quite straightforward and there is little room for dispute about who does it best. Playing a symphony is more complicated and standards of performance depend more on judgement.

There are two reasons for the subjectivity of criteria used in the evaluation of complex phenomena. One is that the phenomen is such that there is no widely agreed criterion of quality. The second is that complex phenomena are measureable along many different dimensions. In order to arrive at an overall evaluation of the quality of the performance of a symphony orchestra it is necessary to consider the performance of the instrumentalists as individuals as well as the power of the conductor to persuade them to combine together and perform complex compositions. To assess the performance of a university requires the balancing of an even wider variety of objectives and performance indicators.

In artistic and sporting activities, it is the end result that is normally deemed to indicate the standard of performance and hence the distribution of prizes. In business, the board of directors of a commercial organization is usually most interested in the bottom line showing overall profit and loss. If the management can keep that slightly ahead of the competition the Board will let them get away with almost anything. Not surprisingly, many economists find it easiest to interpret the performance of organizations when competitive markets provide the framework for the allocation of resources. Where resource allocation is based on criteria of 'worth' other than those provided by markets there are almost irresistible incentives to use simplistic formulae based on easily identifiable criteria – such as size of family, or number of rooms in the house –, or to resort to political bargaining, which ultimately means the struggle for dominance of different groups using criteria other than market performance. Military might, the strike weapon, parliamentary rhetoric, moral suasion, performance on television are in this respect all equivalent. They are all substitutes for Adam Smith's 'Invisible Hand' and are ultimately unpredictable and arbitrary in their outcomes. This is not of course to deny that some people, possibly even some deserving ones amongst them, will find such arbitrary outcomes preferable to those that result from market interactions. To many economists, however, markets have the merit of rewarding individuals and groups according to the value of their contribution to general economic welfare, while most other systems of allocation are based on an arbitrary relationship between extent and quality of inputs and the rewards obtained.

A slightly different basis for resource allocation is provided by expert judgement. 'Experts' are individuals who stand above the conflict and whose decisions have a legitimacy based on special knowledge. Only good chemists know what good chemistry is: therefore only good chemists should be involved in decisions about how much resource chemistry needs and how it should be allocated between departments of chemistry. The only problem is that no entirely satisfactory way has yet been discovered of separating the expert knowledge of any group of specialists from the special interests of that group. It is only by applying some external test, such as the employability of its graduates – or the desire of appropriately qualified students to study the subject – that it is possible to compare the competing claims of the chemistry specialists and physics specialists. The fact that in practice the chemists and the physicists often combine to claim that more resources are needed for 'science' as a whole merely obfuscates the issue.

All these ways of setting standards and assessing performance are observable within education. Objective standards of performance are widely used in the simpler educational activities. These are often, but by no means always, at the lower end of the educational spectrum. The speed with which a pupil can answer 50 simple multiplication problems or write a piece of verse 10 lines long with alternate lines rhyming are both measurable with a fair amount of objectivity.[2] So is the student's knowledge of the physiology of the digestive system or changes in statute law since 1945. There are, of course, problems in aggregating the combined score on each of these simple activities to determine an overall standard of achievement in primary school mathematics or first year law. It is even more difficult to combine scores of different individuals along several dimensions to determine the overall standard of achievement of a primary school or a department of medicine. However, these are technical problems and a system of weighting individual scores can be agreed – at least in principle.

In most parts of higher education, however, the basic elements of such criteria have not yet been found. Anyone who has had the problem of explaining to a student why an MA dissertation merits a 'C+' rather than a 'B−' is very pleased to be able to say that x,y,z have been left out or that a particular piece of analysis is wrong. More frequently, however, the real answer is that to the 'expert' some pieces of work have a 'B' feeling about them and others do not. One of the most powerful conventions of British higher education is that if three, and often two, examiners agree that a piece of work has a 'C' feel about it then the students must accept their judgement. This is not necessarily indefensible. A student essay is a complex thing. Some of the component parts can be judged in a more or less objective way against explicit standards. Statistical analysis should not contain arithmetic errors; conclusions should follow logically from premises and each stage of the argument should be laid out; there should be evidence of acquaintance with relevant previous work and so on. Provided that the examiners are subject to no other influences such expert judgement is probably the best way of passing on expertise and of selecting those students who seem to be most likely to be able to continue successfully to higher levels of education. But where resources may depend on the judgement there is a need for extra care. When students from overseas paying a full cost fee are known to want to proceed to a PhD, and when a department suspects that competitors in Britain or in the United States are willing to offer the student a place then there may be a temptation to bend the usual criteria. This type of dilemma merits careful consideration because it is not infrequent and because the issues are not clear cut. After all, if standards are really subjective why should a student not be given a chance of getting a British degree at a good university rather than a second rate degree at one of the lesser American institutions?

If the setting of standards or the evaluation of performance against these standards depends on expert judgement, the expertise of the experts is of paramount importance, but so is the way they are chosen and the influences to which they are subject in arriving at their assessments. *'Quis custodiet custodies?'* or, more appropriately, *'Quomodo custodient custodies?'* 'how are the guardians chosen?' It is the *process* by which standards are set and the *mechanisms* of evaluation that should be the focus of attention in any activity where evaluation depends upon expert judgement. This is particularly important if the result of an evaluation determines rewards or the allocation of resources, whether it be the employment available to students, the income of academic staff members, or the resources allocated to departments or institutions.

The Reynolds Report on the external examiner system and the Lindop Report on arrangements for the maintenance of quality in the public sector have both given rise to discussion about the validity of the mechanisms by which the academic standards of students are assessed and maintained. At the level of departments and institutions increasing financial stringency is resulting in more and more selectivity by funding agencies. This has led to debate about the resource allocation criteria used by the agencies and the legitimacy of the agencies themselves. By the time this paper is published the report of the Croham Committee on the UGC is likely to have appeared and it will have failed if it has not confronted the issue of how universities can reasonably be evaluated and if it has not pointed a way forward that reflects a reasonable balance between the interests of universities and the claims of society for accountability.

Standards of performance of individual members of academic staff have not been subject to such explicit consideration, although evaluations are made at least implicitly every time a new appointment is made, or someone is promoted or considered for early retirement. Staff appraisal has become an important issue in schools, and is likely to become so in higher education – not, it is hoped, in the threatening atmosphere of redundancy and termination of tenured appointments but as part of coherent staff development programmes designed with the interests of students, staff and institutions in mind.

Evaluations of performance can rely on self-monitoring by individuals or institutions, or they can be made collectively, with the system as a whole making arrangements for the evaluation of individual staff members or individual institutions. The British system of higher education has traditionally relied very largely on rigorous selection before admitting individuals to the academic profession and before allowing institutions to become self-governing, but there has been little systematic evaluation afterwards. Once an individual or institution has been admitted to membership of the 'college' the setting and regulation of standards has been achieved largely through individual self-regulation. The external examiner system operates in such a way as to buttress self-regulation rather than apply collectively agreed standards. It is not unreasonable for polytechnic directors to see this right of self-regulation as a privilege to which they ought to have as much access as the universities.

In the public sector, however, a different tradition has evolved. Institutions have always been much more directly accountable to external agencies and there have been more conscious attempts to agree collectively on criteria for the appraisal of students, staff and institutions. It is an interesting question whether the emphasis on self-regulation in the universities ultimately results in higher or lower standards than the more collective approach of the public sector. Individual self-regulation has many advantages: relevance and flexibility of response to changing circumstances; the capacity to assess performance according to many different criteria; and internalization of these criteria such that internal conflict is minimized.[3]

Nevertheless, professional self-regulation also suffers fom the major disadvantage that without effective collective or external monitoring there is often conflict between self-regulation and self-interest. Adam Smith's strictures about the academic staff of the University of Oxford in the eighteenth century are well known. 'if the authority to which he [the college fellow] is subject resides in the body corporate of which he himself is a member... they are likely to make common course to be all very indulgent to one another.... The discipline of colleges and universities is in general contrived, not for the benefit of students, but for the interests, or more properly the ease, of the masters' (Adam Smith, *Wealth of Nations* Book V). At about the same period Edward Gibbon claimed that his tutors neither gave him nor sought to give him more than one lesson. The modern university teacher has been selected far more rigorously and is less able to hide away in an ivory tower than was an eighteenth-century Oxford don. However, at the same time the vastly increased resources of the higher education system and its role as gateway to virtually all worthwhile employment has legitimately increased claims for external accountability and hence of objectively observable indicators of performance.

Resources and Performance Indicators

If there are objective or collectively agreed criteria or standards, indicators of performance present few conceptual problems.[4] There may be technical problems about how a particular standard can best be measured, or political problems about who should have access to a particular indicator, not to mention the administrative problem that individuals and institutions will manipulate any indicator in order to enhance outside perceptions of their performance. If the agreed criteria are not in practice adequate surrogates for what really need to be measured, there is the much more serious problem that actual performance may be distorted in order to achieve high scores. This is the real problem with examinations. If examinations really measured what they purported to measure the Diploma Disease could not exist.

A recent example of the distorting effect of indicators is the growth of computing in universities at a time when substantial demand for computer experts in other occupations makes it very difficult for higher education institutions to appoint high quality recruits. It is widely believed that a measure of the commitment of a university to progress and modern technology is the proportion of its resources that it devotes to information technology. There has consequently been headlong expansion of computer science departments at a time when substantial demand for computer experts in other occupations is making it very difficult for higher education institutions to make high quality appointments at the available salaries. There has been little consideration of whether a better development would not have been a wide dispersion of computing facilities and expertise across the university rather than concentrating them in special departments. A systems analyst in a sociology department is just one more negatively scoring sociologist whereas the same person in a department of computing scores plus points and attracts a higher grant for the university.

There is obviously a link between performance indicators and allocation of resources. An interesting paradox is that resources nowadays are both a reward for good performance and the means of achieving better performance. So far in this paper resources have been treated as the former. Institutions that are doing well get more resources to enable them to do even better. This is how markets allocate them and it is how funding agencies have increasingly been behaving. However, organizations that use resources usually see them as being necessary in order to be able to achieve certain levels of performance. Poor performance can thus be a justification for increased resources. This is one implication of several recent reports on schools by the Inspectorate: standards are suffering because resources are inadequate. There is no necessary contradiction between the two positions but there are frequently misinterpretations. The most important example of this conflict in higher education at present is the difference of opinion between the university sector and the public sector of higher education over the unit of resource per student. Representatives of public sector institutions point to their levels of income per student and claim that this justifies increased funding in order to bring their standards up to those of the universities. Representatives of universities imply that their high levels of expenditure reflect the higher quality of university level education, particularly through their research activities. The conflict between increased resources to improve performance and resources as a reward for high performance is likely to be one of the central issues of higher education policy for the foreseeable future. It is worth exploring in some detail.

First, it is apparent that there is *some* relationship between resources and performance. A university system that spends £500 per student per year will certainly be inferior to one which is able to spend £3000 per student per year. In order of importance the main deficiencies of the former system are likely to be:

   i   The quality of academic staff
   ii The quantity of academic staff
   iii The quality of students
   iv The pattern of subjects offered within higher education
   v The quality and quantity of plant and equipment.

The Quality of Academic Staff

In order to achieve high levels of performance, universities, polytechnics and colleges must have the resources to recruit staff who are capable of achieving the highest levels of performance in any other high-level professional activity. People who are going to be responsible for training future leaders of national life must themselves have the knowledge and understanding that would enable them to perform well in industry, commerce, public administration, the professions and the world of the arts. It is not of course necessary for all academic staff to be able to turn their hand to all of these, nor for them all to be paid like captains of industry. There are other compensations, including a formal work load that allows a varied and flexible lifestyle, esteem and prestige resulting from being seen to be doing a worthwhile job, and freedom to indulge personal peccadilloes in the broad interests of the world of scholarship. All these non-pecuniary advantages of academic life are likely to be diminished in a higher education system that is seriously under-financed.

The Quantity of Academic Staff

An under-financed system of higher education will have unfavourable staff/student ratios. Students will have little personal contact with members of staff and staff will not have time for proper preparation of their teaching. These will add to the list of reasons in the previous paragraph for low morale.

The Quality of Students

Lack of finance and poor quality staff with low morale are likely to reduce the attractiveness of higher education institutions both to able young people and to adults seeking continuing education. The example of continuing education is instructive. Much of the demand for continuing education is not spontaneous, nor is it a result of inertia, as it may be in the case of the initial higher education of school-leavers. Much of the latent demand for continuing education necessary in order to keep abreast of new technological developments and their professional and social implications will be realized only if supply is able to run ahead of demand. A post-compulsory education system that has no spare capacity for innovation and new developments is unlikely to be in a position to stimulate new demands. The problem is a particularly insidious one because the damage resulting from failure to maintain a high quality labour force becomes apparent only over a very long period. The results of failing to make proper provision for continuing education now are likely to become apparent only in the 1990s and thereafter.

The Pattern of Subjects Offered

If higher education is seriously under-financed it is likely that those areas of study which are intrinsically expensive, for example much of technology and medicine, will become divorced from the rest of the higher education system. Large enterprises will undertake a greater proportion of their own research: they will also find it worthwhile to train their own scientists and technologists. Modern knowledge will tend to be limited to those economic enterprises that are able to keep abreast of advances in knowledge.

The Quality of Equipment

In any organization that is seriously short of finance the least painful way of saving money is to delay replacement of equipment and to reduce the amount of equipment to a minimum. This means incomplete library collections and single instead of multiple copies of text books, out of date laboratories, and generally unattractive learning environments.

Detailed performance indicators are not needed in order to observe the deficiencies of a higher education institution or system that is seriously short of the resources needed to perform its essential functions. However, few higher education systems in the Western world, certainly not the British, are so short of resources. This makes it difficult to determine the point at which lack of resources begins to be the primary reason for poor standards. The quality of the output of higher education is a function not only of the amount of resources available but also of the way they are used. If the allocation of resources is not directly related to the provision of specific services there will be no strong incentive within an institution to shift resources between activities as circumstances change. Such shifts of resources are particularly difficult in institutions with participatory systems of management. Therefore it can well happen that although an institution or system is not seriously under-financed overall, the areas of growth and development certainly are.

Scarcity and Growth

It is instructive to consider each of the above areas of deficiency in the context of a higher institution or system which is not *obviously* under-financed, in the way previously assumed, but is apparently short of resources in that desirable developments are not able to take place and there are signs of strain in the recruitment of staff and students and the acquisition of new facilities.

Quality of Staff

While it is certainly true that higher education institutions need some staff who are potential high fliers in any walk of life it is not clear that all staff need to fulfil this requirement or that all the staff who do need to be full-time in the institution concerned. Team teaching and research, proper use of new information technology and intelligent use of joint appointments and part-time staff can all help education institutions to make more effective use of their most able people. It is often argued that such an approach will diminish collegiality and hence the quality of the learning enviroment, since some people will be perceived as performing more important roles than others, and will probably be paid more. The first criticism is certainly not valid. In a genuine team approach all members would see their roles as equally important and as opening up equivalent career prospects. The second may have some validity: it is unfortunately true that some skills are more in demand than others. Within limits, however, explicit income differentials based on accepted criteria that do not imply intrinsic academic worth are unlikely to be more damaging to collegiality than arrangements which allow some members of staff whose services are much in demand outside the university or polytechnic to acquire considerable external consultancy income. It is a fragile sort of collegiality that requires everyone to be treated exactly the same, regardless of their capacities and interests.

Quantity of Staff

The interpretation of staff/student ratios in higher education depends very much on the extent and form of contact between staff and students. Quantitative models can easily be developed to show the relationship between staff numbers, formal contact hours per week (or year), student numbers, their formal contact hours and the average number of students per class. One of the main reasons why staff often feel overworked despite relatively favourable staff/student ratios is that much of the teaching takes place in unnecessarily small groups. It is a basic tenet of British higher education that individual contact between students and staff is essential. I myself hold this belief very strongly. However, the effectiveness of formal lecturing is virtually independent of the number of people attending a lecture and with the development of audio-visual recordings it is now possible to repeat such teaching activities to successive groups of students with relatively little additional input. The Open University has brilliantly demonstrated some of the possibilities.

However, any simple calculation of the constituents of staff teaching loads will show that individual tutorials are extremely time consuming. A group of twenty students each requiring a one-hour tutorial every week will take twenty hours of staff time, whereas those twenty students joining five other such groups in a lecture hall will require the equivalent only of twelve minutes of formal teaching. Even if the twelve minutes require four times as much preparation time the students will still require only one hour of staff time. This is the reason why, in practice, individual tutorials now have little place in undergraduate teaching in most universities. However, individual tutorial work does not on the whole require the permanent attention of the most experienced staff. It can quite easily, and often more successfully, be done by postgraduate students, research assistants and others who are learning the academic trade. This is a large topic and not strictly relevant here. Specialists in university teaching can determine the appropriate balance between lectures, workshops and tutorials in undergraduate teaching programmes. The relevant issue is that any evaluation of relationships between resources and performance depends on the answers to such questions. Whatever the right balance of teaching activities for any individual student there is no unique way of meeting these needs. For any specified learning package some ways of delivering it are much more economical than others.

Quality of Students

The issue here is whether an under-financed higher education system need necessarily suffer from a decline in the quality of its student intake. The morale and intellectual climate of an institution is more important in attracting students than the amount of its resources. The research on the ethos of academic departments shows it is possible for departments to have very different learning enviroments with the same level of resources. This does not mean that serious under-funding does not lead to a deterioration in the academic climate available for students: it does mean that within broad limits the learning environment is a function of patterns of resource utilization as well as level.

Subject Distribution

Here the analysis is less clear. A university which does not have sufficient resources to teach medicine or engineering is unable to teach medicine or engineering. The main question which arises is whether there needs to be separate funding for such expensive activities. In practice there always has been, and it is likely to continue. The only important aspect of university resources in which there has not been differential funding in favour of the more expensive subjects is in the level of staff salaries. Even here, clinical teachers have differentials to bring them more in line with their colleagues in the National Health Service. This has not been felt appropriate in other subjects: to some extent adjustments have been made in the form of higher consultancy earnings by members of staff who have skills and knowledge which are demanded outside the institution. Such an equilibrating mechanism does not always work: some subjects, particularly some of the sciences, which require intensive input from high-level staff, do not necessarily offer large amounts of consultancy income.

Quality of Equipment

This is an area that was examined by the Jarratt Committee for the Universities and by the Audit Commission for the public sector. The general conclusion appears to be that there is scope for improved performance in purchasing arrangements and in the management and utilization of equipment through central services.

Conclusion

The purpose of the above discussion is to show that there is no hard and fast relationship between level of resource provision and the performance of institutions, departments or individuals. This makes the management of publicly financed institutions a delicate art, particularly when the political climate is one of financial stringency. An institution which shows that it is able to cope with reductions in expenditure without doing irretrievable damage to the quality of its education may be thought to have been previously operating inefficiently. This discourages efforts to adapt to financial stringency. It is likely to be more rewarding to demonstrate the damage done in the areas where this is obvious than to attempt to shift resources out of activities where further improvements in efficiency are still possible.

Most serious economic analyses of the finance of higher education ultimately come to the conclusion that there is a choice between centralized bureaucratic control, with resources and tasks centrally allocated to institutions and individuals, and a diversified system with a variety of sources of finance each corresponding to particular sets of institutional functions. In broad terms the former is the model favoured in much of continental Europe and the latter the one in the United States. I have no doubt that if we wish to maintain the traditional British independence of higher education institutions the latter route is the only viable one. Only a university that in the last analysis is able to ignore UGC advice or a polytechnic that can afford to turn down a NAB allocation can really claim academic independence. The strength of United States higher education derives mainly from its great variety (of standards as of everything else) and from the enormous amounts raised from a wide variety of public and private agencies, even in many public sector institutions. An institution that is dependent on a single source of funds is ultimately dependent on that agency for the criteria it uses for admitting students, for awarding qualifications, for the research it does, for the staff it appoints and for the subjects it teaches.

The last ten years have shown that British higher education can wield little power when it tries to play a political or collective bargaining game. At the same time there is no doubt that many of its activities, if performed well, do have considerable economic value to students, to government and to the world of industry and commerce. To respond to demands from such a variety of groups would make the life of administrators much more difficult. But ultimately it would lead to a healthier higher education system. The notion that high academic standards depend only on academics having the freedom and the resources to do their own thing in their own way is one of the many myths of the 1960s that provides little guidance as we approach the 1990s.

Notes

1   It is not a concern of this paper to examine the concept of intelligence, important as it is in considering many aspects of educational standards. Recent developments in the idea of intelligence do, however, highlight some of the problems in examining standards in education. Home computers can now do in a fraction of a second all the problems it took me at least an hour to do in my 11+ examination and they can in a real sense *learn* how to improve their performance. It is possible to define a standard of such artificial intelligence in virtually the same way as standard units of electricity are expressed. However, many psychologists now tell us that this is not really intelligence at all. I am not sure whether this shifting of the goalposts corresponds to the shift from Newtonion to Einsteinian physics or whether it is a habit peculiar to the soft sciences.

2   Of course the use that is made of the information is another matter.

3   An example of the conflicts generated by attempts to enforce external criteria on higher education institutions is the reaction within university departments of education to the proposals by the Council for the Accreditation of Teacher Education for certain standards in initial teacher education. Although these criteria would probably be supported by any honest teacher educator, the fact that they have come from outside has generated considerable hostility.

4   The many problems in identifying and measuring the outputs of higher education have been well known in the economics of education literature for twenty years but largely ignored in the practical world until very recently. There are useful discussions in Verry and Davies (1976), Bear (1974), Archibald (1974) and Johnson (1974).

References

Archibald, G.C. (1974) On the measurement of inputs and outputs. In Lumsden (1974)

Bear, D.V.T. (1974) The university as a multi-product firm. In Lumsden (1974)

Lumsden, K. (1974) *Efficiency in Universities: the La Paz Papers* Elsevier

Johnson, H. (1974) The university and the social welfare: A taxonomic exercise. In Lumsden (1974)

Verry, D. and Davies, B. (1976) *University Costs and Outputs* Elsevier

4

The UGC and Standards

M.L. Shattock

The creation of the universities preceded that of the University Grants Committee, and when the UGC was set up it did not see its role as maintaining standards but as acting as a somewhat unorthodox piece of machinery to channel government funds to deserving universities and colleges. In time the machinery justified itself to such an extent that though remaining constitutionally unorthodox within Whitehall it became the most widely approved and envied method, within international university circles, of distributing state monies to universities. But the UGC never took on the 'quality control' aspects embodied in the constitutions of the University Grants Commission of India, the UGC in New Zealand or the Nigerian Universities Commission, where each body was formally charged to maintain standards in university education, nor has it ever embarked on academic programme reviews like many state co-ordinating boards in the USA. The UGC's role has always been primarily financial, and its use of the block grant system for the allocation of recurrent funds has essentially passed the maintenance of standards issue down to the institutions themselves. In Britain, from the earliest Charters, it has been the university examining institutions which have been responsible for the award of degrees and even where a period of 'tutelage' was required before new foundations could confer their own degrees, the external bodies were universities rather than external statutory bodies like the Council for National Academic Awards. It is the institutions either collectively or individually which have been responsible for maintaining the standards of degrees through their own mechanisms of self-criticism and by the use of external examiners. In research, standards are maintained by the operation of the 'free market' of publication or by the exercise of peer review through the research councils.

The UGC thus has no formal role in these matters, but its influence on standards has been pervasive throughout the British university system. Primarily this influence has operated at the system level, and has only taken on an institutional or departmental dimension when comparisons have been necessary across the university system as a whole. The UGC's international reputation is based on its effectiveness in distributing government funds, the guarantee it provides for institutional autonomy, and its success as a 'buffer' or 'intermediary' standing between government and universities. Too little attention has in fact been paid to the UGC's role in maintaining the standards, and standing, of the British university system, the ways in which this has been achieved, the benefits and failings of the British approach, and the UGC's successes and occasional failures. Within the limitations of space available this chapter will seek to examine the UGC's role in the main-tenance of standards, first in historical context and then in relation to the most searching tests of its ability to make academic judgements in the 1980-81 and 1985-86 resource allocation exercises.

Any consideration of the University Grants Committee must start from a recognition of its longevity and of the continuity in the procedures it employs. In some cases these procedures pre-date the UGC itself and derive from the advisory committees that preceded it. Thus the formal UGC institutional Visitation, dignified at various times in the UGC's history with much pomp and academic significance appears to derive from the nineteenth-century Inspections carried out on any educational institution in direct receipt of government funds. Such inspections were necessarily impressionistic, to put it optimistically, in regard to educational matters, but could be searching over matters of finance and maintenance of grounds and property. Certainly such visitations were of considerable importance from well before the turn of the century (Shinn 1983). The quinquennial funding system stretched back to 1908 and although a regular sequence was not established until 1924-25 the linkage between visitations, UGC advice to Government, Government response and UGC distribution of funds on a five-year time scale, became an essential element in the UGC system until brought abruptly to an end in 1974. There can be no doubt that the continuity of such procedures and, after 1919, the regular publication of UGC reports and of university financial and student returns (in standard format) and the informality and familiarity of dealings between the chairmen of the Committee and individual vice-chan-cellors, combined to create an atmosphere of clubby benevolence which survived unaffected the re-constitution of the Committee's membership and terms of reference in 1946. Indeed between 1919 and 1964 the UGC had only four chairmen, and of their five successors three have been vice-chancellors and have, therefore, been drawn from the same inner circle of the higher education establishment. Similarly the secretariat, at least up until the transfer of the Committee to the DES, maintained the continuity of membership and style that was fostered within the Treasury, and to a considerable extent this characteristic ethos was bequeathed to their successors.

The UGC of the inter-War years took a relatively uncomplicated view of its remit. It saw the universities at the top of an educational pyramid: 'Universities first and above all, stand for quality; they aim at providing the highest type of education attainable.' Below them, but on the next rung, were to be found the local technical colleges administered and funded by the Board of Education and the local authorities (UGC 1925). The chief expression of this view in practice was in respect to the admission of colleges on to the UGC grant list. Here, although the words 'academic quality' or 'high quality' often occur in the UGC's records, the evidence suggests that the admission of Reading, Southampton and Nottingham to the grant list was very much dependent on the extent they could rely on private funding, the amount of local support, the degree to which autonomy was already present in matters of governance, and the size of the staff and student body. Nottingham, for example, lacked UGC support for its Charter for some time not because of the standard of its teaching and research but because the Committee was dissatisfied with the over strong element of lay control. Applications from Leicester, Hull, Exeter, and, more emphatically, Bradford, Heriot-Watt, Lampeter, Croydon and Huddersfield, were resisted because of their insufficient external finance and their inability to measure up to the overall criteria of university status described in the quotation above (Shinn 1983) To the UGC, private funding and absence of debt spelt institutional autonomy, and autonomy, when combined with size of plant and student numbers, was almost synonymous with academic quality. Some thirty years later the UGC was seeking assurances from cities and counties aspiring to found new universities not about the academic programmes envisaged but about the adequacy of local financial support and the provision of a site of a minimum of 200 acres.

Curiously neither of these criteria seem to have played a great part in the approval for the foundation of the University College of North Staffordshire (Keele), which was 'sold' to the UGC and to the Treasury on the experimental nature of its academic programme, in spite of the opposition of the Vice-Chancellors' Committee. Their objection was spelt out as follows:

> There is no prospect of gain from new institutions which would justify the diversion to them of human and material resources which could be employed with greater advantage to the national interest in enabling the existing university institutions to fulfil the programmes on which they have already embarked. (CVCP 1946)

This was the kind of objection which, on its record before and since, the UGC might have been expected to have fully supported. The printed evidence does not make clear why the UGC made what can only be described as an aberrant decision not to oppose the College's application for a Charter. Was it the length of time the application had been on the table, was it the intervention of Hugh Dalton, then Chancellor of the Exchequer, was it the personal and moral qualities of the Rev. Thomas Horwood, the leader of the Labour group on the Stoke City Council (which might have appealed to the then Chairman of the UGC), was it the presence of R.H. Tawney on the UGC's membership (as he would have supported the adult education side of the case), or was it simply the passion and commitment which the sponsors demonstrated for a radical departure from the traditional approach to university education in an unfashionable part of the country? Whatever the reason, it is clear that the proposed experimental academic programme was a decisive factor, and that in supporting it the UGC was parting company with established university opinion, as represented by the Vice-Chancellors' Committee, which took the view that: 'The suggested basis [of academic studies] seems to provide not a new type of University institution but a new type of Technical College' (CVCP 1946).

Whether the experiment can, with the benefit of hindsight, be regarded as a success may be open to question, though the ideas that launched Keele were widely reinvoked in the case of the new universities ten years later. The

UGC's decision to go ahead with the project must be seen as the Committee stepping outside its normal persona, which on the whole was cautious, pragmatic and closely aligned with general university opinion. In a somewhat comparable case some three years later the UGC faced a Government proposal that a new technical university should be founded, and responded with a recommendation that, on the contrary, Imperial College should be strengthened, on the grounds that 'the isolation of an institution confined to a narrow range of subjects [would be] unfavourable to the highest attainment' (UGC 1957).

Throughout its history the UGC, while strongly upholding the universities' autonomy, has tended to emphasize the homogeneity of the system. It is perhaps inevitable that a central bureaucracy, armed with the power of the purse, should unconsciously guide individual institutions down a common path and it would only be proper to acknowledge that the UGC's intention has always been to encourage institutional individuality. Thus on the academic side the UGC has, until recently, declined to reveal such criteria or formulae which it has developed to assist in resource allocation because of a concern that they would become a substitute for the exercise of discrimination and individual judgement at the institutional level. But the system of resource allocation, both capital and recurrent, the use of full-time student equivalents as the 'currency' for recurrent grant, the categorization of student targets into Arts, Science and Medical, the emphasis on first degree and postgraduate study, and the use of norms to control the proportion of senior to junior academic staff or the allocation of capital grant, have all had the effect of providing a university model that is easier for universities to fit into than to depart from. The model has been severely criticized by Lord Beloff, who accused the UGC of imposing 'the dead hand of conformity' on to the university system (Beloff 1967), and by the Institute of Economic Affairs, which suggested that 'the UGC designed originally to preserve the independence of the universities has become an agency for their enfeeblement' (Ferns 1982). Whether or not such criticisms are fair it must be recognized that one of the inevitable consequences of the UGC's maintenance of consistent standards of resource allocation, and of its concern for the overall effectiveness of the university system, from which both the system and the institutions have benefited, is that the system suffers from a tidyness and a homogenity which has discouraged innovation outside the conventional university model.

Most of the administrative pressures for homogenity have stemmed more from Whitehall or the Public Accounts Committee, operating through the UGC, than from the UGC itself (Shattock and Berdahl 1984). Nevertheless the UGC must be judged guilty in giving insufficient sympathy to attempts to break out of the conventional university model. Thus it declined to take over the Royal College of Art or the Cranfield Institute of Technology in the mid-1960s because it said that their roles were distinct from the traditional university model. In the 1980s it discouraged the idea that the Open University should come under the UGC. In 1964 it recommended, against the advice of the Robbins Committee, that the colleges of education should not be transferred from the public sector to the universities, and in 1966 it discouraged the Universities of Sussex and Warwick from merging with or developing special collaborative arrangements with their local colleges of technology. It accepted the transfer of the colleges of advanced technology to university status but took no serious steps to encourage them to maintain a separate 'mission' from the rest of the system and indeed supported their aspirations to model themselves increasingly on existing university patterns. In effect it stood aside while substantial changes occurred outside the university system and, whilst preserving the 'standards' of the universities, it served to isolate them, and inhibit them from embarking on radical new departures.

Moreover, in emphasing its concern for the university system as a whole the UGC was forced to act against the interests of individual institutions. Thus when in 1972 the DES cut the UGC's proposed postgraduate target for the system as a whole by 40% the UGC allocated the remaining numbers in such a way that all universities got a share, irrespective of the relative quality of the programmes offered. Cambridge suffered (and complained) while Salford benefited. Nine years later some of those decisions had to be sharply reversed. Throughout the 1970s, when the unit of resource was falling, the UGC was facing extremely difficult decisions as to whether to strengthen further the most successful institutions at the expense of others or whether, as it normally chose to do, to spread its resources thinly across the system as a whole so as to ensure that all universities had academic facilities at an acceptable level. In maintaining the 'standards' of the system as a whole it had to deny resources to some institutions which could individually have used them to raise their own 'standards'. In a very real sense the 'good' became sometimes the enemy of the 'best'.

By the mid-1970s the UGC had been highly successful in maintaining the standards of the university system, judging by the international respect that the university system, and indeed the UGC itself, was accorded. The cost of this success was that the system had failed to diversify; indeed its homogeneity was increased by a network of university-created agencies like the Universities Central Council on Admissions (UCCA), the Standing Conference on University Entrance (SCUE), the University Council for Non-teaching Staff (UCNS) and others. Most universities were locked into a 1960s mould from which they showed few signs of breaking out. Throughout the 1970s funding became progressively less generous and, with the collapse of the quinquennial system and the reversion to the uncertainties of annual budgeting, the UGC system, whilst retaining the outward bureaucratic forms, had fallen into considerable disrepair. Between 1979 and 1985, however, the UGC has shown remarkable resilience under extreme pressure from budgeting reductions imposed by Government, severe criticisms by some universities, and widespread public questioning of the performance of the Committee and of the university system. This period has not seen the UGC encouraging radical departures from the traditional university model, though some movements at the margin offer promise for the future. But it has illustrated that when faced with severe financial retrenchment the UGC has been able to take determined and, in the university world, very controversial decisions to protect the academic base of the university system. No one could argue that the operation in 1981-5 was completed wholly successfully or that its 1986-90 successor will be a model of perfection, but against the concurrent background of large-scale, system-wide reductions in the coal, steel and textile industries, to quote but three examples, it is impossible not to conclude that the UGC has conducted its contraction with less fuss and greater effectiveness.

One measure of the scale of the UGC's task was the size of the reduction of resources available to the university system. Between 1970 and 1980 it calculated that the unit of resource had fallen by 10 per cent. The 1981 cuts led to a further reduction of 15 per cent and on present forecasts a further 10 per cent reduction can be anticipated for the period 1986 to 1990. Over the period 1970 to 1980 the UGC simply passed on the fall in the unit of resource to the universities, making what marginal adjustments in recurrent grants seemed appropriate to individual institutions' particular needs. In the post-1974 years, after the breakdown of the quinquennial system, it was more concerned to mitigate the effects of high inflation and re-establish some longer-term financial horizon than to undertake any major assessment of the basis on which it was funding the institutions. The UGC could have continued this approach in the period after 1980 but it is a measure of its sense of responsibility to the university system that it chose to review and re-allocate resources rather than continue to weaken the system as a whole by passing the cuts on pro-rata. In fact even if the Government's promise of level funding for the system had been honoured (after the once and for all withdrawal of funding for overseas students) the UGC had decided to undertake such a review because it diagnosed 'genuine symptoms of malaise in the university system' (Parkes 1982a). Once it became clear, however, that further cuts were to be imposed, the UGC weighed 'a three month struggle to get a three year financial horizon covering the whole period of contraction' (Parkes 1982a) so that it could carry out its review of the system with a full knowledge of the scale of the reduction planned. The UGC was publicly concerned about 'the disorder and diseconomies in many universities' (UGC 1984a) caused by such abrupt changes in funding levels which 'threatened the orderly development of the system' (UGC 1981b).

By 1984-85, towards the end of the funding period, it became clear to the UGC that the Government was planning a further round of cuts, less severe than those of 1981 but, at a level of 2 per cent per annum, double the rate for the 1970s. This prompted a decision to undertake a further review of the system and a further re-assessment of the allocation of recurrent grant. Thus in a period of five years the UGC has carried out two major reviews of the university system. It is too early to offer a proper assessment of the effects of the reviews, or to judge the extent to which the UGC has been successful in maintaining the quality of the system, but a comparison of the two very different approaches to the exercise offers considerable insights into the way a central resource allocation agency, albeit one almost entirely reflecting academic priorities and prejudices, can re-shape a university system in a period of acute financial stringency in order to preserve or enhance the quality of the system at the expense of lower quality institutions.

In its 1981 exercise the UGC had two, sometimes competing, fundamental criteria: the first was that it wanted every institution 'to be good at *some* things' (Parkes 1980); the second was that, bearing in mind 'the national economic interest', it wanted to see a shift of student numbers towards physical science, engineering, technology, mathematics/computer science, some aspects of biological sciences and business studies (UGC 1981b). Both criteria were directed towards providing 'a healthy, flexible and innovative university system' (Parkes 1980). At the outset the UGC considered three strategies for dealing with the cuts: closing some institutions; moving to a tiered system with, at the top, a group of institutions liberally funded and staffed for research and a second tier primarily devoted to teaching; or applying the cuts pro-rata to each institution (UGC 1981b). The last alternative was ruled out, for the reasons given above. The closure and tiering options were also rejected, for reasons which reflect very clearly the way the UGC regarded the university system. The closure option, for example, seemed an obvious solution to some of us outside the UGC. Closures of colleges of education had already taken place in the public sector of higher education, and, while there were obvious questions of fairness to students on course or in the admissions pipeline, such problems could be resolved. There were, however, serious technical problems: closure of a university would take five or six years to accomplish and the administrative problems and costs would be formidable and would continue well beyond the period in which the cuts had to take effect; to make a significant financial impact the UGC would have to close one of the large civic universities, but none was conceivably on anyone's 'hit-list' and all had medical schools which were contributing to nationally planned medical manpower requirements; closure of one of the smaller institutions would have made no significant contribution to the cuts. Moreover university closures would raise serious political problems, and the Secretary of State later made it clear that, while he would 'listen to advice' from the UGC on closing a university, his decision would depend on whether it would 'be better for the quality and standards of higher education as a whole' (Joseph 1981). This took the decision outside the UGC's remit and made it clear that political acceptance of a closure policy was unlikely.

But in fact the UGC had other grounds for rejecting both the closure and the tiering options, which the Chairman described later to the Parliamentary and Scientific Committee. Universities, he said, varied from 1:3 to 3:1 in the ratio of science and technology to arts but some of the applied science in the 1:3 institutions was very valuable as was some of the arts in the 3:1 institutions. Looked at from the student choice point of view and ignoring the extremes of education and medicine (the one low and the other high), the average 'A' level entry scores differed by only about seven points on a fifteen point scale between individual universities. Within universities with a low average 'A' level score there were some courses with very high points and vice versa. The institutional 'A' level pecking order was often different to an order based on research. There were some universities where all the indicators were positive, but none where none were. 'Even our weakest universities had, at this level of cut, sufficient parts worth preserving' (Parkes 1982a). But, if the UGC was not to proceed to close universities or to tier them, some system-wide reduction had to be made even before the strengths and weaknesses of institutions could be tackled. The fall in the unit of resource always looked more serious to the UGC than to individual institutions, mainly because it was a crucial element in UGC negotiations with the DES and the Treasury, but it amounted to no more than a marginal issue for individual institutions. The Chairman of the UGC had been considerably exercised by the 3 per cent student number overshoot across the system in 1978-79 and accused universities, somewhat unwisely, 'of scraping the barrel in the belief that money follows numbers' (Parkes 1980). An obvious first move, therefore, in confronting the cuts was to impose a 5 per cent cut in student numbers on the system as a whole.

Concern about student numbers was symptomatic of the wider problem the UGC had to face in the 1980-81 exercise, namely that twenty years of growth in higher education had created a momentum within institutions which was seemingly impossible to check, even when the resources were no longer available to support it. It was this inability, outside the UGC, to recognize the radical nature of the universities' change of fortunes which led the Chairman of the UGC to address the assembled Vice-Chancellors in such colourful terms in October 1980. But in that speech he also set out some of the crucial problems for the position of the UGC and the universities in the new situation. In a period of expansion the system could be steered 'almost entirely covertly' by 'selective addition', but in contraction 'steerage necessarily becomes more overt'. Instead of adhering to 'a philosophy of laissez faire with regard to the development of all but the most expensive subjects', the UGC wanted universities to concentrate on their strengths and not 'to support pallid growths which are now never likely to reach maturity'. If universities were unable to take such painful decisions themselves the UGC in its new 'dirigiste' role would feel bound to assist them (Parkes 1980). Six months later the UGC wrote to universities putting forward an additional argument, that in order to maintain the ability of the system to foster new developments or to reinforce existing work, the range of subjects available at some universities would have to be reduced and there would be consequential implications for the conduct of postgraduate study and research in some fields (UGC 1981a).

We must now examine the machinery which the UGC had available to carry out the task it had set itself. Initially the UGC launched what became known as 'the dialogue' exercise whereby each university was asked to prepare plans based on a 2 per cent increase in funding, level funding, or a 5 per cent decrease. This was followed by an interview at the UGC's offices in Park Crescent. Although the Chairman was later to claim that the results of this exercise was 'the base for the whole of the Committee's work' (UGC 1981b), it had in fact been carried out before the full realization of the magnitude of the cuts involved had been perceived either by the UGC or the universities, and the 5 per cent decrease, ignored by many universities, was to turn out to be an optimistic hypothesis for the majority.

A far more important element in the process was played by the UGC's subject committees. The UGC had had subject committees of various kinds since 1921, when it had set up the first Technology Sub-Committee (Shinn 1983). For forty years, except for the Medical Sub-Committee, which until 1981 acted semi-autonomously, none of the many subject committees was anything but a standing committee meeting now and again when required. In 1964, however, Wolfenden reformed the system to create a network of committees which he described as his 'eyes and ears' into the university system (Carswell 1986). In 1980-81 there were eleven such committees, each chaired by a member of the main Committee, spread on a 7:4 science:arts basis, the higher concentration on the science side reflecting the more costly and specialist nature of the subjects involved. These committees were given a broad remit of responsibility for their subjects across the university system and were expected to develop their own programme of university visits and other consultations. If one were seeking the conventional structures whereby the UGC might be expected to maintain 'standards' in the system it would be in the operation of the subject committee system, and in a notably lukewarm passage in its 1984 Strategy Advice the UGC did concede such a role to the sub-committees (UGC 1984b).

In practice, however, the history of the subject committee system had not been an especially happy one and there is evidence that during the 1970s their performance had been very variable in their approach to universities: some mounted mini-visitations; some held occasional regional conferences; some seemed unwilling to move out of Park Crescent itself. A particular failing of many of the committees was their lack of follow up of the subject-based advice contained in the main Committee's Memoranda of Guidance to universities issued in 1967, 1973 and 1977 to accompany statements of recurrent grant. The example of Russian studies is perhaps the most notable: in each Memorandum the UGC had expressed concern about the proliferation of small courses and departments in Russian, with no discernable result. The 1979 UGC Report on Russian, which reviewed the state of Russian in universities, contained a statement on the need for the rationalization of small subject provision which could serve as a text for the UGC's approach to this aspect of the maintenance of standards in the 1980-81 exercise:

58. A large number of small or very small teaching groups leads to obvious waste, both financial and academic. Financially it is cheaper to house and service, say, six teachers in one place than two groups of three in separate places. Moreover, duplication of basic library materials can be avoided, either with a consequent net saving or, alternatively, with a better use of the aggregated funds to secure a wider range of more specialised material, particularly for research. Above all, more satisfactory provision could be made for teaching and research in larger units.

59. On the academic side the advantages of larger, but fewer, teaching groups are:
   (a)   courses of wider scope, with a more attractive range of options and a greater number of teachers in contact with each individual student;
   (b)   a more favourable atmosphere for research, more diverse supervision of postgraduate students, and the creative interaction between teaching and research which is so prominent a feature of Arts disciplines;
   (c)   closer links between language and non-language work and greater opportunities for the permeation of Russian ideas within a University;
   (d)   better library facilities;
   (e)   improved opportunities for study leave, since at present much leave is obtained at additional cost through temporary replacements. We attach particular importance to this in a static or contracting University system;
   (f)   greater effective weight (or less vulnerability) in the local allocation of resources, and the possibility of academic leadership from an

established Chair. We note that of the current forty teaching groups only seventeen have one or more Chairs, some of which are personal Chairs;

(g) more resources, both teaching and administrative, to support the University's extra-mural teaching, and the development of links with schools and relations with outside bodies. (UGC 1979)

What the Report was asserting was the UGC's responsibility for protecting the standards and the development of a subject, if necessary, at the expense of the interests of institutions and staff. It was unfortunate that the UGC did not give wider emphasis to its proper concern for the way academic developments had often taken place in the past. Any such emphasis would, of course, have reflected on previous UGC performance. The Report, which recommended the closure of courses or departments at six institutions, the possible phasing out of Russian-based studies at seven others and the freezing of any staff vacancies in six others, was greeted with a chorus of predictable protest, and the essential rationale of the exercise became lost in a furore about the Report's accuracy in selecting particular departments for closure.

As back up to the work of the sub-committees the UGC also consulted the Research Councils, the Royal Society, the British Academy, employers' organizations and the Chief HMI. Of these the most important were the Research Councils which could provide much more detailed information on individual disciplines or sub-disciplines within each subject group than the UGC's rather broad-brush data which had been gathered historically for reporting purposes. A major contribution by the Research Councils was the provision of a list of departments which they felt warranted special protection.

The Chairman later gave a clear indication of the priority which he attached to the subject rather than the institutional basis for the Committee's approach. 'Students', he said, 'selected the subject of their choice first and then took a decision about which university to apply to not the other way round.' Senates and Councils might be concerned with institutional values but 'we have made no value judgements about institutions at all. We have worked on a subject basis' (Parkes 1982a). Each sub-committee was provided with data about 'A' level scores, unit costs, distribution of academic staff, their ages and the relevant student numbers, as well as the material submitted by each university, and was given a target for student numbers, and asked to rank universities according to academic criteria. Because of the priority accorded to subjects over institutions, the sub-committees had first go at handling the cuts, and their conclusions were considered by a small Resources Sub-Committee. It is no secret that in spite of the Chairman's statement that 'the UGC are much more interested in subject provision across the whole system and our interest in institutions is secondary' (Parkes 1982a), the conflation of the sub-committees' first round of recommendations into institutional profiles caused the Resources Sub-Committee to draw back because the effect of the recommendations on some institutions would have been so catastrophic. The actual decisions conveyed in the UGC's letter of 1 July, drastic as some appeared to be to the outside world, represented, therefore, a watering down of the original assessments by the sub-committees.

An important element, not so far discussed, was the targets fixed for each of the sub-committees. One of the two basic criteria referred to above was to increase the science, technology and management studies component in the university system. Strategic decisions of this kind were made doubly difficult because of the unit costs of the subjects involved. The first problem was medicine. Throughout the 1970s medical education had been protected from the decline in the unit of resource for the system as a whole and the overall intake target had been determined by Government in order to conform with a nationally planned doctor output. Medical and dental places cost about six times as much as an arts place and about twice as much as a science/ engineering and technology place. The UGC concluded that the priority previously so slavishly accorded to medicine could no longer be continued, but even the decision to peg the intake at 1979-80 levels produced a 5 per cent growth. Eventually the UGC rejected the idea of closing one particular 'highly prestigious but highly expensive provincial medical school' in order to produce savings to avoid making cuts elsewhere. Similar, though less fraught, decisions had to be taken over each sub-committee area. In engineering and technology a 3 per cent increase was agreed. It is illustrative of the sub-committees' approach to their task that the Technology Sub-Committee in its assessment of engineering and technology courses both favoured broader degrees, which it saw as promoting greater flexibility in adapting to new technology, and took into account the difficulty for sandwich courses in finding industrial placements and the overlap with the polytechnics. In the final result about half of the forty-four institutions which had engineering received an increase, about half were given unchanged numbers and two were required to reduce numbers. Unfortunately for the reception of these decisions the UGC worked on 1979-80 data and the result of some increase in intakes in 1979-80 was that the universities, given an increase, saw it as a pegging of their intakes, and those who were unchanged found it to be a reduction. Decisions, therefore, which looked significant to the UGC in expensive subjects like medicine and engineering looked modest outside and yet, because of the costs involved, compelled major reductions in arts and social studies. In education, where numbers were linked to teaching manpower requirements the UGC was unable to issue targets because the DES had yet to complete its calculations of need, and targets had to be issued later in the year.

The result of the UGC's review of the university system are well known. Some universities, notably Salford, Aston, Bradford, Stirling and Keele suffered in percentage terms very severe cuts of more than 25 per cent, others like Loughborough and Bath emerged relatively unscathed. In every university the differential nature of the decisions between subjects, which were described in somewhat foggy prose in the accompanying letter, caused acute problems of internal decision-making. Immediate reactions were predictably hostile. At Aston where the Senate had been meeting when the letter was issued 'we suddenly had brought home to us what good energetic students must feel like to get grudging thirds.... Colleagues whose whole working lives had been invested in the university looked as if their moral worth had been questioned... and it had' (Bell 1981). In Government and in the country at large there was acute surprise that the UGC had taken such selective decisions and the CVCP opened a campaign to persuade the DES both to produce additional funding to cover redundancy costs and to extend the period of run down.

We are not concerned here with the political and other fall-out or with the longer-run consequences of the UGC's decisions, for the UGC as well as for the university system. It is, however, worth examining the basis for and the main criticisms of the UGC's strategy. The first strategic question relates to the subject-based approach and to the low priority given to institutional profiles. Even accepting the academic integrity of the subject-based approach it is difficult not to believe that the UGC undervalued institutional character, and an institution's ability to manage its resources, promote innovation, maintain flexibility and sustain research. To look at the university system simply as a federation of subject groups is to miss an essential element, the diversity of institutions and their ability on occasion, through unique combinations of subjects or particular chacteristics, to be better than the sum of their parts might suggest. Had institutional factors been given more weight a number of considerations might have come into focus.

One effect of the cuts was so greatly to reduce the size of some institutions as to make them vulnerable in any future cuts exercise. In the 1960s the minimum economically variable size for a British university urged upon them by the UGC was 3000 students while, more recently, the Williams Report on Australian higher education suggested 4000. The result of the 1981 exercise was that twelve universities were condemned to have less than 2500 home students by 1984-85, and were probably, therefore, committed to higher unit costs and a greater element of vulnerability if the prospect of a decline in student numbers materialized in the 1990s. Another aspect was location. As a number of Members of Parliament pointed out in a series of Commons debates, some of the universities most severely cut were in areas of high unemployment and industrial decline where they might be expected to play a particularly significant role in the local economy. Some universities were in close proximity to one another but rationalization between institutions was never comprehensively considered.

A further criticism which can be levelled at such heavy reliance on the subject-based approach is that the machinery to make it effective was not available. The sub-committees had been variable in their performance in the 1970s and their recommendations were often not based on first-hand information. Thus Aston was recommended to close its Biological Sciences Department when the relevant sub-committee had failed to visit the University for a decade. Stirling produced a full statement of its interchanges with UGC and its sub-committees since 1971 which contained convincing evidence to support its contention that 'although the UGC's advice over the period lacked total consistency and in some instances is very much at variance with their latest advice, the University has generally accepted the UGC's guidance and has implemented their advice in a constructive way' (Stirling 1982). The UGC gave detailed advice with an often spurious precision which it simply did not have the data to support. Two universities were asked to collaborate in a particular field when one did not even teach it; statistics, applied mathematics and computer science were confused and recommendations for closures and transfers had to be unscrambled; courses were recommended for closure which had already been closed. Because each chairman seemed to have been left to transcribe his own sub-committee's recommendations without editorial guidance the CVCP produced a concordat which illustrated a bizarre and confusing range of phrases of varying firmness which served to render debate within institutions that much more difficult.

A further difficulty lay in the definitions of subjects which the UGC sub-committee structure impelled it to adopt, which affected the allocations in complex ways. Subjects like medicine and education benefited because of the relative homogeneity of the field but sub-committee covering areas like arts or social studies had much more disparate fields to tackle. Inevitably they lacked expertise in all of them and there was a danger that a particular individual could exercise a disproportionate influence. This especially affected classics, religious studies, sociology and drama where closures and rationalizations were extensively recommended. In other fields the subject boundaries adopted by the UGC did not match what was happening on the ground. Accountancy, for example, fell to the social studies sub-committee while business studies had its own, although in many universities accountancy and business management were taught by the same department. As a result, the two subjects could be asked simultaneously to contract and expand in the same letter. The Chairman defended the sub-committees and their performance in two ways: arguing that 'senior people in a given discipline have a pretty good and up-to-date idea of what is happening to their speciality in all universities' (Parkes 1981), and that the absence of visitations could not be regarded as significant because what a visitation 'does not do and was never intended to do is to provide us with information in relation to an individual university, and only rarely in relation to an individual department' (Parkes 1982a). Neither defence is convincing. The UGC's decisions had significant effects on the lives of individuals and for the belief to be abroad that those decisions were taken in a less than fully professional way did the UGC no good. As for the visits, whatever the UGC thought, the institutions thought they were visitations, and prepared accordingly, and took careful note of the points made by the chairman in his summing up at the end of them.

The post-1981 decisions debate threw up another range of comments which went to the heart of the UGC system. Unfortunately those who made them could be accused of special pleading and the comments tended not to make much headway in the academic world. Essentially they concentrated on the UGC's over-conventional view of the university system and on its inability to recognize and reward diversity. The most comprehensive case was put forward by Professor Marquand of Salford. He suggested that the technological universities were 'growth points to be nurtured: small, hopeful candles of innovation and practicality, lighting up a university world dominated by the conventional, the stuffy and the precious'. In the 1960s the UGC felt we could afford 'the luxury of a new kind of university' but now 'we must draw in our horns and concentrate on doing the old familiar things in the old familiar way'. He concluded that 'the UGC has proved that universities are too serious to be left to the professors' (Marquand 1981). The argument was taken up by Professor Ashworth, the new Vice-Chancellor of Salford who claimed that the UGC was not structured to take into account institutional diversity and that the subject committees 'have tended to favour the convergence of the separate universities... so that institutional diversity both in subject range and I suspect "others" has diminished' (Ashworth

1982). Another variation was to argue that the UGC had paid insufficient attention to the employment record of graduates from certain universities (for example Aston and Salford, which appeared at the top of *The Financial Times* employment league table) or had paid too much attention to the 'A' level entry scores and not enough to the value added by those universities which attracted less well qualified students but graduated them in good grades.

The strength of these criticisms depends on the extent to which certain universities had consistently pursued priorities which were different from those of the main body of the university system. It is likely that this cherished 'separate mission' was exaggerated in the heat of the argument about the cuts, but the questions raised remain. Nothing in the UGC's history suggests that it was capable of encouraging or rewarding radical departures from the university norm and all the evidence of the way the UGC managed the cuts points to a tendency to reduce diversity rather than increase it. The UGC reply to criticism is best summed up by a letter from Sir Edward Parkes to *The Times* where he bluntly defended the Technology Sub-Committee 'for taking money away from moribund and out-of-date departments' and giving it to the leading technological universities and to universities in the forefront of modern electronics (Parkes 1985). Many of the basic criticisms of the UGC performance, quoted above, can be simply answered by reference to the absurdly foreshortened time-scale of six months which the UGC was forced to work to by the Government's timetable for the reduction in public expenditure. Given more time more care could have been taken, more procedures and facts double checked. But more time would not, one suspects, have amended the broad strategy, which was in a sense implicit in the UGC's constitution and history.

When the UGC girded its loins for a second round of cuts in 1985-86 it had the experience of the first round imprinted on its memory. Much had happened in the interim. The 'new blood' scheme had come and gone, offering some additional evidence on the quality of various departments, and the Engineering and Technology Programme had established a new pecking order in engineering and computer science. The cuts proposed were less drastic in impact, allowing a longer time-scale for run-down. On the other hand the university system was still digesting the 1981 cuts and some of the universities had and were still having acute problems of adjustment. The effect of the 1981 exercise, together with the two initiatives quoted above, had been greatly to increase the differentiation between institutions in terms of perceived quality· and the weaker universities were now more obviously weaker both because of their reduced size and in some cases because of a loss of morale.

In 1980-81 universities wer ill-prepared for the cuts after two decades of expansion, but in 1984-85 and 1985-86 they were almost inured to the climate of retrenchment and the Government's new programme of cuts was greeted with less emotion and more resignation. The UGC, too, had learnt some important lessons from 1981, in terms both of presentation and methodology. But the external climate had also changed, particularly with the arrival of the National Advisory Body (NAB). The creation of a parallel body to the UGC for the public sector of higher education forced the universities to ask hard questions of themselves about how they were different from public sector institutions. The 1981 exercise had not only re-shaped the university system but had also established an internal pecking order of some importance. The most obvious differentiation between the two sectors was in research capability and the UGC in its Strategy Document had emphasized the need for further selectivity in research within the university sector.

The 1985-86 exercise accordingly took on a different complexion to that of 1980-81. In 1980-81 the UGC was undertaking an exercise primarily to distribute cuts in recurrent grant, while in 1985-86 it was concerned more with outright selectivity so as to establish appropriately funded centres of excellence in research: in its May 1985 letter the Committee stressed that its policy was 'to be more selective in its support for research [in order] to maintain the quality of university research and the strength of the dual support system as far as possible within the resources available.' Although 'it should be possible for every university to be strong in some subjects both in teaching and research... the extent to which excellence can be preserved in all subjects and in all universities depends on the resources available. It is to be expected that there will be increasing differences among universities in the range of subjects they cover, in the nature of the research they do and in teaching styles' (UGC 1985a). These differences were to be accentuated by the formula funding approach the Committee was later to adopt which could lead to some institutions being funded for undergraduate teaching alone (UGC 1985a). Thus in adopting research excellence as the fundamental criterion, the UGC was moving towards the tiering option rejected in 1980-81 and somewhat away from the concept of every university being strong in some area. Again, unlike in 1980-81, the UGC explicitly rejected the idea of shifting student numbers towards science so that the exercise could concentrate on a single major criterion.

The UGC also very much refined its methodology. First, it was made clear that while the subject committees would take 'a full role' in examining universities' plans, it was intended 'to give special attention to institutions as a whole at the beginning and the end of the allocation process', and a new mechanism of 'territorial groups' was to be set up for the purpose. These groups would offer comments about institutions at the beginning of the process and again after the sub-committees had made their reports. Although the subject committees would recommend student numbers and resources final decisions would be made on the advice of the territorial groups (UGC 1985c). This marked a significant shift of power away from the subject committees.

Secondly, the UGC was able to go much further than it had been able to do in 1980-81 in advising on subject rationalization. Not only did it lay down criteria and appropriate measures to be used but it also spelt out minimum viable sizes for each subject group. It encouraged an increase in collaboration between institutions and indicated its willingness to appoint impartial outsiders to assist in discussions about departmental mergers (UGC 1985b). Within institutions the detailed guidance was often criticized as over-mechanical but the UGC was careful to emphasize that responsibility for rationalization lay with the institutions and that it would intervene itself only exceptionally.

Thirdly, the UGC was able to issue a full description of the resource allocation process, detailing both the machinery and the formulae to be used.

The chief innovation here was the distinction drawn between teaching, research and special institutional factors. In each case the subject committees were asked to determine the teaching cost. When a total teaching figure was arrived at the sub-committee would divide it pro-rata against planned numbers, leaving the research element to serve as the area for selectivity. Universities were asked to provide research plans for each subject group as the basis for these decisions, for assessment by the subject committee. To emphasize the new concern for institutional management universities were asked to provide descriptions of the basis on which they allocated funds for research between departments.

These provisions reflected the fact that the UGC had more time to devote to the exercise than in 1980-81, and that it had learnt the value of a greater degree of openness than had been used in the past. Similarly, the time-scale for the implementation of the cuts was less hectic than in 1981 and the Chairman was able to assure institutions that it had decided to limit the reduction of grant in the first year to no more than 1.5 per cent of the average loss for all institutions. However, the subsequent rate of loss would depend on discussions between the Committee and the institutions as to how quickly they could adapt themselves to lower funding levels. Sensible and well planned as these provisions were they drove the university system irrevocably further down a common route. Although more emphasis was given to part-time and continuing education students, the selectivity criteria pointed firmly towards a more structured university system, where the differentials were more to do with academic strengths than the kind of broader criteria that Professor Marquand was concerned with above. It is true that the effect of the cuts since 1981 had been to encourage universities to embark on extensive income generating activities and that this had tended to introduce a new element of diversification. On the other hand, since the UGC's recurrent grant was by far the largest element in any university's budget, the diversification introduced by income generation remained fairly peripheral. So the end product of two rounds of severe cuts differentially administered on the university system was that in seeking to maintain standards the UGC had enhanced the traditional and conventional aspects of British universities, and had probably increased the homogeneity of the system. While it had increased the differences between universities, in size, in research capability and in reputation, so that universities were much less equal than before, it had done very little to increase the diversification of the system.

The UGC is in many ways superbly constructed to maintain the standards of the university system although that has not been its explicit historical function. In 1980-81 and 1985-86 one hundred and fourteen or so senior academics (including the sub-committee members) were engaged collaboratively in the allocation of the resources required to run the university system against criteria that were almost wholly academic. If the university system has to be re-shaped to reflect a reduction in resources most academics would prefer it to be undertaken by those best equipped to make academic judgements. But there is another view, which tends unfortunately to be voiced more by the extremes of the political right and left than by the academic community, that academic criteria are not the only criteria that should be employed. The UGC's terms of reference include ensuring that universities' plans 'are fully adequate to national needs', but in the replies to the UGC's strategy exercise a few universities suggested that the UGC's influence was 'too persuasive and inhibiting' (UGC 1984b) and that the UGC had indeed failed to take sufficient account of national needs. The question implicitly raised is whether academic criteria are enough, and whether a body so effectively under academic control could ever have a wide enough vision of national need to be able to guide the university system adequately in this respect.

The problem, of course, lies in the definition of national need. The UGC could argue that by acquiescing for a period of more than a decade to the Government's requirements for medical ouput it was responding to national need. (A critic might argue in reply that the UGC had never in that time considered alternatives to the high cost of medical education, had not evaluated alternative approaches to medical training and had not reviewed the arbitrary divisions in many medical schools between NHS and UGC funding responsibilities.) But those most concerned to press the argument about national need in the post-1981 period were from the technological universities which had suffered the greatest cuts. Their plight illustrated another problem for the UGC, that the university system has been created by many initiatives over many years. The 1980-81 Committee inherited a situation created in 1964 when the Government accepted the Robbins Committee's recommendation to absorb the colleges of advanced technology into the university system, without clear guidance being given as to whether their separate 'mission' was to be maintained. To most academic opinion outside Aston and Salford there was more than a suspicion that arguments in the post-1981 period about them having a different mission represented little more than a justification for academic mediocrity. But the principle lying behind the arguments remains valid. Historically it has been assumed that universities have common standards and conform to a common model and, with its strongly academic membership, the UGC has been an effective instrument to maintain that position.

It could be argued that when expansion and resources went hand in hand there was a greater possibility that universities might experiment and diversify, but in fact this did not happen, and the UGC offered no incentives to assist the process. In 1982 an editorial in *Nature* accused the UGC of showing 'very little sign of advocating the changes in the machanisms of financial support for universities that will be necessary if flexibility is ultimately to be achieved' (Nature 1982), an accusation that could and should have been levelled at the UGC throughout the post-Robbins period. When resources contracted sharply in 1980-1981 the UGC had to establish criteria by which to assess universities, and it was only natural, bearing in mind its membership and past history, that academic criteria should predominate. The cumulative effect of 1980-81 and 1985-86 will probably be viewed in the longer term as raising the standards of the university system but may also have the effect of freezing the system ever more solidly into a particular mode. It might be argued that the pressure to seek alternative sources of funds will force universities to diversify, but then we face the paradox that while the UGC's influence, on past record, is likely to be towards a greater homogeneity in the system, it will be left to external funding mechanisms to provide institutions with the stimulus to meet an increasingly diverse set of national needs. National need, therefore, will increasingly be defined by the market place rather than by central government or the UGC. Some critics on the right might welcome this but it portends a university system overreactive to short-term needs and a UGC increasingly concerned with the assessment of academic quality and unconcerned with the wider questions of the universities' place in society. If the UGC is truly to maintain a university system 'of outstanding quality' (UGC 1984b) it needs to broaden its own 'mission'. Academic criteria and the maintenance of academic quality, essential though they are, cannot be the only basis for the management of the system.

References

Ashworth, J. (1982) *Re-Structuring Higher Education in Britain* Edmund Rich Memorial Lecture, Royal Society of Arts, 19 May

Bell, C. (1981) At the sharp end *New Society* 9 July

Beloff, M. (1977) British universities and the public purse *Minerva* 5 (4)

Carswell, J (1986) *Government and Universities in Britain 1960-1980* CUP

CVCP (1946) Note on university policy and finance. Quoted in J. Mountford *Keele:An Historical Critique* RKP, p.57

Ferns, H.S. (1982) *How much Freedom for Universities* Institute of Economic Affairs

Joseph, Sir Keith (1981) Evidence to House of Commons Select Committee on Education, Science and Arts, 11 November 1981 (HC 24)

Marquand, D. (1981) The university cuts we cannot afford *The Guardian* 3 September

Nature (1982) Uneconomic savings. Vol.296, 18 March, Editorial

Parkes, Sir Edward (1980) Address by the Chairman of the UGC to the CVCP, 24 October

Parkes, Sir Edward (1981) Evidence to the House of Commons Select Committee on Education, Science and Arts, 23 July

Parkes, Sir Edward (1982a) Address to the Parliamentary and Scientific Committee, Science in Parliament, Vol 40, No.73

Parkes, Sir Edward (1982b) Evidence to the Public Accounts Committee, 3 February, Session 1981-82 (HC 175) 11th Report

Parkes, Sir Edward (1985) Letter to *The Times*, 4 September

Shattock, M.L. and Berdahl, R.O. (1984) The British University Grants Committee 1919-83: Changing relationships with Government and the Universities *Higher Education* 13

Shinn, C.H. (1983) *A study of the Evolution of the UGC in respect of the English University Institutions between 1919 and 1946* Doctoral thesis, University of Nottingham

(I am grateful to Dr. Shinn for helpful comments and advice on the origins and effectiveness of the early days of the UGC)

UGC (1925) *Returns from Universities and University Colleges in Receipt of Treasury Grant for the Academic Year 1923-24* London:HMSO

UGC (1957) *University Development, Interim Report on the Years 1952 to 1956* Cmnd 79 London:HMSO

UGC (1979) *Report on Russian and Russian Studies in British Universities*
UGC (1980a) *The Functions and Operation of the University Grants Committee* Memorandum to House of Commons Select Committee on Education, Science and Arts, Session 1979-80, 5th Report (HC 787-II) Vol.2
UGC (1980b) *The readjustment of the University System to Changing Resources and Demands* Letter to universities, 30 December
UGC (1981a) *The Future pattern of Resources for Universities* Letter to universities, 15 May
UGC (1981b) *Procedure Leading to UGC 1981-82 Grant distribution* Memorandum to House of Commons Select Committee on Education, Science and Arts, 2 November
UGC (1984a) *UGC Annual Survey 1982-83* Cmnd 9234 London:HMSO
UGC (1984b) *A Strategy for Higher Education into the 1990s* London:HMSO
UGC (1985a) *Planning for the late 1980s* Letter to universities, 9 May
UGC (1985b) *Rationalization* Letter to universities, 8 August
UGC (1985c) *Planning for the late 1980s: The Resource Allocation Process* Letter to universities, 19 November
University of Stirling (1982) Minutes of Evidence to House of Commons Select Committee on Education, Science and Arts, 29 March (HC 274)

5

Judging Institutions

David Billing

Before we can judge institutions of higher education, we must make up our minds what they are for. Before they can judge themselves, institutions must decide what they are for. This paper is first, therefore, about, institutional goals and plans. Thereafter, it explores possible indicators of effectiveness or measures of performance with respect to institutions' self-evaluations of their whole function and organization, and appraisals of institutions carried out by such external bodies as the Council for National Academic Awards (CNAA), the University Grants Committee (UGC) and the National Advisory Body for Public Sector Higher Education (NAB). Throughout, we shall deal mainly with UK experience, and in particular with the public sector, where many of these processes are most developed.

Institutional Goals and Plans

We begin, as we will end, with the government's consultative Green Paper, *The Development of Higher Education into the 1990's* (HMSO 1985a). Not only was this the first major government paper on the whole of the higher educational system in the UK since the Robbins Report (HMSO 1963), but, in spite of its much criticized narrowness, it also contained valuable points. Among them is its insistence that:

> each type of institution has a valuable contribution to make, provided that what each does is fit for the purpose which it serves. (para 1.8)

The notion of 'fitness for purpose' is taken up by the Chairman of the NAB Board, when referring to quality (Ball 1985, p.95):

> Faced with the resource constraints of the 80s, and the demographic trends at 18+ in the 90s, institutions – like the planning bodies – must address the issue of fitness for purpose. I doubt whether the idea of excellence in education has much meaning unless it is related to educational purpose.

The importance, and difficulty, of spelling out purpose in the form of objectives is also clearly stated in the Green Paper (para 7.4). Thus one

UK polytechnic, in preparing to review its academic plan and organization in 1984, began to redefine its objectives by examining the aims of its local education authority. After several meetings, and discussion at various levels in the institution, the Academic Board and Governing Body eventually arrived at a list of ten objectives, of which the shortest was 'to contribute to the cultural life of the metropolitan area,' and the longest was, 'to deploy and develop staff, physical and financial resources effectively in the support of high quality and innovation in education, including the applications of new technologies, the development of teaching methods and the exploitation of these learning opportunities by the maximum numbers of students consistent with maintenance of such quality and innovation.'

Taken together, the list of objectives reflected the characteristics of a polytechnic as defined in the Government's 1966 White Paper (HMSO 1966), the principles of the Council for National Academic Awards (CNAA 1979a) and the criteria of the National Advisory Body (NAB 1982). This range demonstrates that the institution is attempting simultaneously to respond to the expectations of students, community, local authority, governors, staff and validators. These aims can be broadly grouped according to their sources, namely students, staff (including subject discipline), and external (including employment and the local community), as Lane (1975, p.69) and Billing (1973a, 1983b) have previously noted. The potential conflicts between these emphases are also significant, and are graphically indicated in Lane's triangular diagram. The similarities and differences in the priorities actually accorded various goals have been mapped by Romney (1978), who looked at twenty goal areas in forty-five US instititutions, as rated by trustees (ie governors), administrators, and faculty staff. There were notable similarities as well as differences in the rankings, leading Romney to stress the tension between goal congruence and goal conflict.

Goal consensus is not a characteristic of most higher educational institutions in the UK (Yorke 1984). They are characterized by conflict and plurality, only giving an impression of order and consensus (Adelman and Alexander 1981). The result of this conflict, as the Jarratt Report (CVCP 1985a) demonstrated, is that 'objectives and aims in universities are defined only in very broad terms', from which plans and specific priorities for implementation cannot be derived. Hinman (1980) found in the USA that goal statements which have widespread agreement must be ambiguous, and if they are concrete and measurable they either provoke dissension or are too mundane. The inconsistencies between competing interests become apparent when attempts are made to implement such agreements (Bredo and Bredo 1975).

What are produced (CVCP 1985a) are simply statements of intent to maintain all existing subjects; long-term planning is largely ignored and there are no corporate strategic plans that are regularly reviewed and updated. Limited forward planning is done generally on the margins, with no evidence of thorough consideration of options. There are perhaps two reasons for this situation: the wish to preserve institutional cohesion; and uncertainty about future exernal influences. Similar conclusions were reached by Davies and Morgan (1982) in their institutional case studies of policy-making. Given uncertainty and economic reality, policy decisions are increasingly concerned with *marginal* decisions, and not with the grand fixed strategy of a development plan. The future of *whole* institutions cannot be easily imagined or planned, and even if future projections can be made, their variability prevents consensus about any one of them.

The National Data Study (CVCP 1985b) was based upon discussions with twenty national bodies, visits to five universities, and efficiency studies of six universities. What emerged was a reluctance to set priorities, not only between objectives, but between academic departments. The Jarratt Report found that resource allocation did not take into explicit account the relative strengths of departments. For lack of any other, the basis for resource allocation has to be historical; planning and resource allocation therefore tend to be incremental, pragmatic responses to short-term political pressures. There is little systematic use of performance indicators, and resources tend to be allocated in a fragmented way. Given Baldridge and Tierney's (1979) finding that management innovations fail if they do not link planning activities with budgeting strategies, it is disturbing that resource allocation in universities is quite separate from planning (CVCP 1985b). There is also very little formal accountability for the actual use of resources and especially not for staff time. This view has been forcibly put by the Audit Commission's study of further education in the UK (HMSO 1985c).

The series of structural proposals which follow in the Jarratt Report (CVCP 1985a) may nevertheless be inadequate means to the report's ends: to speed up corporate and strategic planning decisions so as to meet external requirements for change. This is because the report is, in Burns and Stalker's (1966) phrase, 'mechanistic' and completely ignores the 'organismic', political aspects of decision-making. As Morris (1974) said:

> universities are politically rational organisations, not economically rational organisations...[with a need] to anticipate behavioural response to change and to seek a coincidence of that with the pursuit of economic efficiency in the prosecution of politically determined activity.

Morris advocated formalizing tensions between competing activities so that they could openly compete and negotiate. Cuthbert and Birch (1980) also asked for an examination of the political structure in which decisions are reached and power and responsibility assigned and withdrawn.

As Davies and Morgan (1982) reminded us, collective policy-making is slow and problematic in the face of external requirements for budget cuts, since these must be made on a time-scale that does not allow for consensus building. Enderud (1977) suggested that the ambiguities arising from uncertainty and search for consensus can be used positively, by recognizing them in evolving policy and planning processes. Davies and Morgan's (1982) approach is similar. Their model for policy formation usefully identifies a number of critical processes which must be carried out early enough if proposed strategies are not eventually to fall at the Senate or Academic Board level, and places particular stress on the political dimensions and on the consequent need for such activities as informal briefing by officials, bargaining, brokerage between interest groups, and alliance building.

The *possibility* of consensus building is an optimistic prognosis not shared by those like Adelman and Alexander (1981) and Morris (1974), who see plurality and conflict as the reality, and consensus only as rherotic. Adelman and Alexander (1982) nevertheless set out an ideal, which they thought could be approached:

> What we have termed the *'theorising institution'*...imbues *all* its day-to-day decision-making processes, not merely those at the classroom level, with reflection not only on action but also, and initially, on the educational need and justification for actions of particular sorts.(p.148)...[In their eyes] [evaluation] is premissed on a view of...improved professional practice [which requires] a climate of critical commitment leading to what we term the 'theorising institution'.(p.28)

In such an institution 'policies can most usefully be regarded as hypotheses, theories or predictions', and therefore:

> policy formulation and institutional decision-making ought to be subject to an approach analogous to scientific inquiry, namely, one of constant critical examination using the experience of implementing policy not as a means of proving, whatever the cost, that the policy was right but as a means of testing its validity, strengths and weaknesses. (p.171)

This is the language of the evaluator rather than the manager; but their values, these authors point out, are in conflict. Is the prescription of Adelman and Alexander's 'theorising institution' any more realistic, as opposed to rhetorical, than Davies and Morgan's essential of consensus building? Baldridge (1971), based on studies of New York University, suggested that conflict is endemic and the notion of an academic community is fiction; the criterion of success is the extent to which an institution is better than a zero sum.

Another view is that institutions are not static in their organizational type. Clark (1972), based on case studies in the USA, introduced the notion of an 'institutional saga'. Broad goals, such as service to the community, are key components of the collective conventional wisdom; this, together with the relatively cohesive set of publicly held beliefs and values (rooted in the institution's history and its unique accomplishments) is the 'organizational saga'. The development of a strong 'saga' depends both on a strong cause pressed by a visionary leader (or small group) and on a setting in which progress can be made. Quinn and Cameron (1980) suggested that organizations proceed through life-cycles in which the creative and collective ideation are subordinated to the requirements of the organization, and Yorke (1984) saw the saga as likely to erode. Davies and Morgan (1982) also believed that a weakly held organizational saga quickly disintegrates as the environment moves from one of slowed growth through one of moderate contraction. Strongly held sagas, on the other hand, appear to be one of the most important variables in determining institutional response, for example to contraction. While Davies and Morgan expected to see evidence of this in the variable resilience of UK universities' in face of UGC cuts, there is similar evidence to be sought in the influence of NAB's successive planning processes in the UK public sector institutions.

In 1982-83 most of these institutions avoided conflict, and kept their organizational sagas, by proposing to spread evenly the 1984 reductions in expenditure projected by NAB, rather than give priority to some activities and reduce others; indeed, they mostly sought to expand student numbers with a reduced 'unit of resource'. Initial proposals to close specific courses were fiercely resisted both within institutions and externally, but this may not be possible in the most recent major NAB planning exercise (aimed at 1987) which requires institutions to produce a plan, both of immediate priorities for growth or contraction, and of aspirations for the end of the decade.

The NAB guidance (1984, 1985) on preferred subject areas (reflecting the Green Paper's vocationalism), more part-time, continuing education and sub-degree programmes and more 'non-standard' student entrants, offers no additional resources to match the greater costs of most of these activities, which seems likely to make consensus building more difficult, as it simultaneously encourages a number of conflicting planning directions. Thus one institution stressed the preservation of a 'balance between types of work, that is between nature of the student intake, modes, subjects and levels of study, and vocational or non-vocational character'. Attempts to build uncertainties into its 1984 plan had failed to produce workable planning parameters. The best position was felt to be one of maximum responsiveness to opportunities. Three versions of the plan later, in its 1985 response to NAB, this institution defined a 'priority mission':

To concentrate on the imaginative education of qualified persons for employment in industrial, commercial, professional and public services and to provide high quality routes to such qualifications for the widest possible spectrum of potential students.

Resources would be channelled, over a period of time, towards enterprises which enhanced the 'priority mission' and the service of the community, and exploited the unique local environment; other activities would only be maintained in so far as they utilized the same resources, without distorting their priority use. The immediate effect of the adoption of this planning document by the Academic Board was justification for all the existing work of the institution under the criterion of service to the community, and a search for a very broad interpretation of the professional/vocational emphasis of the 'priority mission'. The major problem which then arose was the conversion of the general policy into specific target numbers of students for each course.

The final agreed figures derived from political and pragmatic interactions, and the pragmatic criterion which counted most was the protection of resources, demonstrating the ease with which planning and resourcing become separated and eventually have to be brought together in an uneasy compromise. Once again, reference to goals and objectives proved an inadequate touchstone for detailed decision-making.

Institutional Self-Evaluations

Yorke (1984) has reviewed effectiveness in higher education, and supports the Pennings and Goodman (1977) categorization of methods, criteria and analyses into goal achievement measures and internal process criteria.

Goal Achievements

Work on goal achievement is mainly concerned with indicators of performance, and much of it was reviewed by Sizer (1981, 1982). He saw the development of numerous partial indicators (such as accessibility, efficiency, acceptability) as an inevitable consequence of the many and various dimensions of institutions' work, the lack of consensus on objectives and indicators for the whole institution (see above), and the tendency to highlight those aspects which can be quantified. Calvert (1980) identified four which needed measuring: efficiency, effectiveness, resource commitment and utilization. Of these, effectiveness was identified with extent of goal achievement and efficiency with the economy of goal achievement. He believed that quality (students, staff, environment) had been ignored in efficiency measures of teaching activity: a conspicuous example being the Audit Commission's report (HMSO 1985c). There are many competing approaches to categorizing indicators of performance (see Yorke 1984), but they do not map on to each other. Thus Romney (1978) preferred progress measures of the impact of the institution on society, but highlighted the difficulty of incorporating these into management information systems which would lead to actual decisions.

The most active line of development with performance indicators concerns the analysis of courses and subject areas within an institution. Doyle and Lynch (1979) located each course on a 2 x 2 matrix according to its proportion of the national 'market' for such courses and the proportion of the total market which that subject area commanded. Sizer (1982) modified this approach to produce the 3 x 3 matrix shown in Figure 1.

The basis of this 'portfolio analysis' is subject areas, rather than courses, since resources are normally allocated to subject areas (departments), enabling the quality of resources and links to the community to be taken into account. Such a 'directional policy matrix' reveals strengths and weaknesses and suggests which areas should grow, which should be consolidated and which should be phased out. Sizer also attempted to depict the extent of the institution's existing resource deployment in each subject area, as a measure of its adaptability. This approach was taken up by Billing (1983a), who suggested a three-dimensional matrix, with the third axis being revenue expenditure for the subject area. He looked at courses, with the two major dimensions of analysis being academic quality (instead of Sizer's 'institutional strengths') and viability in terms of recruitment (equals 'subject area attractiveness'). There was a significant difficulty in the identification of academic quality, since objective measures could not readily be obtained by a panel of staff internal to the institution. This echoes the finding of Becher and Kogan (1980), and Billing suggested that the views of students might be a better starting point.

The authors of the National Data Study (CVCP 1985b) found that the major omission in management data was any attempt to measure costs of outputs, as opposed to inputs; this would entail apportioning the costs of activities to departments, including a proportion of central overheads. Birch and Latcham (1985a) also took up the relation of inputs, according to the system shown in Figure 2, which is taken from Beer (1979).

The major problems lie in defining the objectives of the system, in the lack

SUBJECT AREA ATTRACTIVENESS

- Market size
- Market growth rate
- Market diversity
- Competitive structure
- Cost structure
- Optimal department size
- Demographic trends
- Scientific importance

- Technological trends
- Social/political and economic trends
- Environmental trends
- Government attitudes
- Employment prospects
- Cultural importance
- Etc.

UNIVERSITY STRENGTHS IN THE SUBJECT AREA		High	Medium	Low
• Size of department • Market share • Market position • Number of applications • Quality of student intake	**High**	Growth	Selective growth or consolidation	Consolidation
• Graduate employment • Cost per FTE student • Reputation • Quality & age of staff • Research record	**Medium**	Selective growth or consolidation	Consolidation	Planned withdrawal & redeployment
• Research capability • Image • Publications record • Resources: availability and mobility • Etc.	**Low**	Consolidation or planned withdrawal & redepolyment	Planned withdrawal & redeployment	Planned withdrawal & redeployment

Figure 1
University directional policy matrix.

of general agreement on output measures (CIPFA 1980) and the lack of an obvious definition of the boundaries of the institutional system – for example, how much of the community it should contain. A manager's first task, according to these authors, is not to track down causes, but to detect instability in the system. Figure 2 shows the importance of the comparator, ie the instrument which monitors all variable outputs that are sufficiently important to hurt the system if they change significantly from some intended range of values; this approach ignores conflicts among output variables which may not be optimized independently. There are no acceptable measures of the quality of teaching activity, according to Birch and Latcham (1985b).

Input measures have been much criticized, and most of the findings about them are fairly commonplace. Burnip, Durrands and Lindsell (1980) downgraded unit costs as a measure, and queried staff/student ratios as well as the clear-cut nature of economies of scale. Bottomley (1972) did find evidence of economies of scale, while Verry and Davies (1976) produced regression equations. Calvert's graphs (1980) showed economies of scale for research activity, but few for teaching activities. Cuthbert and Birch (1980) found limitations with staff/student ratios and went on to list the difficulties in

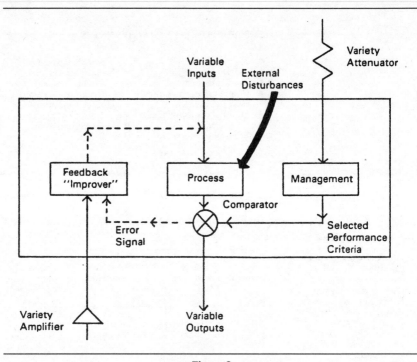

Figure 2
A management unit system.

searching for all-embracing performance criteria, in particular, those in the way of specifying objectives tightly enough to be operationally useful without squeezing out valuable diversities of view, the length of time needed, and the need to make the results comprehensible to those who could use them.

Perhaps the most useful, and simplest, of goal-based approaches to performance measures of the teaching function remains that of Porter (1978). He suggested a profile of several partial indicators for each of a series of critical areas. Figure 3 shows these compared with comparative data on norms.

Porter also considered the several purposes of performance measures: comparison; improving efficiency and effectiveness; identification of 'bottlenecks'; testing policy; providing management information and advice; conflict avoidance or resolution; information and control. They neither necessarily nor invariably sit comfortably together.

Internal Process Criteria

Cameron and Whetton (1981) found from a simulation that there was a dependence of institutional effectiveness on internal processes, irrespective of the developmental stage of the institution. For Ford and Schellenberg (1982)

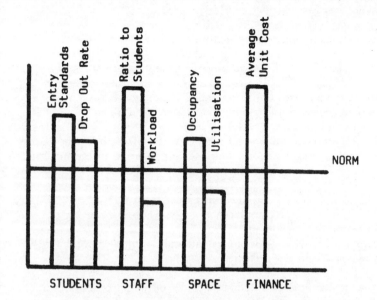

Entry Standards: Average A level score as a ratio of accepted standard

Drop-Out Rate: Percentage of relevant cohort not obtaining a degree as ratio of accepted standard.

Ratio to Student: Staff in post as a ratio of entitlement based on accepted allocation ratios as applied to teaching load.

Workload: Average workload of academic staff as a ratio of accepted standard.

Occupancy: Space currently occupied as a ratio of entitlement based on accepted accommodation norms as applied to teaching load.

Utilisation: Average utilisation of teaching space expressed as a ratio of timetabled hours to desirable standard.

Unit Cost: Average cost of unit of student load as a ratio of average national unit for relevant peer group.

Figure 3
Goal based approaches to performance measures of the teaching function (Porter 1978).

the major aspects of the processes to be considered could be categorized in the following way (as amended by Yorke 1984):

a   the relationship between an institution and its environment;
b   the institution's structures and processes
    – their match with the environment's beliefs about the institution
    – the extent to which formal and operative structures converge
    – the various processes linking policy, action and output; and
c   outcomes, in terms of both personnel and materials.

Lindsay (1981) gave a managerial perspective, showing how the process of evolution (rather than its product) causes intervention in the institutional processes themselves. Institutional assessment can be:

a   a political process aimed at conflict resolution;
b   a means of reducing complacency;
c   an impetus for change; or
d   a ritual to provide a picture of rationality and accountability which promotes a feeling of security.

This list, which comprises a 'hidden agenda' of the purposes of evaluation, should be compared with Porter's (1978) explicit list of the purposes of performance measures; there is not much correspondence.

Dressel (1976) considered US work on institutional self-study, and offered guidance on the operation of evaluations. He saw the need for a properly constituted committee to undertake to:

– determine institutional purposes;
– measure educational and other outcomes;
– evaluate learning experiences;
– evaluate adequacy and utilization of resources;
– evaluate planning and decision-making; and
– interpret the objectives to new staff, students and the public.

Dressel found that the key to successful implementation of the recommendations of such evaluations was to keep the entire institution apprised of progress, preparing the ground for the impact of the recommendations:

> The success of the endeavour depends upon imbedding review, evaluation, and renewal into the institution and upon the development of ways of both involving the students, faculty, and general public and communicating to them the nature of the commitment and its results.

We look now at an example of one such UK self-evaluation, in Dressel's term a 'comprehensive institutional current status self-study'. The purpose was to improve efficiency and effectiveness, although the hidden agenda might be said to be to reduce complacency before an institutional review by the CNAA. A year before this review visit, the Director appointed an Institutional Evaluation Group (IEG) consisting of a new (and therefore relatively detached) assistant director as chair, two faculty deans, two heads of department, the President of the Students' Union, and the Academic Registrar; its task was to conduct the self-evaluation and to oversee the documentation and programme for the CNAA review visit.

The IEG worked responsively over nine months, meeting various groups within the institution, circulating two consultative documents and putting its final report through the normal Faculty and committee system for decisions. During this process it met staff and students representing each Faculty, representatives of course leaders, the Academic Board and all of its major committees (using external consultants at these points), senior administrative staff, and representatives of the major support units (library, computer centre, audio-visual, student services). The summary report, agreed by the Academic Board and Governing Body, formed an important section in the institutional review document, and the final CNAA visit was intended to concentrate on this self-evaluation. In the event, the report of the visiting party commended the consultative nature of the self-appraisal and recorded the wish of the institution to implement the IEG report's recommendations on new structures and procedures. The visiting party's conclusions focused on the institution's commitment to continuing self-appraisal, through a standing committee of the Academic Board with a performance monitoring function.

Inside this institution, the interactive manner in which the appraisal had been carried out, together with the impact of the distribution of its consultative papers and the final report, had prepared staff for recommended changes – as suggested by Dressel (1976). Many of these changes were implemented before the final report was completed. The major recommendation was accepted and consolidated from the start of the consultative process:

i The Academic Board agrees that it should act urgently to strengthen the academic community of the institution and to develop, in interaction with the Faculties, an agreed framework of policies, plans and processes to provide the structure by means of which faculty and centrally-based committees and executives can interrelate. This framework, aspects of which already exist, should include:

a an academic Development Plan for the institution with means of implementation, monitoring and regular review, and incorporating specific targets for faculties and central units (it is recognised that the administrative support implications of this recommendation will require further discussion);

b a translation of that academic plan into a comprehensive institutional resource plan, regularly reviewed, and covering staffing, accommodation and money;

c recognition that executive decisions throughout the institution must normally be taken in the context of the implementation of policies agreed and regularly reviewed by the academic decision-making bodies (nevertheless it is recognised that circumstances may occasionally necessitate ad-hoc decision-making and that this in itself has a role to play in policy formation);

d policies in key areas (such as staffing targets, staff development, admissions, student numbers, accommodation, information technology, student welfare, access course interlinking, and course review) which are sufficiently specific to enable their implementation and review;

e   the effecting of the accountability of executives to the committee structure and of committees to the Academic Board through monitoring processes covering policy implementation, resource deployment, and educational standards;

f   a comprehensive and easily accessible database and management information service.

ii   every attempt should be made to reduce the geographical isolation of units, should opportunities arise; in the meantime the Academic Board will examine means of promoting inter-faculty developments and the interchange of ideas, experiences and perspectives among staff and students.

Momentum decreased, however, following the visit, so that a year afterwards some recommendations were still being worked through.

Shortly after the last CNAA visit, the IEG met, finally, to review the whole process, having sought comments from all involved. Some staff saw the self-evaluation as a camouflage for executive actions and resource cuts; some faculties saw the interaction with the IEG as interrogation. At the same time as the self-evaluation, the institution was implementing a new departmental structure, causing pain in some of its parts. Although, unfortunately, this removed the vital area of executive structure from the self-evaluation, it did not remove the suspicion with which staff viewed central bodies (including the IEG); in these circumstances, the IEG was pleasantly surprised that it got as far as it did. Besides the executive structure, the IEG noted important omissions from its purview in the areas of the effectiveness of the Directorate and of the governing body; in fact, there was virtually no interaction between the IEG and the governors or the local education authority (LEA). In addition, the IEG felt that it had not adequately appraised non-teaching activities, student services and subject groupings. In spite of efforts to the contrary, there had been 'distance' between the IEG and the experiences and views of students and junior staff. Another disappointment was that neither Faculties nor most central committees had carried out their own self-appraisals before interacting with the IEG (in spite of guidance on this). On the positive side, the IEG confirmed the usefulness of meetings (rather than paperwork) and of well chosen external advisers, and recommended that the next institutional self-appraisal should also be carried out by a small, independent, group.

Was the IEG task all too easy?

Adelman and Alexander (1982; p.182) questioned the adequacy of painless evaluation: how comprehensive was the focus, did it grapple with value issues, who was it disseminated to, were all the findings published, did the method identify different analyses of 'facts', would all the institution accept the validity?

Where evaluation findings are accorded the finite status of objective fact, accepted with little debate, they have far less potential for promoting such development than if they are treated as partial evidence of hypotheses in a continuing process of appraisal and modification....

If it is to have any use other than as a purely cosmetic device for satisfying the demands of a validating body, or for servicing the power requirements of institutional oligarchies, evaluation has to be accepted as challenging, uncomfortable, untidy and potentially disturbing to an institution's equilibrium. (p.161)

Perhaps, in Dressel's (1976) terms, the reasons for the IEG's success were that external imperatives and deadlines (CNAA, NAB, LEA) had generated high motivation, that the consultative process did prepare the institution for the recommendations, and that the review was imbedded in the institution. In Adelman and Alexander's terms (1982, p.183), the IEG succeeded perhaps because its evaluative process was collective and open. On the other hand, perhaps the IEG did not succeed, and in Lindsay's (1981) terms, the hidden agenda was actually a 'ritual to provide a picture of rationality and accountability which promotes a feeling of security'. Institutional 'health' criteria can be fulfilled procedurally, without coming near to having a collective 'theorising institution' (Adelman and Alexander 1981), and in these cases institutional evaluation is justified only by external requirements. Again, success is a relative term, depends upon who is asked, and is time dependent (Adelman and Alexander 1982, p.29). It is probably too early to judge the success of the IEG example.

One of the major themes of Adelman and Alexander (1982) was accountability and its relationship to evaluation and management. They were concerned, in relation to the control of evaluation, not so much with the independence of evaluators, but with the integrity of the evaluation process: which has 'somehow to be upheld in the face of strong contrary pressures and constraints– time, limited resources, organisational problems, for example, but above all the risk of evaluation's use, abuse or neutralisation to further or protect individual or section interests.'

In two senses all evaluations are *political*: firstly they are value judgements on effectiveness, which may have resource consequences: and secondly they can be used intentionally by one group to serve interests and prevent a change of power. We can choose whether to make evaluation consistent with the claimed ideology (eg democracy) or with organizational reality (eg bureaucracy); if the latter, then evaluation will be non-problematical because it will be an extension of management practices (Adelman and Alexander 1982, p.163).

Returning to the IEG example, was its integrity as an evaluation upheld against contrary pressures? The IEG believed that it was, in spite of being seen by some Faculties as unwanted interrogation, in spite of not probing areas like the Directorate and the governors, and in spite of the absence of appraisals from particular units. Does the non-problematic nature of this evaluation flow, as Adelman and Alexander (1982) suggest, from its being simply an extension of existing management practices? Certainly it does, in the sense that management practices used a comparable working party with a clear remit, yet it was not true in the sense that the IEG worked through participative processes and that its outcomes in fact changed some management practices. However, while the IEG projected an ethos of self-criticism at all levels (including management), this was not forthcoming. Finally, the IEG was not able to look at educational quality directly, and relied on meetings with the bodies which did undertake course monitoring and course evaluation.

Appraisals by External Bodies

There is a very clear product/process distinction in the manner in which external bodies have appraised the work of higher educational institutions. This corresponds to the distinction made between internal process and goal achievement in the previous section. Those bodies which have concentrated on *quality* have designed ways in which they can look at the processes for maintaining quality. Those bodies which have concentrated on *cost-effectiveness* have ignored processes and looked only at indicators of performance as measures of the product. This mirrors Phaedrus' discovery (Pirsig 1974): 'If Quality exists in the object, why can't scientific instruments measure it....Quality is not a *thing*. It is an *event*.'

Processes Linked to Quality

The Council for National Academic Awards is the major body exhibiting a single-minded pursuit of quality; no other UK validating bodies consider institutional matters. Although the prime purpose of the CNAA is the approval of courses, Davis (1979), in his history of the first ten years, saw the development of CNAA quinquennial reviews of institutions (*c.*1967) as inescapable, in order to explore resource relationships between departments, even though not mentioned in the CNAA's charter or statutes. He offered no commentary on their effectiveness. Billing (1983a) referred to CNAA institutional reviews as complex, major events with no clear remit to form polices. He considered that they were intended to concentrate on effectiveness in two areas – resource allocation processes, and internal course validation and evaluation processes – but was concerned that at all levels there was inadequate probing of the institution to check out the veracity of the descriptions of processes, and their validity. The IEG described above was also disappointed by the CNAA's lack of vigour in probing the institution's self-evaluation. Ball (1985, p.8), in a significant speech at Thames Polytechnic in 1981, saw CNAA institutional validation as 'impractical, unreal, impertinent and unprofessional'. Adelman and Alexander (1981, 1982) believed that the CNAA assumed bureaucratic, consensus, closed, 'mechanistic', institutional solutions; institutional autonomy might be advanced but at the expense of the individual.

A search for the purposes of institutional reviews is not helped by the CNAA's own notes (1983a), which, like the FOCII report (CNAA 1984a), simply list the information expected in review documents. Other references are *Developments in Partnership in Validation* (CNAA 1979b, A2.6) and the *Degree Regulations* (CNAA 1979a, para.2), but, like the new Reviews

Coordinating Sub-Committee (CNAA 1984c), they highlight only the need for a relationship between course visits and institutional visits. Glanville (1981), the CNAA's Registrar for Institutional Reviews, justified such visits: 'the rationale for institutional reviews has developed by a process which has aggregated those aspects of course approval, conditions for course approval and necessary background to course approval which could not be handled adequately at the level of activity of individual subject Boards.' Earlier, Glanville (1979) spelled out some CNAA purposes:

i   to assess the academic environment common to any CNAA course which is to run in an institution;

ii to satisfy itself that the institution is capable of maintaining the standard of any approved course which it continues to run; and

iii to ensure that the Council's validation and review of a course is informed by a knowledge of the institution at which the course is to run, or has been running, and of its internal course validation and monitoring procedures.

While the form and scope of CNAA institutional reviews has changed considerably since 1967, first towards elaboration and intervention, and more recently towards focusing and consultation, the Lindop Report (HMSO 1985b, p.58) on validation in the public sector found them to be one of the most contentious issues in the responses which it received. The report suggests (paras 9.13-9.14) that four elements should be added to the institution's self-analysis, if institutional accreditation is to be granted: external assessors should be members of internal validation panels; the CNAA should be free to sample internal validation procedures; annual reports (to an agreed format) from external examiners should be included; and transbinary comparative statistical data should be used. As to the criteria for determining whether to grant accreditation, the report recommends (annex 5):

i   sufficient number of staff working at the appropriate level;

ii   sufficient range of degree-level work;

iii   academic community cohesive enough to achieve consensus, and act on it effectively;

iv   high quality of teachers and students, so that appropriate standards are expected and achieved;

v   effectiveness–both established and predicted–of the institution's internal validation and review processes;

vi   external confidence shown in the institution; and

vii satisfactory relationship with its local education authority.

It is interesting that item iii reiterates the CNAA's own assumptions that academic community and consensus are possible, assumptions which have been questioned earlier in this paper.

With the single exception of course review, the above Lindop criteria do *not* map on to the CNAA's own recent attempts (CNAA 1984b) to set out the conditions for a freer relationship with a given institution ('Mode B'):

a   that its proven concern is for the maintenance and wherever possible the enhancement of the quality and relevance of the educational experience of its students, and of the standard of the awards for which they are candidates;

b that it has the means and the will to decide, across the range of its courses, when external advice is needed, and how best to assess and use it;

c that it is prepared to take difficult decisions in order to maintain standards;

d that its policies have been developed and implemented in ways which stimulate, as well as control, the development of the work of the institution;

e that it has the means to analyse course delivery, including questions of teaching, learning and assessment, and to take action to improve performance as an integral part of course evaluation and review;

f that it has the capacity and will to generate course development and improvement based on a sufficient commitment to research and allied activity and to staff development, as a support to teaching and learning;

g that it is efficient in the conduct of procedures such as those for examinations and assessment, and the effective servicing of its consultative and deliberative machinery.

It is strange that neither the Lindop nor the CNAA criteria make any direct reference to the institution's resource base or the effectiveness of its deployment, with the exception of Lindop's interest in the number of staff. This is a far cry from CNAA papers of the 1970s on the adverse effects of resource constraints (see CNAA 1977), and a number of well publicized, very critical, institutional reviews whose aftermaths involved the LEAs in resource discussions. It seems that the CNAA's interest in total institutional resources has become vulnerable to political forces.

At no point does any of the evidence bring us any closer to being able to appraise the effectiveness of CNAA institutional reviews, let alone provide a basis for endorsement of either of the above two sets of criteria. In contrast, nothing at all has been published analysing the activities of Her Majesty's Inspectorate (HMI) or advisors/inspectors employed by local authorities. What is well known is that unlike CNAA members they do directly observe teaching. In secondary education, HMI do report to LEAs on individual schools and colleges and they also survey the effects of resourcing trends; in higher education, the former is not now often carried out, and instead there are surveys of subject areas and types of course. One particularly useful report has been that on first degree courses (Department of Education and Science 1983), which highlights problems of overteaching and a lack of staff development by updating in industry. The most recent report on the effects of resource policies (DES 1985) covers 1984 and summarizes a total of 111 visits to institutions concerned with advanced further education (AFE); a total of 108 sessions were observed. Overall, the levels of teaching and non-teaching staffing and other resource provisions were satisfactory in the vast majority of AFE institutions. The most significant problem areas were in non-teaching staffing (20 per cent of classes affected) and poor or limited accommodation (30 per cent). The only comment on institutional processes was that in one-sixth of visits the management and deployment of teaching resources were less than satisfactory.

Certain independent bodies have looked at the higher education system in the UK: the Nuffield Foundation (1976), for example, through its Group for Research and Innovation in Higher Education, and the Society for Research into Higher Education through its Leverhulme Programme (1983). The conclusion of the Nuffield Report (1976) was concerned with general issues like access to learning materials, use of staff time, credit transfer, admission of mature students, professional development of staff, and a network of subject interest-groups; the only points which related to institutions, as such, were the need for course monitoring and for protection of innovations. The SRHE Leverhulme Report was also pitched at general issues such as access, funding mechanisms, and the need for recognition of two-year courses; at institutional level, the major points were the need for reviews of institutions, courses and staff, for academic and non-academic decision-making to be brought together, for more lay participation in academic affairs, for an academic development plan recognized by its funding body, and for a research policy. A number of these points, concerning access, credit transfer, and the duration of courses, were also discussed in the CNAA's consultative paper (1983b) on future development of academic policies at undergraduate level.

Indicators of Performance

The major UK bodies carrying out external appraisals are the National Advisory Body for Public Sector Higher Education, the University Grants Committee, the Committee of Vice-Chancellors and Principals (CVCP), the Audit Commission for Local Authorities, local authorities themselves (LEAs), and the Government (DES).

NAB planning has concentrated on first-year student number intakes to courses grouped into 'programme areas' (of which there are now 19). The criteria for the first major planning exercise (for 1984/85 intakes) can be seen to be (NAB 1982):

a   special place of sub-degree and part-time higher education;
b   balance between student numbers at lower unit costs and reducing student numbers;
c   academic quality of courses;
d   relevance to regional and local needs;
e   interrelationships between courses, in terms of mutual support of a viable academic community with a sound teaching base; and
f   advanced study and/or research on the part of academic staff, as a necessary support for teaching.

Institutions were asked how they would plan with a 10 per cent reduction in real income. Their responses about projected student numbers were treated as 'bids' by NAB, and each institution was then allocated maximum targets for FTE (full-time equivalent) students in programme areas, for the full-time/sandwich total, and for the first degree/postgraduate total. The 'all years' numbers of FTE students, weighted by programme area, and multiplied by the 'unit of resource', determined the financial allocation to each institution for AFE work. In view of the link between numbers and income, all institutions sought to negotiate higher numbers, and the result was a lower 'unit of resource'. A number of specific course closure proposals (eg in town planning) were also made by NAB, but intense pressure, and late inputs of information on quality from the CNAA and HMI, caused them to be severely modified. The process did not improve confidence in NAB.

There was a complete lack of institutional perspective in NAB's decision-making, with no account taken of the interrelationships between numbers and decisions across programme areas. The lack persisted in NAB's advice to the government (NAB 1984) on strategy for the 1990s: although there were chapters on the characteristics of the public sector and on the needs of society (jointly with the UGC), the strategy document said nothing about institutions, as such.

A number of additional course closures were agreed in 1984: a multidisciplinary BA course at the Hertfordshire College of Higher Education, for example, without ostensible thought as to the effect of that decision on the viability of the other major area of work – teacher education. The LEA provided a report in 1985, as requested, on a merger of the college with Hatfield Polytechnic – only to be overtaken by a proposal from NAB's Teacher Education Group to report on its initial teacher training work according to a number of criteria. In practice, the merger proposal from the LEA was ignored and NAB recommended to the Secretary of State no intakes of initial teacher training after 1985, ie effective closure of the college. By this time, pressure groups had caused NAB to remove all but the Hertfordshire College from its primary teacher education list; the Secretary of State found the reductions inadequate and referred them back to NAB, which reinstated the 1986 intake. Most recently, NAB has been unable to meet the Government's timetable for the further primary education review, and the Secretary of State has taken over such decisions himself. A similar fate was accorded to NAB's attempt to reduce numbers of Part I degree students in architecture, which singled out the department at North East London Polytechnic.

NAB's Board contains representatives of institutional interests, and its Committee is dominated by local authorities; it is arguable whether anything other than these sorts of political compromises could have emerged from such a body. Further, throughout the period, the Hertfordshire LEA was held at arms length by NAB in relation to the *actual* reasons for its decisions. Without such information, many college staff saw the termination of the BA as the means of weakening the college prior to complete closure. (Such a hidden agenda would, however, mean that NAB did have an institutional perspective.) Many other criticisms of NAB's processes and decisions have been forcefully made by Knight (1985).

With its request to institutions for 1987/88 student projections, based on ±5 per cent variations in first-year numbers, NAB (1985) gave guidance on its priorities (part-time and sub-degree provisions, vocational and technological programme areas, continuing education and access), and sought translations of these into 'a statement of how (the institutions) view their role and activity at the end of the decade.' Here, at last, NAB echoed the view of the Price Report (HMSO 1980), which was its origin, that all institutions should submit (to UGC or NAB) statements on their objectives, course provisions and structures, study patterns, intended student profile, balance between teaching and research, and relationship of the academic programme to the available facilities: in effect an institutional academic development plan. It remains to be seen whether NAB will learn to use such plans and to work with institutions in developing them. Most recently, NAB has agreed to undertake ten case studies of good management practice in institutions (NAB 1986).

NAB's preoccupation has not been with quality, but with numbers and regional distribution. However, it has sought to obtain authoritative information on course quality from the CNAA. The CNAA's ranking of town planning courses into three categories in 1983 led to so much criticism and misunderstanding, however, that it is no longer prepared to give comparative views on courses (CNAA 1984d).

Turning, now, to the analogous university body, little has been published on UGC visits. Their purpose has been vaguely defined (UGC 1978): 'to obtain an up-to-date and direct impression of the work and intentions of each institution as an individual centre of teaching and research.' The notes only discuss composition of groups of staff to meet the UGC party. The UGC's Form 3, which is used to collect statistics, has been criticized (CVCP 1985b) because it has led universities to allocate resources in undesirably small parcels. The statistical digests produced by UGC officers rarely highlight points for the Committee and there is said to be no attempt to evaluate performance or out-turn. The National Data Study suggested (CVCP 1985b) that the UGC needed:

i   some way of evaluating information on national needs;
ii to produce policy advice about the teaching/research balance;
iii to decide on the extent to which it will focus its attention on institutions as a whole, as opposed to departments or subjects; and
iv an understanding of what each university is trying to do, together with a means of judging how well it is doing it.

Like NAB, the UGC does not appear to consider an institution as a whole. Its advice to Government (UGC 1984) on higher education strategy for the 1990s was related to collections of departments. The only comprehensive suggestions were that every university should acquire a deliberate bias towards change and should examine the effectiveness of its decision-making. There was nothing in the advice about cost-effectiveness and some fairly complacent and mundane observations about standards. Also, according to the Jarratt Report, the UGC, like NAB, has no intention of taking into account the *quality* of teaching because there is no reliable way of assessing it (CVCP 1985a). The report suggested that more direct UGC intervention in spending grants could achieve greater value for money, that the UGC should monitor the outcomes of its advice, and that the CVCP and UGC should develop performance indicators. The UGC has said little about its own effectiveness (UGC 1984), except an intention to be more open and to review the organization of its visits.

The Jarratt Committee also made comments on the universities themselves (CVCP 1985a). They should search for value for money as a vital part of any plan for change, but staff tenure was a major impediment to rapid change and to matching staffing to objectives and student numbers. The final recommendations are deliberately confined to questions of efficiency and, consequently, do not acknowledge or identify their possible effect on academic standards. They are:

We recommend that all universities examine their structures and develop plans within the next twelve months to meet certain key requirements. These are:

a Councils to assert their responsibilities in governing their institutions notably in respect of strategic plans to underpin academic decisions and structures which bring planning, resource allocation and accountability together into one corporate process linking academic, financial and physical aspects.

b Senates to continue to play their essential role in co-ordinating and endorsing detailed academic work and as the main forum for generating an academic view and giving advice on broad issues to Council.

c Developing a rolling academic and institutional plan, which will be reviewed regularly and against which resources will be allocated.

d Recognising the Vice-Chancellor not only as academic leader but also as chief executive of the university.

e Establishing a planning and resources committee of strictly limited size reporting to Council and Senate with the Vice-Chancellor as Chairman and both academic and lay members.

f Budget delegation to appropriate centres which are held responsible to the planning and resources committee for what they have achieved against their budget.

g Developing reliable and consistent performance indicators, greater awareness of costs and more full cost charging.

h Appointing Heads of Departments by Councils, on the recommend-ation of the Vice-Chancellor after appropriate consultation, with clear duties and responsibility for the performance of their departments and their use of resources.

i Introducing arrangements for staff development, appraisal and accountability.

j Saving academic and other time by having fewer committee meetings involving fewer people, and more delegation of authority to officers of the university – especially for non-academic matters.

Value for money was a concern of the Jarratt Report and, in the public sector, also of the Audit Commission (HMSO 1985c). According to Lindop (1981), educational quality gets excluded from criteria of efficiency when external constraints increase; which highlights a yawning gap in the Audit Report, based as it was on visits to 165 of the 550 polytechnics and colleges of further education. The Audit Commission spent 30-40 man-days at each selected institution, interviewing staff and collecting data during 1984, data which included average student hours, average class size, average lecturer hours, student completion rates, and non-academic costs. The report was very critical of the lack of proper market research and made major suggestions also on tailoring teaching resources more closely to demand, better cost-recovery and tight control over non-teaching costs. There was particular concern about the extent of remission of lecturing staff from agreed class 'contact hours'; but in this, the Commission misunderstood the nature of the academic communities and the management of staff time. The closest the report came to considering quality was to refer to the possible link between student completion rate and the 'attractiveness with which a course is presented', before linking it to effective marking. It is difficult to see how the Audit Commission carried out its intention to 'avoid making educational policy judgements', or how its report is consistent with its own statement that 'value for money is not synonymous with economy'. In fact, it is hard not to conclude that the Commission equated 'value' with maximum numbers of students and, in so doing, leaned very heavily on educational policy-making, without any understanding of its dynamics or of institutional purposes. Birch and Latcham (1985b) were also critical of the Commission's neglect of the effects of different institutional mixes of work, and of its pursuit of intricate details of hours when the prime cost criterion should be student/staff ratio.

Perhaps individual local authorities can be more sensitive than their government-appointed financial inquisitor. The Inner London Education Authority sought institutional self-evaluation in its colleges (ILEA 1983a), anticipating that the benefits would include everyone thinking more systematically about improving their performance, the college facing its principal tasks, regeneration of the quality of college life and professionalism, motivation to implement recommendations on quality, effectiveness and efficiency, and an information base for college central decision-making and planning. The guidance notes were simply a list of headings for appraisal, and nothing appears to have been published about methods or about the results or effectiveness of such evaluations, or indeed whether any have taken place.

In the field of advanced further education, the ILEA published a consultative paper (ILEA 1983b), proposals based upon the responses to this (ILEA 1983c), and a set of recommendations (ILEA 1984) based on consideration of the review by committees and institutions. Re-location of various departments was the major outcome for a number of institutions, but the authority itself has set up an AFE strategy section and inter-institutional subject groupings. The strategy section meets each institution annually to discuss its plans and advises the Authority. The subject panels advise the Authority and the institutions on subject level needs, developments and possible collaboration and rationalization. The review also caused the ILEA to rethink and publish the aims of higher education in Inner London (ILEA 1983b, 1983c).

The UK Government has said rather less in its recent Green Paper (HMSO 1985a) about how it sees the aims of higher education, except in the sense of linking them primarily to the generation of wealth. However, the Green Paper has a chapter on institutions, in which it goes further than the visions in either the NAB or the UGC advice, in seeking specific objectives for whole institutions and their monitoring. Much is also said about academic staff appraisal and updating professional skills and knowledge. Finally, the Green Paper endorses the Jarratt Report's (CVCP 1985a) search for reliable and consistent institutional performance indicators. However, the measures listed in Annex B discount research outputs and social benefits, and elaborate only the output of 'highly qualified manpower'. The measures of recurrent costs per student, non-completion rates, entry qualifications, first destination statistics, and social rate of return on investment are not significantly developed there for the purposes of institutional self-appraisal or comparison.

Conclusions

The major conclusion is not very different from the last point: that none of the process or performance criteria are yet sufficiently developed or proven, nor are their limitations properly understood or taken into account in use. No fully convincing studies have been done on the appraisal of institutions; they lack substantiation on the effects and effectiveness of such appraisals. At all levels there is more dark than light, and more conflict than consensus.

References

Adelman, C. and Alexander, R. (1981) Who wants to know that? Aspects of institutional self-evaluation. In R. Oxtoby (Ed.) *Higher Education at the Cross Roads* Guildford: Society for Research into Higher Education

Adelman, C. and Alexander, R.J. (1982) *The Self-Evaluating Institution – Practice and Principles in the Management of Educational Change* London: Methuen

Baldridge, J.V. (1971) *Power and Conflict in the University* New York: Wiley

Baldridge, J.V. and Tierney, M.L. (1979) *New Approaches to Management* San Francisco: Jossey-Bass

Ball, C. (1985) *Fitness for Purpose* Guildford: SRHE & NFER-NELSON

Becher, A.R. and Kogan, M. (1980) *Process and Structure in Higher Education* London: Heinemann Educational Books

Beer, S. (1979) *The Heart of the Enterprise* New York: Wiley

Billing, D. (1983a) Practice and criteria in validation under the CNAA. In C. Church (Ed.) *Practice and Perspective in Validation* Guildford: Society for Research into Higher Education

Billing, D. (1983b) Appraising academic priorities *Evaluation Newsletter* 7(2) 42-53

Birch, D. and Latcham, J. (1985a) Measuring college performance. In *Assessing Educational Effectiveness and Efficiency* Coombe Lodge Report 18(3) 97-121

Birch, D. and Latcham J. (1985b) The Audit Commission and FE: Value for money and the audit ratios. In *Assessing Educational Effectiveness and Efficiency* Coombe Lodge Report 18(3) 122-137

Bottomley, J. et al. (1972) *Costs and Potential Economies* Paris: OECD

Bradley, J., Chesson, A. and Silverleaf, J. (1983) *Inside Staff Development* London: NFER-NELSON

Bredo, A.E. and Bredo, E.R. (1975) Effects of environment and structure on the process of innovation. In J.V. Baldridge and T.E. Deal (Eds.) *Managing Change in Educational Organizations* Berkeley: McCutchan

Burnip, M.S., Durrands, K. and Lindsell, S. (1980) Indicators in polytechnics. In D. Billing (Ed.) *Indicators of Performance* Guildford: Society for Research into Higher Education

Burns, T. and Stalker, G.M. (1966) *The Management of Innovation* London: Tavistock

Calvert, J.R. (1980) Relative performance. In D. Billing (Ed.) *Indicators of Performance* Guildford: Society for Research into Higher Education

Cameron, K.S., and Whetton, D.A. (1981) Perceptions of organizational effectiveness over organizational life cycles *Administrative Science Quarterly* 26,525-544

Chartered Institute of Public Finance and Accountancy (CIPFA) (1980) *Financial Information System for Institutions of Higher and Further Education in the Maintained Sector: Manual of Guidance*

Clark, B.R. (1972) The organizational saga in higher education *Administrative Science Quarterly* June, 178-184

Committee of Vice-Chancellors and Principals (CVCP) (1985a) *Report of the Steering Committee for Efficiency Studies in Universities*

Committee of Vice-Chancellors and Principals (CVCP) (1985b) *National Data Study* Foster, C. and Thompson, Q. for Coopers and Lybrand Associates and the CVCP

Council for National Academic Awards (CNAA) (1979a) *Principles and Regulations for the Award of the Council's First Degrees and Diploma of Higher Education*

Council for National Academic Awards (CNAA) (1979b) *Developments in Partnership in Validation*

Council for National Academic Awards (CNAA) (1983a) *Notes on Institutional Reviews*

Council for National Academic Awards (CNAA) (1983b) *Future Development of CNAA's Academic Policies at Undergraduate Level* Consultative Paper

Council for National Academic Awards (CNAA) (1984a) *Files on Courses in Institutions (FOCII): Policy and Operation* Development Services Publication No.8

Council for National Academic Awards (CNAA) (1984b) *Development of the Council's Relationships with Institutions* Consultative Paper.

Council for National Academic Awards (CNAA) (1984c) *Reviews Coordinating Sub-Committee*

Council for National Academic Awards (CNAA) (1984d) *Future Arrangements for Relationships Between the CNAA and NAB* Consultative Paper. Also Chief Officer's letters, with attachments, to institutions 20 January 1984 and 13 September 1984; and CNAA letter 12 July 1985 and appendix 'The streamlining of validation and review'

Cuthbert, R.E. and Birch, D.W. (1980) Limitations of the student-staff ratio as a resource control. In D. Billing (Ed.) *Indicators of Performance* Guildford: Society for Research into Higher Education

Davies, J.L. and Morgan, A.W. (1982) The politics of institutional change. In L. Wagner (Ed.) *Agenda for Institutional Change in Higher Education* Guildford: Society for Research into Higher Education

Davis, M.C. (1979) *The Development of the CNAA 1964-74* PhD Thesis, Loughborough

Department of Education and Science (DES) (1985) *Report by Her Majesty's Inspectors on the Effects of Local Authority Expenditure Policies on Education Provision in England – 1984*

Dressel, P.L. (1976) *Handbook of Academic Evaluation* Chapter on Institutional Self-Study, pp.401-432. San Francisco: Jossey-Bass

Doyle, P. and Lynch, J.E. (1979) A strategic model for university planning *Journal of the Operational Research Society* 30(7) 603-609

Enderud, H.G. (1977) *Four Faces of Leadership in the Academic Organization* Copenhagen: Nyt. Nordisk Forlag

Ford, J.D., and Schellenberg, D.A. (1982) Conceptual issues of linkage in the assessment of organizational performance *Academy of Management Review* 7(1) 49-58

Glanville, H. (1979) *Institutional Reviews* Cyclostyled. London: CNAA

Glanville, H. (1981) *The Institutional Review Process: An Appraisal* Evidence to the Council's Working Party on Longer Term Developments, cyclostyled, CNAA

Her Majesty's Stationery Office (HMSO) (1963) *Higher Education: Report of the Committee under the Chairmanship of Lord Robbins* Cmnd 2154

Her Majesty's Stationery Office (HMSO) (1966) *A Plan for Polytechnics and Other Colleges* White Paper, Cmnd 3006

Her Majesty's Stationery Office (HMSO) (1980) *The Funding and Organisation of Courses in Higher Education* Fifth report from the Education, Science and Arts Committee (Price Report) (HC 787-1)

Her Majesty's Stationery Office (HMSO) (1985a) *The Development of Higher Education into the 1990s* Cmnd 9524

Her Majesty's Stationery Office (HMSO) (1985b) *Academic Validation in Public Sector Higher Education* (Lindop Report) Cmnd 9501

Her Majesty's Stationery Office (HMSO) (1985c) *Obtaining Better Value from Further Education* Report by the Audit Commission for Local Authorities in England and Wales

Inner London Education Authority (ILEA) (1983a) *Keeping the College Under Review: A Method of Self-Assessment for Colleges Devised by the ILEA Inspectorate*

Inner London Education Authority (ILEA) (1983b) *Consultative Paper: Review of Advanced Further Education in Inner London*

Inner London Education Authority (ILEA) (1983c) *Review of Advanced Further Education in Inner London: Education Officer's Proposals*

Inner London Education Authority (ILEA) (1984) *Review of Advanced Further Education in Inner London: Education Officer's Recommendations*

Knight, P. (1985) Unfair helpings? *Times Higher Educational Supplement* 30 August, No. 669, p.12; Messages from above and below *THES* 6 September, No. 670, p.14; All for one and one for all *THES* 13 September, No. 671, p.12.

Lane, M. (1975) *Design for Degrees: New Degree Courses under the CNAA 1964-74* London: Macmillan

Leverhulme Report (1983) *Excellence in Diversity* Guildford: Society for Research into Higher Education

Lindop, N. (1981) Seeking a middle poly way *Times Higher Education Supplement* No. 467, p.190

Lindsay, A. (1981) Assessing institutional performance in higher education: A management perspective *Higher Education* 10(6) 687-706

Morris, A. (1974) The context and process of university planning *Higher Education Bulletin* 3(1) 3-15

National Advisory Body (NAB) (1982) *Letter to Institutions* 26 July

National Advisory Body (NAB) (1984) *A Strategy for Higher Education in the Late 1980s and Beyond*

National Advisory Body (NAB) (1985) Letter to Institutions 29 March

National Advisory Body (NAB) (1986) *Letter to all Institutions* 2 January

Nuffield Foundation (1976) *Making the Best of it* Final report of the Group for Research and Innovation in Higher Education, London

Pennings, J.M. and Goodman, P.S. (1977) Towards a workable framework, In P.S. Goodman et al; *New Perspectives on Organizational Effectiveness* San Francisco: Jossey-Bass

Pirsig, R.M. (1974) *Zen and the Art of Motorbike Maintenance* London: The Bodley Head

Porter, D. (1978) Developing performance indicators for the teaching function *Workshop on Performance Indicators for Institutions of Higher Education* Programme on Institutional Management in Higher Education. Paris: OECD/CERI

Quinn, R.E. and Cameron, K.S. (1980) Organizational life cycles and shifting criteria of effectiveness: Some preliminary evidence. Quoted in K.S. Cameron and D.A. Whetton (1981) Perceptions of organizational effectiveness over organizational life cycles *Administrative Science Quarterly* 26,525-544

Romney, L. (1978) *Measures of Institutional Goal Achievement* National Centre for Higher Education Management Systems Research Report, Denver

Sizer, J. (1981) Indicators of institutional performance. In *Measuring Up to the Future: Institutional Evaluation and Renewal* Manchester Polytechnic Conference Paper No. 40

Sizer, J. (1982) Assessing institutional performance and progress. In L. Wagner (Ed.) *Agenda for Institutional Change in Higher Education* Guildford: Society for Research into Higher Education

University Grants Committee (UGC) (1978) *Notes for Guidance on Quinquennial Visitations*

University Grants Committee (UGC) (1984) *Strategy for Higher Education into the 1990s* London: HMSO

Verry, D. and Davies, B. (1976) *University Costs and Output* Elsevier Scientific Publishing Ltd

Yorke, M. (1984) *Effectiveness in Higher Education* A Review. London: Council for National Academic Awards

6

Staff and Standards

John Nisbet

Once upon a time (to start as all good fairy tales do) just to be a university lecturer or professor was itself evidence of quality. As with the aristocracy in a pre-democratic age, any incompetence or indolence in a member of university staff tended to be regarded tolerantly, as a form of eccentricity. In days when a degree secured admission to membership of an exclusive social group, concern about standards was not seen as appropriate among those who had secured membership. Tolerating possible weaknesses among a minority could be justified as a price worth paying for the security and autonomy of the rest; besides, had not history shown that some of the most creative original work was done by those whose life styles or modes of working did not match conventional expectations? Even Adam Smith (1776) author of *The Wealth of Nations* commented favourably on students' liberal judgements on the essential qualities of a university teacher:

> Such is the generosity of the greater part of young men, that so far from being disposed to neglect or despise the instructions of their master, provided he shows some serious intention of being of use to them, they are generally inclined to pardon a great deal of incorrectness in the performance of his duty, and sometimes even to conceal from the public a good deal of gross negligence.

In Adam Smith's day in Scotland a professor's salary was determined by how many students he could attract to pay the fees for his class. His point is that even in this crude system, students' choice was not based on any simple formula for 'correct performance'.

These fairy-tale days, however, are now gone. Quality of staff in higher education is a matter of public concern, for we depend on public money; it is no longer a private concern internal to the profession. The reason for the change is not just the increased public share in the costs of higher education, and not the occasional abuse of privileged freedom by some professors and lecturers in the bad old days. Public attitudes to professions generally have changed. The quality of teaching in schools is subject to similar scrutiny. Public sector institutions are required to submit to a validation procedure which includes a review of staff. The rapid pace of development in university subjects demands a continuing effort to keep up. No longer can a good first degree at age 21 be accepted as proof of competence throughout life: the concept of innate intelligence on which that myth depended is now discredited. There are many contributing factors which have eroded the old idea of an intellectual élite, not least the enormous growth in the numbers of university teachers. Some form of checking standards of performance and effort among academic staff is not merely a safeguard against indolence, but will also provide a stimulus to motivation of staff at all levels, or so it may be claimed.

Thus staff appraisal in higher education has emerged from the shadows in recent years to become an issue of open debate in Britain. The debate, however, tends to be about the method of its introduction rather than the principles involved. To question the principle of staff appraisal in the present climate of opinion is likely to be seen as unrealistic. The common attitude is that appraisal is coming whether we like it or not; it is only a question of how and how soon, not whether or why. Consequently, so the argument runs, let us introduce our own scheme before a worse one is forced upon us. Various strategies have been suggested:

a leave staff appraisal to heads of departments and keep it an internal and private matter;

b design a self-appraisal procedure, for departments or for whole institutions or for individuals, so that standards can be discussed more openly, but still privately within the institution; or

c wrap up the appraisal procedure in a positively worded programme of 'staff development' in which planning ahead is discussed as well as assessing past performance, thus minimizing the implicit threat – though in some appraisal schemes the wrapping of 'staff development' only thinly covers a strong element of compulsion and authoritative scrutiny.

Discussion at the level of method, however, is merely a patching exercise. It is necessary to try to establish underlying principles in the assessment of standards of academic staff, and this is not as simple a task as is assumed by those who draw up lists of 'performance indicators'. Any process of assessment of people affects relationships, and therefore the way in which the system operates is often more important than the specific components.

Appraisal is nothing new, of course: at the end of probation or for promotion from one salary scale to a higher status, a formal, fully documented review is a conventionally accepted procedure. Some criticize it as ineffective and publicly unconvincing, and recommend instead a system of annual appraisal, with sanctions for those who fail to match standards determined by their 'superiors' in the hierarchy of office. This could well prove self-defeating, making matters worse, not better, if it resulted in staff working cautiously to satisfy or avoid offending a senior 'manager'.

What we want is a system which will be beneficial. In the end, it may have to be a system in which the benefits will no more than outweigh the bad effects, but the solution is not to be found in a simple balance of plus and minus. The system should be designed so as to allow the beneficial effects to grow and the harmful effects to be eliminated, as people become more used to and more skilled in applying the system. This line of reasoning is already familiar in respect of examinations, and perhaps what has happened with examinations is a warning for staff appraisal schemes.

In the second half of the nineteenth century there was a similar public demand for more rigorous examination procedures, at all levels of education from elementary school to university. At university level examinations probably helped to raise standards of student performance. At school level, and especially in elementary school with the introduction of Payments by Results in 1861, examinations came to tyrannize the curriculum and to destroy interest and originality. Staff appraisal has similar potential for good or for evil. As with examinations, it could have beneficial effects in motivating, setting targets, giving feedback, diagnostically identifying areas of weakness for remediation. But it could also damage commitment, morale and relationships among academic staff, exercise a restrictive influence on their work and waste time in elaborate bureaucratic procedures. Probably it would also prove to be an inefficient system for identifying the alleged 'incompetence'. The analogy with examinations is helpful. Examinations tend to distort the curriculum, but the solution is to improve them, not to abolish them. Staff appraisal has a contribution to make to academic standards, but its effect will depend on what form it takes and what resources are provided in support.

If the appraisal of staff in higher education is to avoid a comparable damaging effect on relationships and morale, the model on which an appraisal procedure is based must be considered very carefully. The model assumed in the current debate is often an industrial model, based on a hierarchical staffing structure and a simple criterion of quality of output. Arguably, the application of this style of appraisal will tend to discourage divergent thinking which a university can turn to advantage but an industrial organization cannot tolerate as readily. The traditional model in higher education is a collegiate model, the university or college being seen as a community of scholars in which there is accountability to one's peers. As a means of ensuring academic standards, this style of accountability has lost favour in recent years, presumably because there is evidence that it is too tolerant of incompetence and indolence. Or is it because of a feeling that accountability should be more public and open? Or, perhaps most likely, is it out of favour because a collegiate system does not change quickly enough when conditions require change? If the inertia of the traditional system is the underlying cause, then the industrial model is attractive in that it can (or claims to) implement change more quickly, operating through a management structure in which the decisions of those at the top do not have to wait for the persuasion of the rest. Thus an appraisal system can readily become a mechanism of control, a matter of compliance not of standards.

But if the aim of an appraisal system is to encourage higher standards by raising awareness of quality among academic staff and bringing issues of standards into a more open forum for discussion, a hierarchical structure of authority is not required – nor indeed should it involve dependent relationships. Studies of innovation and change in education show that top-down growth does not work: changes imposed from above do not last. The argument in this chapter is that the beneficial effects of appraisal can be got through a collegiate, peer-accountable system, accepting that changes will be needed. In the present climate in Britain, an argument on these lines is unlikely to win acceptance; but possibly after some disasters, this is the kind of appraisal system which will eventually emerge.

Staff Appraisal: Universities

Concern over standards in university teaching was conspicuously lacking until the Robbins (1963) and Hale (UGC 1964) Reports. In the Robbins Report, training was seen as appropriate only for new staff ('for all newly-appointed junior teachers', recommendation 123) and no proposals were made about appraisal. The Hale Report urged that training 'should be given as a matter of course to all newly appointed staff, without waiting until complaints are heard or mistakes have hardened into habits' (para.392). But the Hale Committee also suggested that new staff 'should undergo some test as a matter of course' (para.345), by a colleague sitting in on a lecture or by recording.

In 1968, the Prices and Incomes Board, commenting on university salaries, recommended extra discretionary payments to teaching staff for 'exacting loads' or 'quality of teaching', without being able to suggest how teaching might be assessed. When the Universities Authorities Panel and the Association of University Teachers drafted their 'agreement on probation' in 1971 (finally agreed in 1974), appraisal at the end of the probationary period was included unquestioningly. The UAP were untroubled by doubts about how to assess lecturers:

> Assessment...depends inevitably on subjective estimate. It is however in just this class of assessment, the assessment of academic worth and potential, that senior university teachers are most experienced and most skilled.

Such complacency is now clearly outdated, inviting the criticism of 'a cosy solidarity which inhibits scrutiny' (*THES* 1985). In the 1970s concern over standards was limited to teaching; research could be appraised by the traditional criterion of publication, and even that, if assessed only by quantity of output, was viewed by many as antagonistic to true qualities of scholarship. In the humanities especially, a scholar's life-time work could be justified by the publication of one major definitive book. By 1978, some 20 of the 45 universities in Britain had established centres or units to provide courses in university teaching (Nisbet and McAleese, in Teather 1979) but until recently none had even considered a system of regular staff appraisal other than for promotion.

Between then and 1983 the attitude to appraisal changed dramatically. The reasons for this change are obviously to be found in government policy, in the cuts of 1981, the end of expansion and recruitment of new staff and consequent pressures on existing staff to justify their continued employment; but the 'accountability' movement began long before the 1979 General Election and affected other sectors in education much earlier. The surprising fact is that the universities escaped this pressure for as long as they did. By 1983, attitudes had changed so much that no one expressed dissent from or even surprise at the cautious concession made in the Leverhulme Report (1983):

Prime responsibility for standards must rest with the higher education community.... Nevertheless, there is a legitimate external interest, and the higher education community benefits when its quality is clearly visible.

By the time when the University Grants Committee (UGC) published its advice to Government in 1984, there had been a significant move nearer to acceptance of a staff appraisal system. The document, *A Strategy for Higher Education into the 1990s* (UGC 1984), devotes two pages to 'Academic standards'. It reviews four aspects, research, curricula, teaching and examining, and on teaching (para.6.5) states:

It is the responsibility of departments to monitor teaching and make sure it is effective.... Staff appraisal has become much more searching and constructive for professional staff in many organizations. In the universities there are modest staff development programmes and some systematic induction for new staff is now common. This is not sufficient.

Paragraph 7.15, headed 'Effectiveness of existing staff', does not refer to appraisal, but mentions staff development, retraining, mobility and transfers, and study leave.

The Jarratt Report on 'Efficiency Studies in Universities' (March 1985) was the next to appear. In its section on 'Academic staff', the advice is stronger and more blunt:

Universities are unusual in that little formal attempt is made on a regular basis to appraise academic staff with a view to their personal development and to succession (sic) planning within the institution. We believe this to be of crucial importance.... A regular review procedure, handled with sensitivity, would be of benefit to staff, and to the university as a whole.

The report goes on to specify in some detail what should be done:

In considering the form of staff appraisal system for a university, three main objectives can be identified:

a   Recognition of the contribution made by individuals,
b   Assistance for individuals to develop their full potential as quickly as possible,
c   Assistance for the university to make the most effective use of its academic staff.

We commend an annual review on this basis as is the practice in the best staff development systems used elsewhere.

The report also recommends that 'there should be some central responsibility for coordinating staff reporting procedures'.

With this by way of preparing the ground, it is perhaps surprising that the Government Green Paper (May 1985a), *The Development of Higher Education into the 1990s*, contains only one reference to staff appraisal, in a relatively short paragraph (7.9) headed 'Staff development':

All teachers in higher education should have opportunity and encouragement to develop and update professional skills and knowledge.... Effective staff development will not happen without a formal institutional framework for evaluating performance and for responding to development and training needs. Institutions and employers should develop their arrangements in these areas and should adopt a more systematic approach to raising the professionalism and adaptability of their staff.

The paragraph ends with a reference to the Jarratt Report recommendation 'for staff development, appraisal and accountability as part of... planning and management structures'. An earlier paragraph (6.11) on 'Quality' states that standards depend 'first and foremost on the quality, competence and attitudes of the academic staff'. A less friendly tone is struck in the concluding paragraph (6.15) of the chapter:

> Meanwhile, however, there are outstanding questions about the answerability of the universities when there are complaints from students, staff or the public....The Government is concerned about the present apparent lack of accountability and is discussing with the CVCP what might be done.

The Committee of Vice-Chancellors and Principals (CVCP) had already taken action in 1983 by setting up an 'Academic Standards Group' with Professor Reynolds, Vice-Chancellor of Lancaster, as chairman. Guidelines on various aspects were published, and in September 1985 the Reynolds Committee produced a draft paper which dealt (among other themes) with the monitoring of standards of staff performance. The paper, *Universities' Internal Procedures for Maintaining and Monitoring Academic Standards*, acknowledges that the quality of academic staff is a crucial factor in standards in higher education:

> The academic standards of courses and the standards which students achieve will above all be affected by the commitment, teaching skills and performance of the staff involved, and, given the interdependence of teaching and research, by their research interests and activities.

However, the Committee appear to regard the quality of staff as unproblematic for they devote only half a page to the section on 'Academic staff', after four pages on procedures for monitoring courses. In that previous section, the Committee sets out 'the components of an effective monitoring system', which include factual data on student performance and research activity, the views of external examiners, employers and students, and 'auditing of the commitment and teaching skills of staff'. Responsibility for 'auditing' is 'normally that of the head of department', who would be expected to send reports 'at appropriate intervals to a higher body for review'. The subsequent comment on staff appraisal is made cautiously and set in the context of staff development:

> Most universities do and all should have appropriate procedures for an effective system of regular appraisal of all staff during their careers to ensure that individuals satisfactorily meet their responsibilities and that any necessary guidance and assistance is given in regard to career development.

For all its soft wording, this sentence expresses the negative functions of appraisal: 'meet responsibilities' implies detecting inefficiency and 'necessary guidance' suggests authoritative direction. It does not mention the recognition and reward of excellence, or promise to improve morale or commitment. It is also vague in not specifying what is 'appropriate', 'effective', 'regular' or 'satisfactorily'.

Staff Appraisal: Polytechnics

In the past ten years, polytechnics have given more attention to appraisal and staff development than the universities. Validation procedures required by the Council for National Academic Awards (CNAA) may have helped to make the concept of staff appraisal more acceptable, since validation includes assessment of institutional resources as well as course content and structure, and staff are a prime element in institutional resources. In respect of staff, however, the validation procedure tends to rely on formal qualifications and possibly research output and consultancies, judged corporately and not individually.

Within the polytechnics and the Scottish central institutions, there is neither standard procedure, nor any national statement of guidelines for staff development or appraisal apart from the conventional reviews for promotion to a higher salary scale. A survey in 1979 by Greenaway and Mortimer (Teather 1979) reported that 'about half a dozen' polytechnics had formulated policies for staff development, with annual meetings between individual lecturers and the head of department (or a nominated person). The schemes were on a voluntary basis, and Warren's (1977) survey in one polytechnic showed that only one third of the staff opted into the scheme. By 1985, though no comprehensive survey has been done, it appears that most institutions in public sector higher education have a formal statement of policy on staff development, and within these there is usually provision for staff appraisal.

In 1978, for example, Trent Polytechnic published a policy (Fox 1978), covering aims, responsibilities, available opportunities and financial support. Most of the document sets out the ways in which staff can 'maintain and increase their effectiveness as educators'. Appraisal is mentioned: it should be 'effective and fair... constructive, compassionate and informative', and may include either interview (annual or biennial) or class observation (or taking part in classes cooperatively) or both of these.

In 1984-5, Trent introduced various changes in its Staff Development Service, which by then had been in existence for some ten years. An important new element was a reporting procedure on staff development plans which was to operate through a network of departmental staff development advisors. Appraisal is on a department basis, setting out 'in broad terms the main areas of staff strengths and weaknesses without identifying individuals'.

In Sunderland Polytechnic, the annual interview 'occupies a central position in the implementation and review of staff development' (Report to Governors, October 1985).

> Each member of staff is required to complete a proforma prior to the interview which is then jointly signed by the Head of Department and the staff member concerned on completion of the interview.

Interview data are collated annually by each Head of Department in an annual staff development report, which is appraised by the Staffing Committee.

Identifying relevant criteria for appraisal is a current concern in both Teesside Polytechnic (Pennington and O'Neil 1985) and Oxford Polytechnic (Gibbs 1983). The Oxford proposal, for example, is based on a 'teaching profile', adapted from a Canadian model, with thirty-three categories; this is limited to appraisal for promotion and is submitted at the initiative of the applicant. Teesside proposals, which are still at the stage of debate favour

> a regular form of staff review... a two-way process... not linked crudely to salary incentives... positive (where weaknesses come to light they are not penalized but are allied to a support mechanism)... based on clearly defined public criteria... and an open appeals procedure.

In Scottish central institutions, staff appraisal is commonly practised in the context of staff development. At Queen's College, Glasgow, all staff are interviewed annually by the Principal; at Dundee College of Technology, annual appraisal is undertaken by the Staff Development Committee; in both institutions the results are used to prepare a programme of secondment.

Many other examples could be given, all differing in detail. The common element is an emphasis on a positive function for staff appraisal, as a basis for promotion, secondment or study leave. In the attempt to play down the hidden threat, policy statements on staff development tend to be idealistic about the good effects of the schemes; they tend to assume that senior staff do not need guidance or training in the skills required in conducting appraisal interviews, and say little about the massive burden of preparing and processing the documentation which is suggested.

Parallel Developments in Schools

The events in higher education in Britain cannot be understood without reference to the pressure towards teacher appraisal and staff development in schools. This dates back to the Ruskin College speech by Prime Minister James Callaghan in October 1976 which initiated publicly the 'accountability' movement:

> Public interest is strong and will be satisfied. It is legitimate. We spend £6 billion a year on education so there will be discussion. If everything is reduced to such phrases as 'educational freedom versus state control' we shall get nowhere.... Where there is a legitimate public concern it will be to the advantage of all involved in the educational field if these concerns are aired and shortcomings righted or fears put to rest.

In succeeding years, the focus of interest was on the concept of 'accountability'. The Inner London Education Authority, along with other authorities, developed procedures for self-evaluation by schools, setting out questions for discussion among staff and criteria for judging success, seeing this both as a means of reporting to parents and also for staff development.

The Open University developed a course on Institutional Self-evaluation and Assessment (Open University 1982) and books were written on the subject (Shipman 1979; Simons 1981; Adelman and Alexander 1982; Eraut 1983).

But self-assessment lacked credibility to a government concerned about standards and pressed by teachers' associations for improved conditions of work. More recently, a succession of papers from the Department of Education and Science have argued more strongly the case for regular teacher appraisal: *Teaching Quality* (DES 1983), *Better Schools* (DES 1985b), *Quality in Schools* (DES 1985c). *Teaching Quality*, for example, stated:

> The Government believe that... formal assessment of teacher performance is necessary and should be based on classroom visiting by the teacher's head or head of department, and an appraisal of both pupils' work and of the teacher's contribution to the life of the school.

In September 1983 (according to *Quality in Schools*) at least fifty-six education authorities reported self-evaluation in their schools, though 'only eleven had mandatory policies requiring evaluation and the production of written reports'. *Better Schools* expressed the belief that 'systematic, nationwide arrangements for appraising teacher performance are essential' and that it may prove 'desirable or even necessary' to introduce statutory requirements for appraisal. The Queen's Speech in November 1985 proposed legislation requiring local education authorities to appraise the performance of all their teachers at regular intervals.

The 1985 paper, *Quality in Schools*, gives detailed accounts of staff appraisal schemes in school. One example specifies annual appraisal (with provision for termly checks) covering fourteen areas of performance, four aspects of personal development and eight aspects of school involvement for each teacher, plus a review of development plans and a career review, resulting in a written record of interviews and a summary review of all twenty-six aspects, signed by the head, the teacher and the inspector involved. The DES selected two local authorities to carry out pilot projects in teacher appraisal: the Suffolk report (*TES* 1985a) warns that a teacher assessment system would be expensive, but argues that it would be worthwhile. The report considers that classroom observation must be 'seen to be central to the process of appraisal'; it urges that excellence should be rewarded, not with merit pay but with sabbatical leave, while poor teachers should not be disciplined directly but offered support and training, at least initially. In a subsequent article (*TES* 1985b) the Chief Education Officer for Suffolk argued against annual appraisal, preferring 'a pattern based on factors related to promotion, on teacher request, on years of service and where doubts about adequacy of performance exist.'

In Scotland, the approach has been more cautious. Only one document has been issued, *Arrangements for the Staff Development of Teachers* (National Committee for the In-Service Training of Teachers 1984). This states explicitly that it is 'not concerned with... machinery for assessing the basic competence of teachers but rather with help... to teachers to maintain and enhance their expertise.' The report recommends 'a periodic review of each teacher's needs... to ensure that every teacher is helped to keep abreast of the considerable changes in the curriculum...,' and asserts that staff development 'must generate teacher commitment (which is) most evident when planned collaboratively.' It warns against 'the creation of a complicated and bureaucratic system of reporting,' condemns the 'deficit model in which teachers are seen as lacking certain professional skills,' and recommends that we 'leave it to the judgement of schools and education authorities as to the form and frequency of the consultation and reporting.' Staff development is defined as 'the planned process whereby the effectiveness of staff, collectively and individually, is enhanced... in order to improve, directly or indirectly, the quality of pupils' education.' Perhaps the universities and polytechnics need a definition like this.

Staff Appraisal in Other Countries

Discussion so far has been limited to Britain. It is beyond the scope of this chapter to attempt to review staff appraisal and staff development in other countries: to review the American scene would require a book on its own, and many have been published in the last ten years. (Elton 1984 quotes three review articles on the evaluation of teaching, each of which gives extensive bibliographies.) The essential point to note is that in most other countries, and especially in USA, there is a more ready acceptance of open, competitive appraisal than in Britain. This acceptance is linked with a broader interpretation of what is conventionally taught in colleges, a wider range of qualifications among college staff and a different attitude to tenure.

The standard form of appraisal in USA is the formal committee procedure presided over by a dean or chairman. Student appraisal is also widely used, usually in combination with the traditional procedure. From a review of 756 American colleges and universities, Centra (1977, in Braskamp 1980) reported that 80 per cent used student ratings for assessing the performance of staff. More recently, in a 1983 survey of 616 liberal arts colleges by Seldin (1984), 67 per cent 'always used' systematic student ratings, and many others used student opinion gathered less formally. There is no clear consensus on procedure (how to obtain ratings, who should collect them, how they should be handled) and some controversy over their value. One of the more serious criticisms is the 'Doctor Fox effect' reported by Naftulin et al. (1973):

> An instructor who can teach charismatically but non-substantively for a brief period on a topic about which he knows nothing can be rated very favourably.

But student ratings are generally seen as a useful element in an appraisal system, a conclusion supported by Flood Page's (1974) balanced assessment of students' evaluation of teaching.

The variety of procedures used in appraisal systems is vividly demonstrated by Seldin's review of practice in American liberal arts colleges (mentioned above). Policies currently in use for evaluating 'overall faculty performance' included reports on:

Classroom teaching, supervision of graduate study, supervision of honors program, research, publication, public service, consultation, activity in professional societies, student advising, campus committee work, length of service in rank, competing job offers, personal attributes.

Similar lengthy lists of 'performance indicators' are presented for the separate assessment of teaching, of scholarship and of 'college service'. The length of the lists demonstrates the variety of roles on which a university teacher may be judged (a point we shall return to later).

Strenuous attempts have been made to develop precise objective measuring instruments for the assessment of staff performance. Miller (1972), for example (to quote only one of many texts on the subject), describes twenty-one appraisal schedules which can be combined into an overall performance rating by allocating percentage rating on a scale 1 to 7, and using weighted addition to get a total out of a maximum 700 points. This is reminiscent of Barzun's (1969) less serious suggestion of a formula for colleges to calculate their Visible Prestige (ViP):

$$ViP = \frac{2p + 5n}{f}$$

– twice the number of Pulitzer prizes plus five times the Nobel prizes divided by the number of faculty.

Across the border, in Canada, the Teaching Dossier (Shore et al. 1978) mentioned above has 45 categories by which a lecturer's academic performance may be judged. Elton's (1984) paper gives references to comparable work in Australia.

In summary, staff appraisal is more common in these other countries and is more detailed, relying more on systematic procedures with schedules or checklists. Whether it is more valid is another matter: objective, 'low inference' data are usually more reliable (in the statistical sense) but often less valid, whereas subjective, 'high inference' judgements have lower reliability but are often more meaningful, more easily communicated and more credible. However, appraisal procedures in these other countries have been more subject to rigorous evaluation. In Britain there is no provision for monitoring the monitors, for analysing the validity of appraisal procedures. Appraisal is seen largely as a matter of academic reputation judged by peers mainly on the basis of published work, with some allowance for other forms of competence such as teaching or administration; and staff development, in the universities, is still essentially the staff member's own responsibility.

Aims and Criteria

The pressure to introduce staff appraisal in a more systematic form in higher education seems unlikely to diminish. Elton (1984) is one of many who warn: 'if... (universities) do not maintain order in their own house, others may insist on doing it for them.' Plans for the introduction of an appraisal system should be based on explicit aims, so that it is clear what function the appraisal is to perform. A statement of aims can lead to a set of criteria which an appraisal procedure must satisfy, and by which the procedure itself can be judged. (Deciding the criteria by which academic performance is to be judged, the 'performance indicators', is a subsequent task.)

In polytechnics, the future pattern seems already to be emerging, though no national policy has been agreed: appraisal is built into a staff development policy, with regular (usually annual) interviews to review the past record and plan a future programme. In universities, staff appraisal at present tends to be limited to probation and promotion, and therefore occurs rarely, with long intervals between. At the end of probation, the procedure is often criticized as perfunctory; at senior lecturer level, so few promotions are now available that the procedure has little to offer to the majority of candidates. The most likely prediction is that universities also will introduce staff development schemes based on interviews and documentation, following the polytechnic example, and some universities have already moved towards this. Before accepting this practice unquestioningly, we should ask what functions an appraisal procedure ought to perform.

Three different categories of function can be distinguished: academic standards, accountability and management. There is considerable overlap among these categories, as can be seen if they are expressed in terms of aims.

The prime aim of appraisal must be to help to improve the quality of teaching and research. Any scheme which does not do this should be resisted. It is not sufficient merely to identify those who fail to come up to expected standards, even if the consequent action proposed is constructive rather than punitive. That would be a deficit model, plugging the gaps, more likely to demoralize the conscientious than to reform the delinquent. The effect should be positive across the whole range of performance, encouraging motivation, ideally by some form of reward or recognition. 'The main currency for the academic is not power (as it is for the politician) nor wealth (as it is for the businessman), but reputation' (Becher and Kogan 1980). Consequently the leverage of an appraisal scheme is through reputation or status among one's peers. In the field of research, the present informal and relatively unstructured system performs this function quite well. At the highest level, there are awards such as fellowships of learned societies or even Nobel Prizes and the like, but for less distinguished researchers publication is a well established route to recognition which has a beneficial motivating influence on the conduct of research. There is no comparable route to recognition in teaching.

The second aim is accountability, to reinforce a sense of responsibility, to allay public misgivings by demonstrating that appropriate checks are made and, in respect of teaching, to give more strength to the clients, whether they are considered to be the students, employers or the public at large. Here too, it is not just a matter of ensuring that the job is not scamped; appraisal should encourage those who are already performing adequately to be responsive to the demand for higher standards.

The third aim is perhaps less readily acceptable but for some of the advocates of appraisal it is an underlying motive, namely, more effective management of the higher education system. As with the first and second aims, management is more than coercing the indolent and getting rid of the incompetent. In a more positive sense, it is coping with change, and appraisal is seen as a means of encouraging staff to respond to new demands, and ensuring that they keep up to date in both teaching and research. From the management point of view the 'raison d'etre... is to expedite the making of decisions and judgements' (Laurillard 1980).

The way in which each of these aims has been expressed brings out the reasons why staff appraisal must be set firmly in the context of staff development. Appraisal is an empty procedure if there is no provision for follow-up or when the outcome can only be to penalize. Setting appraisal within staff development must not be mere rhetoric: it is an essential first principle. The 1985 Green Paper stated:

> Effective staff development will not happen without a formal institutional framework for evaluating performance and for responding to development and training needs.

The point could have been made the other way round: a formal framework for evaluating performance should not happen without effective staff development.

If a statement of aims can be agreed, it is possible to establish criteria by which to judge whether an appraisal system is adequate and appropriate. The seven suggestions made below identify important aspects, though not necessarily in order of importance and not covering all the requirements of an appraisal scheme. The procedure should satisfy the following criteria.

1 It should be *beneficial* in its effect. It should be linked to a development programme which will provide support to improve staff performance. It must not damage or distort the processes of learning, teaching and research. It must not damage morale, destroy relationships and trust, discourage initiative or diminish the wholehearted commitment which many academic staff give to their work far beyond the call of duty, just because the commitment is spontaneous and unforced.

2 It should be *fair*. It must not only operate equitably for all concerned, but also be seen as working fairly. This is an extremely difficult requirement to meet. Since judgements of quality necessarily reflect assumptions about values, one person's judgements on academic quality will necessarily differ from another's. Who makes the appraisal is therefore more important than how it is made. The process will be seen as fair only if there is trust in those who make the judgements, whether peers, heads of departments, students, deans or committees, and also trust in the procedure, which must therefore be widely discussed with the academic faculty before it is introduced.

3 It should be *comprehensive*, covering the full range of work done by academic staff. Seldin's lists, referred to previously, demonstrate the multiple roles which staff perform: teaching, research, publication, supervising research, student advising, consultancies, public service, administration, management, and committee work. An appraisal procedure must not be limited or give undue weight to those activities which have a distinct measurable output, to the neglect of important activities which cannot readily be assessed. How is the assessment of these various roles to be combined: how is one to be balanced against

the other, or how many roles do you have to be good at to deserve promotion? These questions are considered in the next section. At this stage, the argument is simply that any role not included in the review will tend to be neglected.

4   It should be *valid*. Procedures should be checked to see if the conclusions they produce prove to be right in the long term. Thus the monitoring system itself needs to be monitored. Face validity is also important, in that the procedure must have a sound rational basis and must carry conviction among staff.

These four criteria derive mainly from the first of our three aims. The three which follow are more related to the second and third aims.

5   An appraisals procedure should be *open*, in the sense that the procedure is clearly stated and understood: what sources of evidence are used, how decisions are made, and so on. The information should either be factual (objective) or its subjectivity should be explicit, with provision for cross-checking subjective judgements. The procedure should be understandable and communicable, and ideally (though probably this is impracticable because of confidentiality) the decisions should be verifiable: others who may see the evidence should agree that the right decisions have been made.

6   It should be *effective* in producing changes. Also (as before) it should be seen as being effective. This assumes that there is acceptance of the aim that the procedure should encourage staff to be responsive to new demands, but it is arguable that an appraisal procedure is not the best way to achieve this, though it may help to promote awareness of the need for it.

7   It should be *practicable*, a point more easily appreciated if it is expressed negatively, not cumbersome, complex, bureaucratic or time-wasting. Some of the examples quoted earlier in this chapter clearly do not satisfy this criterion.

No doubt there are other criteria which should be added, and some of the seven listed can be sub-divided into separate considerations.

The Unit of Appraisal

The procedure for staff development and appraisal which seems to be currently in favour is based on a series of interviews, with the individual member of staff as the unit of appraisal. It is doubtful if this procedure satisfies criteria 1, 2, 4 and 7 in the list above, and perhaps not 5 and 6 either. The major problem of an individual appraisal system is that academic staff perform multiple roles, and a department needs to maintain a variety and balance in staff qualities. Consequently, different standards and different qualities have to be applied with respect to different individual academics.

For each of the three aims set out above, the department is a more appropriate unit of appraisal than the individual. The academic aim of raising standards involves a balance of effort within a department: it is not essential, nor desirable, that all the staff should be expected to perform all the multiple roles of staff in higher education. The accountability aim is consequently also a department function; and the management aim is more likely to be accepted readily if it is related to corporate achievement and associated with relatively small units within which people feel that there is personal knowledge and mutual trust. As the Scottish report quoted earlier states: 'Staff development must generate teacher commitment which is most evident when planned collaboratively.' This places a heavy responsibility on the head of department, who usually has no training and sometimes little aptitude in this form of management. The case for departmental appraisal is open to other criticisms too. It may not be appropriate to the mode of organization of some departments. Individuals may still be indifferent to the group pressures of their peers. But this may not be altogether a weakness. Rutherford (quoted cynically in Barzun 1969) is alleged to have said:

> Every good laboratory consists of first-rate men working in great harmony to ensure the progress of science; but down at the end of the hall is an unsociable, wrong-headed fellow working on unprofitable lines, and in his hands lies the hope of discovery.

Perhaps the weakest feature is that departmental autonomy is currently out of favour among those who wish to see a powerful line-management structure applied in higher education. But giving departments the responsibility for ensuring the maintenance of the highest academic standards is a surer way to preserve the all-important element of provision for divergence – though that too depends on the capacity of a head of department to hold together a group of individuals with diverse talents.

To argue for a departmental basis of appraisal is not incompatible with the principle which is at the root of all discussion of standards, namely that the scholar works to his or her own standards. Standards are not, and must not be, a step towards standardization. Standards for academic staff are not prescriptions which might be registered with the British Standards Institute, a set of requirements to be ticked off one by one as a means of quality control. Standards are most effective when we set them ourselves. This is the strength of professionalism, also currently under attack. Professionalism requires from us the capacity to apply the highest standards to our work even when there is no one but ourselves to judge. This is what we try to teach our students, to internalize standards, to apply the rigour of professional standards after they have left our tutelage, as a matter of principle. They learn (or do not learn) from our example. In the intellectual and economic climate of the 1980s, this philosophy is dangerously idealistic and so is unlikely to command ready support. But it is in harmony with the trend of the 1970s, and hopefully also of the future, towards a stronger reliance on self-evaluation, set in a context of collegiate effort and shared accountability.

References

Adelman, C. & Alexander, R.J. (1982) *The Self-Evaluating Institution* London: Methuen

Barzun, J. (1969) *The American University: How it runs and where it is going* London: Oxford University Press

Becher, T. & Kogan, M. (1980) *Process and Structure in Higher Education* London: Heinemann

Billing, D. (1980) *Indicators of Performance* Guildford: Society for Research into Higher Education

Braskamp, L.A. (1980) The role of evaluation in faculty development *Studies in Higher Education* 5,45-54

Centra, J.A. (1977) *Reviewing and Evaluating Teaching* San Francisco: Jossey-Bass

Committee of Vice-Chancellors and Principals (March 1985) *Report of the Steering Committee for Efficiency Studies in Universities* (Jarratt Report) London

Committee of Vice-Chancellors and Principals (September 1985) *Universities' Internal Procedures for Maintaining and Monitoring Academic Standards* (Reynolds Committee) London

Department of Education and Science (1983) *Teaching Quality* Cmnd 8836. London: HMSO

Department of Education and Science (1985a) *The Development of Higher Education into the 1990's* Cmnd 9524. London: HMSO

Department of Education and Science (1985b) *Better Schools* Cmnd 9496. London: HMSO

Department of Education and Science (1985c) *Quality in Schools: Evaluation and Appraisal* London: HMSO

Elton, L. (1984) Evaluating teaching and assessing teachers in universities *Assessment and Evaluation in High Education* 9,97-115

Eraut, M. (1983) Within institutions evaluation: perspectives and value issues. In M. Skilbeck (Ed.) *Evaluating the Curriculum in the Eighties* London: Hodder & Stoughton

Flood Page, C. (1974) *Student Evaluation of Teaching: the American experience* London: Society for Research into Higher Education

Fox, D. (1978) *Trent Polytechnic: Policies for Staff Development* Standing Conference on Education Development Services in Polytechnics (SCEDSIP)

Gibbs, G. (1983) *Guide to submitting Teaching Profiles for Promotion* Oxford Polytechnic: Educational Methods Unit

Greenaway, H. & Mortimer, D. (1979) Britain (polytechnics) – a case of rapidly evolving institutions. In Teather (1979)

Laurillard, D.M. (1980) Validity of indicators of performance. In Billing (1980)

Miller, R.I. (1972) *Evaluating Faculty Performance* San Francisco: Jossey-Bass

Naftulin, D.H., Ware, J.H. & Donnelly, F.A. (1973) The Doctor Fox lecture: a paradigm of educational seduction *Journal of Medical Education* 48,630-635

National Committee for the In-Service Training of Teachers (1984) *Arrangements for the Staff Development of Teachers* Scottish Education Department Edinburgh: HMSO

Nisbet, J. & McAleese, R. (1979) Britain (universities). In Teather (1979)

Open University (1982) *Course E364: Curriculum Evaluation and Assessment in Educational Institutions* Milton Keynes: Open University Press

Pennington, R.C. & O'Neil, M.J. (1985) *Appraisal in Higher Education: Mapping the Terrain* Paper presented to the Annual Conference of the Society for Research into Higher Education

Robbins Report (1963) *Higher Education* Cmnd 2154. London: HMSO

Seldin, P. (1984) *Changing Practices in Faculty Evaluation* San Francisco: Jossey-Bass

Shipman, M. (1979) *In-School Evaluation* London: Heinemann

Shore, B.M., Foster, S.F., Knapper, C.K., Nadeau, G.G., Neill, N. and Sim, V. (1978) *Guide to the Teaching Dossier: its Preparation and Use* Canadian Association of University Teachers

Simons, H. (1981) Process evaluation in practice in schools. In C. Lacey & D. Lawton (Eds.) *Issues in Accountability and Evaluation* London: Methuen

Smith, A. (1776) *An Inquiry into the Nature and Causes of the Wealth of Nations* (1976 edition) London: Oxford University Press

Leverhulme Report (1983) *Excellence in Diversity* Guildford: Society for Research into Higher Education

Sunderland Polytechnic (1985) *Report to Governors*

Teather, D.C.B. (1979) *Staff Development in Higher Education* London: Kogan Page

Times Educational Supplement (1985a) Study backs classroom observation of teachers *TES* 12 July

Times Educational Supplement (1985b) Will teacher assessment ever get off the ground? *TES* 23 November

Times Higher Education Supplement (1985) Leader on Lindop Report *TES* 26 April

University Authorities Panel (1971) Agreement on probation. In Teather (1979)

University Grants Committee (1964) *Report of the Committee on University Teaching Methods* (Hale Report) London: HMSO

University Grants Committee (1984) *A Strategy for Higher Education into the 1990s* London: HMSO

Warren, J.W.L. (1977) Institutionalization of staff development in higher education. In L. Elton & K. Simmonds (Eds) *Staff Development in Higher Education* Guildford: Society for Research into Higher Education

Acknowledgements

For assistance with information on staff development schemes thanks are due to Clem Adelman, Colin Biott, George Brown, Graham Gibbs, David Kennedy, Mike O'Neil, Gus Pennington and Harold Silver.

7

Students and Quality

Paul Ramsden

How is it possible that educational experiences so often fail to bring about conceptual changes in the most fundamental respects? The fact is that students may acquire huge bodies of knowledge without appropriating the conceptualizations on which those bodies of knowledge are based.

Ference Marton

Fitness for purpose in undergraduate education, I want to argue here, should be judged by the quality of learning demonstrated by its students. I shall try to show that recent thinking provides a rationale and a language for understanding the quality of learning in higher education; and that the same thinking offers a path towards improving the quality of learning by raising the professional standards of teaching in a particular way.

The biggest pitfall we are likely to encounter in devising ways of maintaining and improving standards and criteria in undergraduate education is one that should be very familiar to teachers. The procedures we use to measure standards may become more important than the things we are measuring, so that we lose sight of the purpose of our measurement. In a moment I summarize some evidence that supports the view that this transformation of means into ends in student assessment is harmful to standards. In particular, because the means of assessment are often quantitative, the qualitative nature of educational change – the fact that learning in higher education invariably involves grasping meaning as well as gaining more information – may be temporarily forgotten.

It is precisely this trap, made seductive by the magic of valuations to which numbers are attached, that discussions of standards in undergraduate education must avoid. Fail to avoid it, and the discussion will concentrate on how much a student, teacher, or institute faithfully and narrowly reproduces the signs that are supposed to indicate excellence. A quite different conception of standards is assumed here. It may be an inconvenient conception: it involves accepting simultaneously that standards are relative and that it is the teacher's responsibility to improve them.

Lest we may be thought to be stating the obvious by arguing for a qualitative conception of standards, let us look at the way in which the output of undergraduate education is typically measured. A usual indicator is the number of honours degrees, and the quality of the product is shown by the proportion of 'good' degrees (firsts and upper seconds) awarded. While other measures have also been suggested (eg employability) this one has a satisfying continuity and simplicity. Certainly a good degree is important: it is stipulated for entry to many careers and required for financial support for postgraduate study; some salary scales are related to the class of degree held. With due allowance for differences in the proportion of good degrees awarded in different subject areas, good degrees may be used to indicate the effectiveness of a department or institution. More efficient institutions will produce good degrees with lower costs (smaller resource inputs: for example staff salaries and student ability) than less efficient ones.

Results from a recent study by Bourner sponsored by the Council for National Academic Awards (summarized in Gold 1985) have been inter-preted as showing that public sector institutions are more efficient than universities in producing graduates; given less able raw material (entering students with lower average 'A' level grades), the polytechnics and colleges produce proportionally more first-class honours graduates than universities. This was in spite of the fact that the more expensive teaching in universities produced more good degrees. The 'value added' by the CNAA institutions was greater. According to these calculations of efficiency, if CNAA institu-tions had taught university students, 9.5 per cent of those students would have obtained first-class degrees. If universities had taught public sector students, they would have gained 4.2 per cent firsts.

Doubts over this kind of analysis begin to creep in when the unreliability and possible invalidity of the major variables as indicators of quality are contemplated: the poor predictive power of 'A' levels and questions about the relative perceived worth of degrees from different institutions. While an undergraduate degree is clearly to some extent a valid indicator of qualitative educational change, the belief that the proportion of good degrees can be used to rank departments or institutions is founded on very shaky ground. Bourner argued that the proportion of good degrees in a subject was a function not of teaching quality, student ability, or resources, but of the distribution of results in previous years. And as Bee and Dolton (1985) have shown, large differences exist in the pattern of degree awards between universities. The differences they discovered could not be explained by subject area ratios, 'A' level grades of students, or staff/student ratios (or other institutional differences considered quantitatively such as library size). However, there was a strong association between the proportion of good degrees awarded by each institution in the year of their study and the proportion awarded in the five previous years. Together these studies suggest that preconceptions of the appropriate proportion of good degrees in an institution and in a subject area determine the actual proportion.

The error involved in the use of degrees as indicators of effectiveness is simply to forget that they are proxies for output, not the output itself. The evidence is clear that they do not measure the same things in different departments and institutions. But what are we trying to measure anyway? The real difficulties in comparing standards by looking at degree results and student or institutional inputs are not technical problems of measurement. They are to do with the fact that quantitative indicators are asked to do an educational task which they are not capable of performing. The conception of standards as being related *directly* to the quality of education is one explored in the rest of this paper. The approach has, in the eyes of some managers, a fatal flaw. It is administratively awkward. It cannot provide indicators of the worth of a department, individual, or institution – at any rate not in such a way that one unit or person can be placed in a single rank order with the rest. It inolves accepting uncertainty and fallibility in human judgement in deciding standards; it also means that teachers will have to take greater professional responsibility for finding out how their students learn and for applying their discoveries. Its weaknesses are also its strengths. We shall see that it provides a way not merely of monitoring standards but also of improving them, in a truly educational sense.

Values and Aims

It is odd that discussion about standards, which are about the values attached to educational outcomes and processes, sometimes proceed as if normative considerations were irrelevant. Teaching in higher education is manifestly not a value-free activity. Teachers cannot say much that is sensible about standards unless they are explicit about the kind of learning they want their students to do. The understanding that they seek to help students to achieve involves grasping the relationship between phenomena and their context, and the relationship depends on the meanings which they as experts attach to those phenomena. This is true of all the disciplines. We try to persuade students to see the meaning in the same way that we do, and perhaps (though rarely in many fields at this level) to explore other meanings.

Academic staff, educationalists, employers and students are in broad agreement about what kind of learning outcomes undergraduate education should produce. The prescriptions (and doubts) of Newman, Pattison, Whitehead, Ashby and others converge with the aims of lecturers to produce a clear picture. Students are expected to learn skills and much detailed knowledge, of course; but superordinate to these things is the development of a quality of learning and thinking within a discipline or profession. We want our students to think 'like historians or biologists or economists think'; to conceptualize phenomena and ideas in the way we do. Lecturers in higher education typically play safe by overrating factual knowledge, to the detriment of what Ashby (1973) has termed 'post-conventional thinking' and others have described as 'critical thinking' or 'high level problem solving' (Entwistle and Percy 1974; Goodlad and Pippard 1982). The testing of hypotheses against evidence, the ability to synthesize and organize complicated ideas, the capacity to copy with uncertain problems requiring judgement: the manner in which such skills manifest themselves will be very different in historical argument and in chemistry, but there is no doubt that these general qualities are celebrated by teachers in higher education and endorsed by the employers of graduates. Students agree with them too; Little (1970), for example, found that undergraduates rated as their highest aim for a university that it 'should develop in its students habits of independent intellectual inquiry'.

How far are these aims achieved? It is plain that the development of critical thinking is incompatible with the poor performance revealed by many students in assessments, which often suggests that the retention and regurgitation of half-understood information rather than the application of knowledge has been paramount in their study methods. Every teacher of undergraduates has at some time felt depressed about the quality of work produced by them. What must surely have been self-evident in the lecture course on probability has been misunderstood in the examination answers; the time-worn ideas of a secondary source on Marx have been presented back again in fifteen nearly identical sociology essays, devoid of any suggestion of insight; the same mistakes that happened last year in understanding the reactions of carbon compounds have been made. Fortunately there are good answers as well – usually. Why are these experiences so common? The most usual response is to explain poor performance in terms of our students' intellectual failings or their laziness. Is this always an accurate and complete explanation?

Students who are highly selected from a large pool of potential entrants to higher education often fail to learn in the ways we would wish. This is serious enough in itself, but recent studies of students' experiences have revealed that, far from their responses to our teaching being signs of intellectual weakness, they are frequently rational and intelligent adaptations to circumstances. Our aims are often not realized because the relation between students and the context of learning in higher education is not what it ought to be. This relation is partly determined by the students' previous educational experiences, especially those school experiences which have reinforced widely-accepted views of learning as the quantitative accretion of information and techniques. But the quality of undergraduate teaching has a decisive influence.

Particular difficulties arise in the assessment process. Elton (1982) surely echoes the feelings of most higher education teachers – and the values assumed in this paper – when he declares that 'the overriding purpose of assessment is that it should encourage learning in consonance with my declared student learning aims' (p.107). Assessment has several purposes, but, unfortunately, two of them, selection and maintaining student standards, do not *encourage* learning at all. They are concerned with the products rather than the processes of student learning. Paradoxically, this may lead to a lowering of standards and less effective selection. The learning activities of students – the processes by which knowledge is gained – determine the very qualities which should be reflected in selection and in standards.

Examples of the invalidity of student assessment provided by Elton cast doubt on whether many of our current practices actually test what we think they do. He provides disturbing evidence from research and anecdote of the effects of conflating grades and of badly designed marking schemes on students' published performance. In view of this evidence it is not at all surprising that a single number (a degree classification) correlates poorly with measures of student ability at entry or with measures of institutional inputs.

Studies of students' experiences of assessment reveal many worrying effects. Laurillard (1984), for example, reports that perceptions of grading schemes may distort students' problem-solving strategies. Swedish investigations show how students' misapprehensions of fundamental concepts in economics and physics may remain untouched by the questions they are asked in assessments, so that students may be certified as passed when they understand very little (Dahlgren 1978; Johansson, Marton, and Svensson 1985). In New Zealand, Crooks and Mahalski (1985) describe the low-level cognitive demands of many university examinations and outline the strategies students use to cope with them. Typically, the students in this investigation adapted by narrowing their attention to material presented in lectures and collecting large quantities of notes which were then rote-learned and reproduced in examinations. Similar unpalatable evidence was reported by Ramsden (1984) in relation to British students.

Taken together, the findings of these and many other studies of student assessment are compelling. Assessment methods provide signals to students about the kinds of learning they are expected to carry out. Inappropriate assessment methods – which are often used out of higher education teachers' ignorance of alternatives – and excessive amounts of assessed curricular material encourage minimalist, reproductive learning strategies and also hide the inadequate understanding which such approaches inexorably lead to. There is also clear evidence that teaching strategies which fail to engage students with subject matter, and in particular which do not permit the use of idiosyncratic pathways through learning materials, are implicated in poor quality student learning (see Entwistle and Ramsden 1983; Marton, Hounsell, and Entwistle 1984). That there is excellence in undergraduate teaching is not in doubt; but these several investigations reveal that the standard often falls below the acceptable. In these circumstances, discussion of standards in terms of criteria such as staff/student ratios and numbers of degrees awarded seems premature.

A Theory of Student Learning

Our discussion of standards now shifts to the question of how we can encourage the kind of learning that will maximize the chances of desirable changes in students. The practices of excellent teachers and of courses which appear to demand and reward close engagement with the subject matter perhaps point the way (see Ramsden and Entwistle 1981). But it is sensible to take a step back from this question. What is meant by 'learning' in higher education is often taken for granted. We regularly assume that students understand phenomena in the same way that we, as teachers, do; or that differences in the standards achieved by students are obvious reflections of their ability to grasp what we want them to grasp; or that differences in how students learn are directly related to their skills and competence as learners. It is instructive to suspend belief in these assumptions. Let us try to find a way of describing differences in learning that does not depend upon conventional assessment criteria and which considers the content of what is learned and the process used to learn it.

Unfortunately most psychological theories of learning do not help us much. The search for general principles of learning has resulted in a methodology which not only provides descriptions of what is learned chiefly in quantitative terms (eg how much is remembered of a text and the degree of isomorphy between the learners' responses and the parts of the text), but which also sees learning processes as issues separate from the content of what is being learned (see Dahlgren 1984, pp.21-23, for an elaboration of these points).

An alternative assumption is that what is learned (the outcome of learning) is inseparably related to how it is learned (the process of learning). At the same time, it can be assumed that the way someone learns represents a relation between the person and aspects of the world around the person (Marton, in press). A number of recent research studies have examined learning in higher education from this point of view, and their findings have implications for improving undergraduate education.

The texts which undergraduates read (and by analogy, other instructional matter to which they are exposed) typically have a hierarchical structure. To subject experts this is an obvious point, and the structure is immediately apparent to them. A common structure consists of a principle (eg a concept) and examples which support or illustrate the principle. Understanding the text involves recognizing the relationship between examples and principle, the fact that the first are subordinate to the second, the fact that the principle is given meaning by the examples. It is particularly important to realize that students may not see the text in this way at all. They may not see that there are superordinate principles and subordinate examples. Although a test may show that they remember and are able to manipulate both concepts and examples, they may not have understood the argument at all.

More generally, students may fail to see the dialectical relation between principles and examples in a topic. For example, a psychological principle may be demonstrated in a textbook by reference to several experiments. The meaning of the principle depends on the experimental results; but, if the results themselves are separately focused on, there is no hope of understanding the principle that links them together. This will not prevent the information constituting the principle, together with supporting examples, being repeated in an essay, however. Fundamental conceptual changes in the apprehension of, say, the phenomenon of price determination (from seeing the price of a commodity as an inherent quality of that commodity to considering it as a relation between supply and demand) may be supposed by lecturers to have taken place after one year of university economics, while in practice no such changes have occurred (see Dahlgren 1978).

Qualitative differences in the outcomes of learning can be understood in terms of the approach to learning students use; that is, in terms of the relation between themselves and the content and context of learning. In Marton's original experiment on reading academic text (see Marton and Säljö 1984), students who did not understand the point of the article (that improving pass rates in Swedish universities would depend on taking selective measures aimed at groups who were doing badly rather than at all students) focused on the text itself, trying to remember as much as possible and not seeing the task as one which required relating the text to its underlying structure or to the real world. Paradoxically, it was the students who were *not* trying hard to remember the text who in fact remembered it very well. They also grasped the main point of it by preserving the article's structure and relating its argument to their experience.

The *approach* to learning is decisive in explaining the quality of learning, not only in reading texts but in a wide variety of different tasks which undergraduates typically perform, including essay writing and problem-solving (see for example Hounsell 1984; Laurillard 1984). It can be seen to have two aspects: a referential and a structural (Marton, in press). Figure 1 gives some examples of the distinctions. The deep-surface distinction is about what the student refers to, or intends – typically, trying to memorize or reproduce and considering the need to fulfil assessment requirements with minimal engagement, versus trying to understand by relating the task to some aspect of reality. The holistic-atomistic dichotomy concerns the way the text or problem is manipulated – thinking about the task in terms of its structure and relations between examples and concepts, versus attending to its unrelated parts.

DEEP-HOLISTIC	SURFACE-ATOMISTIC
Referential aspect (Deep)	**Referential aspect (Surface)**
Try to understand:	Try to memorize:
'I had to think about it and understand it first, relating it to previous work'	'I tried hard to concentrate – too hard – so my attention was on "concentration" to remember it for the exam'
Structural aspect (Holistic)	**Structural aspect (Atomistic)**
Preserve structure, focus on complex relations:	Distort structure, focus on local relations:
'Looking at the system I was thinking of what was actually happening, connecting numbers to features'	'I went through each part in sequence without worrying about the relative importance of the symptoms'

Figure 1
Examples of deep-holistic and surface atomistic approaches.

These rather subtle theoretical distinctions, very sketchily outlined here, repay the effort of reflection in terms of one's own subject and how it is taught. Two points need to be borne in mind. It cannot be assumed that the differences in approach are visible from the point of view of the grade awarded. We cannot assume, given the assessment difficulties referred to above, that a mark reflects the learning process used, even though in an ideal world it always would. Secondly, while it may very well be correct that newcomers to a discipline will treat advanced tasks in an atomistic way, it is not the case that approaches to learning are characteristics of individuals. They are not inside students; they describe only a relationship between an individual and what he or she is learning. The relational character of the concept of approach makes it educational; it reminds us that our focus as teachers (and as researchers into teaching and learning) is properly on learners in the settings in which they learn. The setting consists of the content of what is learned and the way in which the content is taught and evaluated. By understanding more about the complicated association between instruction and students, we may hope to teach and examine in such a way as to encourage the qualities that characterize excellence in undergraduate education.

In concrete terms, this theory of student learning implies that we should give our sharpest attention to setting the right kinds of learning tasks, providing the right kind of teaching support, and assessing the outcomes of learning in appropriate ways. It means we must not take for granted the ways students approach and understand what to us are elementary ideas in our subjects. It does not seek to provide prescriptions or general principles for doing these things, however. Its propositions are, like others in educational research, indeterministic. That does not make it less appropriate; rather the contrary. It offers a way of formalizing our expectations in particular settings and may be reinterpreted by teachers in different situations. It provides a means by which reflection on the effectiveness of teaching can improve standards.

It is clear from this perspective that the quality of learning will not be improved by using either advanced methods of delivering academic content or by supplying students with general learning skills advice. These are good solutions to different problems, perhaps, but not to the problem of the standard of undergraduate learning. We cannot hope to make unambiguous causal statements about how certain inputs will produce certain effects in teaching and learning. It is useless to seek for ways of improving the standard of undergraduate education by focusing on characteristics of students or characteristics of teaching methods, so long as variation in approaches is a result of an interaction between the student and the context of learning.

An instructive illustration of the need to consider this relation when intervening to change students' learning strategies comes from the experience of the learning skills project at Melbourne University (Ramsden, Beswick and Bowden, in press). Six departments organized special learning skills programmes for their first-year students where matters such as organization of study time, reading, writing, and note-taking were discussed. It might be expected that attendance at such non-didactic groups would help students to become more aware of their own approaches to learning and to select wisely among the various strategies available to them. In doing so, they might avoid approaches aimed at reproducing academic content and become more aware of the ways in which deep approaches could be exercised. The students who attended the groups increased their use of surface-atomistic approaches during the year in comparison with the students who did not attend. Interview data supported the interpretation that the learning-skills students used the experience rationally. They recognized that the first-year assessment often tested the accurate reproduction of large quantities of knowledge, and derived useful techniques from the sessions which enabled them to deploy surface approaches successfully.

If the student-context interaction is the source of variation in approaches, then practical educational solutions to improving standards must focus on students and teaching concurrently. It seems clear from recent research into undergraduate learning that contextual conditions for deep approaches can be readily identified, although precise predictions about what will happen in particular learning episodes cannot be made. Perceived interest and relevance in a learning task increase intrinsic motivation and make it more likely that a student will relate to the task at a deep, holistic level (Laurillard

1984; Entwistle and Ramsden 1983, chapter 8; Watkins 1984). A crucial component of 'good teaching' in students' perceptions is help from teaching staff in improving approaches to learning. Teaching which is not simply well-founded in subject knowledge, but which shows empathy for students' misunderstandings and recognizes mistakes in their processing of new material, while permitting students to find personally congenial paths through subject matter, is also associated with deep approaches. Conversely, excessive amounts of curricular material presented unpalatably and assessed inappropriately are a recipe for minimalist, reproductive responses. None of these associations may be a startling revelation to wise teachers, but the strength and reliability of the connections (they have been demonstrated many times in many subject areas in several educational systems) is evidence of their universal importance.

Improving the Standard of Learning

The difficulty remains of how to convert these findings into practical teaching strategies in order to improve the standard of learning. One rapid way of altering students' approaches (although the results may not always turn out as expected) is to change assessment methods. Newble and Jaeger (1983) report an attempt to modify final-year assessment to emphasize the importance of clinical skills in the School of Medicine at Adelaide University. In 1971 final-year assessment was modified to emphasize the importance of clinical skills. Ward-based assessments replaced the traditional clinical viva. However, the new assessments proved to be less critical than expected – few students failed them. Students responded by spending less time in the wards and more in library study for the remaining, more hazardous theoretical component of the course. Thus the effect of the changes was exactly opposite to that intended, students focusing on being able to reproduce the 'right' theoretical answers; a perfectly rational adaptation to circumstances. Subsequently, the faculty introduced a more innovative and demanding form of practical assessment. This time the effect was to improve student learning: study habits were less influenced by the theory test and the form of assessment was perceived to be relevant to practice.

A strength of the theory of student learning advocated here is that it provides the tools to make the analysis of students' learning processes and outcomes possible. Promising examples of this approach can be found in recent developments in the use of computer-assisted learning in science subjects and in undergraduate medical education. Eizenberg (1985) has studied the relation between the pre-clinical anatomy programme and students' approaches to learning in the large medical faculty in which he teaches. The widespread adoption of surface-atomistic approaches by highly able students led to an attempt to improve standards by designing forms of assessment and teaching which were expected to elicit more appropriate types of engagement with the subject matter. Faculty goals for students were explicitly linked to assessment expectations in a published handbook, teaching moved towards a stress on application, incorporated the derivation of anatomical terms, and focused on the relation between concepts and terminology. Assessment is being amended so that 'essential' information is clearly defined: the stress is on what is to be assessed, rather than on what students have to learn (cf Goodlad and Pippard 1982, pp.97-98). Examination questions and marking schemes which are explicit about their testing of understanding are being introduced.

A continuing study of clinical problem-solving by fourth-year students (Whelan 1985, and in progress) illustrates the exciting potential for improving teaching of studies of how students manipulate content. Using a minimal interference interview technique the students are being asked to solve a problem presented as a case summary. Questions aimed at eliciting an outcome (a diagnosis) and a reflection on process (how they went about the problem) were used. Qualitative differences in levels of outcome have been described and are being related to differences in the approaches used to the content of the task. The research has revealed unexpected differences, which had not previously been taken into account in teaching, in the ways students represent the problems to themselves. It is hoped to model the characteristic processes and processing errors in an interactive video format. Students will be given control over the critical steps in the problem-solving and test their reasoning attempts against the model.

In the area of computed-assisted learning (CAL) in science and social science, Laurillard (1985) has described the use of research into students' conceptions as a means of designing CAL simulation programs which incorporate an analysis of the relation between what a student knows and what he or she needs to know. Changes in students' understanding are facilitated by a program which allows them to focus on relationships between phenomena and checks on their analysis:

> [This method] allows the student to come close to what it means to 'act like a scientist'. The hypotheses that are posited by the student in the course of the program are simple, each one is meaningful to them at the time, and each one is testable. Moreover, the feedback is meaningful... it forces them to reason about the relationships involved. That makes it far more likely to be a productive learning experience than the tutorial program that confines students to the straight-jacket of an answer-matching form of interaction.... The development of this kind of simulation program requires research into the common student misconceptions in the topic concerned, and the derivation of crucial experiments necessary to help students decide between their misconception and the received knowledge. (pp.12-13)

We may take a final example of the approach from a quite different subject area. Hounsell (1984) and Biggs (in press) have recently argued that the quality of history essays written by undergraduates is partly a function of the student's conception of what an essay is and what essay writing involves. Biggs maintains that the development of skills in historical (or other types) of writing requires a focus on the interaction between content and language: a good essay results from an understanding of which *genre* is appropriate to the question. Hence teachers should consider explicating the content structures that typically arise in their disciplines; guidance in essay writing which attempts to be content-free or which fails to confront students' current grasp of what is meant by 'an essay' in history or English or psychology is of little use. Martin and Ramsden (1985) report an attempt at intervention to improve writing in a British university department of history which implicitly adopted these suggestuons in a 'learning to learn' programme. Students discussed with their teachers essays written by previous cohorts of students on topics similar to the ones they were preparing at the time. There was some evidence that students who attended these sessions developed more complex conceptions of learning and produced better essays.

The common theme of these studies is the implementation of teaching strategies which take into account students' experiences of learning and involve staff in testing hypotheses about the effects of teaching on the quality of student learning.

Conclusions and Recommendations

Improvements in teaching and learning always begin by questioning something we take for granted (Marton, in press). This essay has put forward the view that we should ask ourselves whether the standard of undergraduate education, considered in terms of the quality of learning demonstrated by its students, is satisfactory. If we reflect on what undergraduates learn and how they learn it, we realize that these aspects of learning are related. Students' ways of learning, seen as relations between them and the context of what is learned, should be the focus of attempts to improve the standard of undergraduate education. It is possible to do this by giving attention to assessment and teaching.

The main changes we expect to occur in students are qualitative ones. We should assess such changes qualitatively. There is evidence that assessment procedures frequently fail to do what we want them to do. Instead they have a negative effect on the quality of student thinking. All too frequently what we really test is the accurate reproduction of parts of topics or even just terminology. The fact that students are aware of this leads them to adopt strategies at variance with our aims. There is some evidence also of unfairness and of academic staff ignorance of assessment processes (see Elton 1982). Vigorous action is needed to remedy the situation. Detailed study of how particular assessment procedures are experienced by students seems inescapable if standards are to be improved. Steps will need to be taken to reduce in many courses the reliance on quantitative criteria of performance, to introduce more detailed reporting of what students are competent to do, and to decrease the amount of assessed material.

Staff development activity should focus on engaging higher education faculty in inquiries into their undergraduate students' *conceptions* of principal ideas and the *processes* they use to manipulate problems in the subject domain. Activity of this kind, when combined with assessment criteria that are perceived to encourage and reward understanding, enables us to plan teaching to maximize the probability of a deep-holistic approach. For example, by finding out about common misconceptions of phenomena in the physical and social sciences we may be able to intervene to devise teaching strategies that encourage students to impose one structure on an observation rather than another. By requiring students to externalize the process of arguing historically when they write an essay, we may identify errors in the way they realize the relation between content and structure in a particular discipline (cf Biggs, in press). Subsequently, we can direct our teaching at these mistakes.

Staff who have been involved in such activities report that they are intrinsically rewarding to experts in professional subjects and academic disciplines. They connect research interests to undergraduate teaching because the study of how intelligent neophytes apprehend a subject reveals its underlying structure from a different perspective and often sheds light on its historical development. Svensson (Svensson and Hogfors 1984; Svensson 1984), for example, reports on how a study of engineering students' understanding of force revealed Aristotelean as well as Newtonian conceptions of motion. These kinds of inquiry are likely to have a positive side-effect: they will probably produce a more relaxed and empathetic relationship between teacher and taught. Staff and undergraduate students become partners in learning, even though they are learning at different levels. It will also be valuable if staff, even if they do not spend large amounts of time in research into students' conceptions and processes of learning, use teaching time to make students more self-conscious about the ways in which they approach particular learning tasks. Reflection on the learning process is all too rare in many courses, yet it may have a dramatic impact on the quality of learning (see Lybeck 1981; Gibbs 1981). Such simple activities as asking students to describe how they arrived at the answer to a calculation, or what steps they went through when writing a report, or how they read a chapter, have the added benefit of providing highly revealing commentaries on students' perceptions of our requirements. As Gibbs has pointed out, involvement in teaching sessions that focus on the process of carrying out realistic tasks in a subject specialism can demonstrate how our assessment demands may be distorting the types of learning we wish students to adopt (see Gibbs 1981).

In the qualitative perspective on standards adopted here, improving teaching and learning must focus on effectiveness (doing things right). What kind of learning do we value? We must learn to celebrate process as well as product in student learning in order to enhance its standard: to see effectiveness in terms of how students manipulate tasks and conceptualize content. An intriguing corollary to these recommendations is that institutional contexts which reward teachers' study of how their students learn and respond to assessment need to be created with some care. Teachers in higher education are not immune to the situational influences that shape their students' learning. Setting formal, general, externally-defined criteria for good teaching and assessment is not likely to encourage reflection on better ways of teaching. It is much more likely to encourage the transformation of means into ends, so that being seen to fulfil the criteria becomes an objective in itself.

The approach to improving teaching and learning that I have tried to argue for here is congruent with a view of standards in undergraduate education in which responsible judgement by a self-critical group of academics (see Lindop 1985) is the chief means of guaranteeing quality. The indeterministic nature of the statements made by research into teaching and learning puts teachers in the best situation to direct the quest for higher standards.

References

Ashby, E. (1973) The structure of higher education: a world view *Higher Education* 2, 242-151

Bee, M. and Dolton, P. (1985) Degree class and pass rates: an inter-university comparison *Higher Education Review* 17, 45-53

Biggs, J.B. (in press) Approaches to learning and essay writing. In R.R. Schmeck (Ed.) *Learning Styles and Learning Strategies* New York: Plenum

Crooks, T.J. and Mahalski, P.A. (1985) Relationships among assessment practices, study methods, and grades obtained. Paper presented at the Annual Conference of the Higher Education Research and Development Society of Australasia, Auckland, August 1985

Dahlgren, L.O. (1978) Qualitative differences in conceptions of basic principles in Economics. Paper presented at the Fourth International Conference on Higher Education, University of Lancaster, 1978

Dahlgren, L.O. (1984) Outcomes of learning. In F. Marton et al (Eds) *The Experience of Learning* Edinburgh: Scottish Academic Press

Eizenberg, N. (1985) Applying student learning research to practice. Paper presented at an invited symposium on student learning and learning skills, Marysville, Victoria, Australia, November 1985

Elton, L.R.B. (1982) Assessment for learning. In D. Bligh (Ed.) *Professionalism and Flexibility in Learning* Guildford: SRHE

Entwistle, N.J. and Percy, K.A. (1974) Critical thinking or conformity? An investigation of the aims and outcomes of higher education. In *Research into Higher Education 1973* London: SRHE

Entwistle, N.J. and Ramsden, P. (1983) *Understanding Student Learning* London: Croom Helm

Gibbs, G. (1981) *Teaching Students to Learn* Milton Keynes: Open University Press

Gold, K. (1985) Measuring by degrees on the performeter *Times Higher Education Supplement* 26 July 1985

Goodlad, S. and Pippard, B. (1982) The curriculum of higher education. In D. Bligh (Ed.) *Professionalism and Flexibility in Learning* Guildford: SRHE

Hounsell, D.J. (1984) Learning and easy-writing. In F. Marton et al (Eds) *The Experience of Learning* Edinburgh: Scottish Academic Press

Johansson, B., Marton, F. and Svensson, L. (1985) An approach to describing learning as change between qualitatively different conceptions. In L.H.T. West and A.L. Pines (Eds) *Cognitive Structure and Conceptual Change* New York: Academic Press

Laurillard, D.M. (1984) Learning from problem-solving. In F. Marton et al (Eds) *The Experience of Learning* Edinburgh: Scottish Academic Press

Laurillard, D.M. (1985) Computers and the emancipation of students: giving control to the learner. Paper presented at the Computer Assisted Learning in Tertiary Education (CALITE) Conference, Melbourne, December 1985

Lindop, N. (1985) Validation revisited *Times Higher Education Supplement* 29 November 1985

Little, G. (1970) *The University Experience: An Australian Study* Melbourne: Melbourne University Press

Lybeck, L. (1981) (Quoted in Marton, F. (in press)) *Arkimedes i Klassen. En Ämnespedagogisk Berättelse*

Martin, E. and Ramsden, P. (1985) Learning skills or skill in learning? Paper presented at the British Psychological Society (Cognitive Psychology Section)/Society for Research into Higher Education Conference on Cognitive Processes in Student Lerning, Lancaster, July 1985

Marton, F. (in press) Describing and improving learning. In R.R. Schmeck (Ed) *Learning Styles and Learning Strategies* New York: Plenum

Marton, F. and Säljö, R. (1984) Approaches to learning. In F. Marton et al (Eds) *The Experience of Learning* Edinburgh: Scottish Academic Press

Marton, F., Hounsell, D.J. and Entwistle, N.J. (Eds) (1984) *The Experience of Learning* Edinburgh: Scottish Academic Press

Newble, D.I. and Jaeger, K. (1983) The effect of assessment and examinations on the learning of medical students *Medical Education* 17, 25-31

Ramsden, P. (1979) Student learning and perceptions of the academic environment *Higher Education* 8, 411-428

Ramsden, P. (1984) The context of learning. In F. Marton et al (Eds) *The Experience of Learning* Edinburgh: Scottish Academic Press

Ramsden, P. and Entwistle, N.J. (1981) Effects of academic departments on students' approaches to studying *British Journal of Educational Psychology* 51, 368-383

Ramsden, P., Beswick, D.G., and Bowden, J.A. (in press) Effects of learning skills interventions on first year university students' learning *Human Learning*

Svensson, L. (1984) Skill in learning. In F. Marton et al (Eds) *The Experience of Learning* Edinburgh: Scottish Academic Press

Svensson, L. and Hogfors, C. (1984) On science learning. Paper presented at the Sixth International Conference on Higher Education, Lancaster, 1984

Watkins, D. (1984) Student perceptions of factors influencing tertiary learning *Higher Education Research and Development* 3, 33-50

Whelan, G. (1985) Fourth year medical students' approaches to clinical problem-solving. Paper presented at Annual Conference of the Australasian and New Zealand Association for Medical Education, Melbourne, August 1985

8

The Case of Architecture

Patrick Nuttgens

However marginal it may once have been in the richly diverse scene of higher education, architecture has become something of a test case in the last few years. Its problems are, I believe, to be found in the history of its fortunes in colleges and universities. It now finds itself on both sides of the binary line and was the subject of the first 'transbinary' group attempting to establish suitable provision on a national scale.

The event that fundamentally altered the scene of architectural education was the Oxford Conference of the Royal Institute of British Architects (RIBA) in 1958. Until that time most schools of architecture had been in colleges of art, themselves developed from the schools of design widely set up following Parliament's Select Committee on Art and Manufacture of 1835. Architecture was not one of the first departments but it was an obvious development, joining departments of graphic and industrial design and then of fine art, which was a later and increasingly specialized offspring.

The main conclusions of the Oxford Conference were far-reaching in their implications. Architectural education should be full-time rather than part-time; entry to courses of architecture must require two 'A' levels rather than the 5 'O' levels that colleges of art normally asked for; and schools of architecture should be in universities whenever possible, either set up anew or transferred from the local college of art.

At the same time the atmosphere and the aspirations of the architects were changed by the arrival in the universities during the fifties of some powerful professors from practice, mainly in public offices. The best known university schools were those in Liverpool (which had acquired international renown under Professor Sir Charles Reilly), Manchester, and University College of London (UCL). Oxford did not have one. Cambridge did but did not offer a tripos and the course gave exemption only from the Intermediate examination of the RIBA. I remember that, because the School which I attended regarded it as unacceptable to go to Cambridge for such a low level course; so I went elsewhere.

The professors who changed the scene were first Robert Matthew, who went to Edinburgh from the LCC (where he had been Architect to the Council and led the team designing the Festival Hall) and Leslie Martin, who went to Cambridge after following Matthew at the LCC. Martin chaired the Oxford Conference and steered it with great clarity and clearness of aim.

The Bartlett School in University College London, after a minor revolution, abandoned the historical studies and stylistic revival designs taught by Sir Albert Richardson, and appointed Richard Llewellyn Davies, later a life peer (the first life peerage given to an architect, thus indicating the high standing of the profession in the swinging sixties). He demanded 'A' level mathematics from entrants, promoted science and research, delayed the teaching of design and recruited a professoriate of recognized experts in every field but architectural design. After some turbulent years, when the West of England Academy was robbed of its school of architecture, Bristol University followed the UCL trend, demanded 'A' level mathematics and introduced the students to computers.

(That was the school which, alone of all the architectural schools, was wound up by its university in the aftermath of the drastic cuts made by the University Grants Committee (UGC) in 1981; it was noted by observers that the Department of Architecture had never really become an integral part of the university and could be discarded without affecting it significantly. The Department had, in other words, remained on the margin.)

The further development in the late sixties and early seventies that affected the schools of architecture was the validation of the non-university courses for degrees. The major colleges of art having been absorbed into the polytechnics, architectural courses were generally removed from the embrace of the new Faculty of Art and Design and became separate entities, joined by town planning and landscape and sometimes by building. Their degrees were validated by the Council for National Academic Awards.

In a few cases a local university entered into an arrangement and validated the courses. That happened mainly in Scotland. In Glasgow, the University of Glasgow validated the architectural courses at the Glasgow School of Art, while those at the Royal College of Science and Technology went with it into the University of Strathclyde. In Edinburgh, the university expanded its own courses in architecture, town planning and landscape, while the college of art obtained validation for its architectural course from the Heriot Watt University, formerly the Heriot Watt Technical College. In Dundee, the course at the Duncan of Jordanstone College of Art was validated by the University of Dundee.

The results of the changes were, being in Britain, mixed. There were now two schools of architecture in Glasgow and Edinburgh, as well as in Liverpool and Manchester. The scene in London was even more diverse – two in universities (UCL and the Royal College of Art, the latter now redesignated as a university), six in polytechnics and one independent. The final pattern nationally, after some twenty years of change and decay, was as follows. Of the thirty-six schools of architecture recognized by the RIBA, thirteen were in universities, nineteen in polytechnics or colleges, three were hybrid (located in a college with courses validated by a local university) and one (the Architectural Association) was independent.

There was therefore an obvious case for the UGC and the recently founded National Advisory Body for Local Authority Higher Education, the NAB, (set up to create some order in the planning of higher education in the non-university sector) to look into the provision of architectural places. The study group chaired by Lord Esher, a former President of the RIBA and Rector of the Royal College of Art, produced a report in 1985 which was quickly followed by the joint report of the UGC and the NAB (*Intakes* 1985) and a response from the RIBA, all of which, with various amendments, added up to recommending the stabilization of the profession, the abolition of three schools and the amalgamation of others, notably where there were two in one city. In the months that followed, all the bodies concerned bowed to various pressures and at the time of writing two schools have been reprieved and one (in a London polytechnic) awaits its verdict.

To add to the confusion of the scene, the RIBA produced a further paper suggesting which schools should be safeguarded and developed and thus by implication which should be ignored. Although it quickly took the paper back when schools angrily started demanding an explanation, it could be assumed that the profession considered itself big enough, and was either going to stabilize the number of architectural students or reduce the number of schools and then allow some to expand so as to keep the numbers steady nationally.

In addition to these reports, which throw light on what the educators as well as the profession expect of architectural education, a further report struck at the schools and raised questions about the courses and their standards. That was the Report by Her Majesty's Inspectors on *Public Sector Education in Architecture* (1985), based on visits to the schools made in 1984. Among the serious criticisms that could be made of all the schools (and it may be noted that although the report concerned only the public sector schools, similar criticisms might have been made of most of the university schools) were poor knowledge of the technology of building and the use of computers, ignorance of other disciplines even when they were taught side by side with the architects, and the need for more laboratory work and for the employment of more part-time staff with practical experience. Students, it appeared, were regularly late for lectures (a characteristic in which they are surely not alone) and frequently worked at home rather than in the studio (a situation familiar to anyone who has been an architectural student).

'There was evidence during the survey,' said the inspectors, 'that an unacceptably high proportion of students passed through the courses without acquiring, or being required to demonstrate, a knowledge of fundamental principles of building science, economics, and practical construction technology.' In a passage that seems surprising from specialists who ought to have experience of the different time-scales of education and daily life, the inspectors pointed out that design projects take some 60 per cent of the students' time in college whereas they occupy far less in an office (it can be as little as 5 per cent). That, as we shall see later, however justified in general, was to ignore one of the special characteristics of architectural education which does demand a considerable amount of time.

But the report made an important point concerning the structure of the course. Two factors had combined to create a general pattern of course provision. On the one hand, RIBA recognition for exemption from its own professional examinations was in two phases – the Intermediate Examination at the end of the third year and the Final at the end of the fifth year (with two years office experience, before and after the fifth year, necessary for professional registration). On the other hand, the typical English degree course lasted three years (four in Scotland). So it became normal to offer a degree (either BA or BSc) at the end of the three years, with exemption from the RIBA Intermediate examination, and then either a professional diploma or another degree (preferably a BArch) at the end of the following two years. An architectural student could therefore come away with two degrees for one course; it was also rather odd that a degree should be only a half-way qualification, appropriate for architectural assistants rather than principals.

In some respects the postgraduate degree or diploma simply repeated, albeit with bigger scale projects, what the undergraduate degree had required in the first three years. Would it not therefore be better to limit the full-time studies to the first three years and let the postgraduate professional work take place mainly in offices and part-time in the schools? Other professions could learn that way; it might be suitable for architects. And since the attitude of the profession had swung almost to the opposite since the Oxford Conference, it was an attractive proposition. Not for the first time in higher education, we were back where we had started.

My own experience in the educating of architects cuts across many of these issues and illustrates some of the questions that have bedevilled the situation in both its academic and professional development.

I enrolled at Edinburgh College of Art in 1948 to study in its School of Architecture. Within a year the college and the University of Edinburgh had entered into an arrangement whereby a matriculated student of the university would take the whole of the course at the college (no remissions were granted) and at the same time take 'out-subjects' in the University so as to provide him or her with a proper university education. I took out English, history of art, moral philosophy and an honours course in aesthetics, ending with a written thesis on an aspect of the history of architecture. Altogether only five students stumbled through the course in the next few years before it was abolished and replaced by a specifically architectural course leading to a BArch.

Apart from the inherent difficulty of the course – the major difficulty being not so much the packed timetable as the psychological problem of changing one's mental set from creative to academic work and back again in a day – it also raised a fundamental question about architectural education. That was caused by the traditional academics' belief that a training in architecture was not educational; to justify graduation as a Master of Arts with honours from the university, it was necessary to study more reputable academic subjects. In short, architecture could not be an education in itself. The opposite belief – that architecture is indeed an education, being after all one of the basic disciplines in a civilization – took some time to establish, but is fundamental to the future of architectural education.

A decade later I joined the few pioneers who were in at the founding of the new University of York, to take part in the academic planning of the institution but more immediately to take over the direction of the Institute of Advanced Architectural Studies which was one of the two component institutes set up by the York Academic Trust preceding the designation of the university. Partly because of the strength of the institute and partly because of the availability of buildings as well as the obvious suitability of the city of York for a school of architecture, it was planned to start an undergraduate school during the second wave of developments in the university. That was rejected by the University Grants Committee, thus throwing light on its declared policy of never interfering with the academic planning of universities. Nor, in the event, was it possible to graft undergraduate courses on to the institute's graduate short courses; the RIBA was not impressed by that proposal, being committed to full-time five-year courses, even though the technical content of the short courses was of an exemplary professional standard.

Meantime I had worked out what was the minimum size for a full-time undergraduate school of architecture. Assuming a staff/student ratio of roughly 1:10, the minimum number of students that could support the necessary specialist as well as general staff was 150. Clearly there would be variations depending on the availability of part-time professional staff; the presence of the institute in York would, I thought, give an exceptional supply of visiting specialist lecturers and tutors.

But I had also developed a line of thought that I had begun in Edinburgh, when taking part in the devising of the new BArch degree for the University. The argument ran like this. If architecture was to be an education in itself, it must be able to prove that it was a specific academic discipline of status comparable to any other respectable university discipline. But the greater part of an architectural course called upon other people's disciplines (as we shall see later in connection with research). The disciplines that architecture specially called upon or exploited included science, philosophy, history and art. But did or could architecture have its own fundamental area of learning? It did; its discipline was that of *design*. And design was a discipline as fundamental as any traditional academic discipline, like philosophy, and of infinitely greater significance in the daily world of affairs, affecting everything we saw or used. It could indeed be argued that it was precisely the lack of an understanding of the fundamental nature of design that had impoverished the intellectual climate both inside and outside the universities.

If so, what was the discipline of design? There were numerous available definitions which tinkered with only the surface of the problem and suggested a superficial activity. In the wider context, design was the imaginative achievement of a unity or totality out of the assembly of differing and sometimes conflicting needs. The end product of design was an artefact or a building. The university would have to recognize that studies led not to an essay or a thesis, but to an object, which would contain within itself the intellectual and moral standards associated with membership of a graduate body. Since the availability of real projects was slight and in any case the time-scale was impossible, the end product was of course a design.

What has happened since the universities began to play a major part in the development of architectural studies? A significant aspect of increasing importance in the universities was research; if architecture was a serious subject, it must pursue research. But what was *architectural* research? A major part of the research that was influential in the design of buildings was other people's research – in science and engineering, in physics, in the increasingly important field of building services – lighting, heating, acoustics, mechanical services, and electronic control systems that could diagnose and correct faults and provide a memory of the behaviour of a building.

The area of research which expanded most noticeably was in the social sciences, especially the study of behaviour and human needs, that ought to provide much of the programme for housing and town planning. The discipline of history had a temporary decline and then came into its own again – but in a different way. Instead of being taught by architects with a love of old buildings, the history of architecture is now usually taught by professional art historians. The theory of architecture died temporarily in the sixties and then became increasingly specialized, employing a specialized language of its own; much of it was devastatingly critical about the modern movement in architecture.

It remained a question whether worthwhile research could be done into architectural design. An attempt was made to systematize and quantify the *process* of design. Systematic Design Method was an area for research in which papers could be written, studies in operational research could be adapted, material could be fed into a computer and an end product would be recognizable as a piece of research. But architectural design is synthetic as well as analytic and there always remained gaps in the study. In short, Systematic Design Method became a specialism remote from the actual business of the design of buildings. In any case, the design of modern buildings seemed to be getting worse. After nearly thirty years of research and development, the standard of the products seemed poorer than ever before. Perhaps orthodox research was not appropriate in the case of architecture.

The fact is that the traditional location for the stimulation of architectural ideas has not been the laboratory or the library but the studio. While some of the university schools for a time played down the role of the studio, the college or polytechnic schools entered into a new liveliness. Critics could see that something significant was happening in the studio even if its participants had not often tried to rationalize it.

In a study under the general heading of Architecture and the Higher Learning, Donald Schon, professor of Urban Affairs and Education at the Massachusetts Institute of Technology, has produced in *The Design Studio, an Exploration of its Traditions and Potential* a methodical account of the significance of the studio in the formation of the minds and capabilities of students of architecture.

In the orthodox academic mode, he points out, professional competence consists in the application of systematic professional knowledge to the instrumental problems of practice. In contrast to that, the architectural studio has developed traditions of learning-by-doing. That is the tradition, influenced by the Beaux Arts, of project-based education, which often seems innovative when it is introduced to other professional schools. Schon argues that 'the schools of other professions have a great deal to learn from the unique institution of architectural education, the studio' (Schon 1985). What makes it especially unique – and I suspect uniquely important in our developing technological society – is that many stages in the design process, far from having the openness and dispassionate independence of mind of speculative investigation, have binding implications for the next move or the next decision. And he asks 'whether it may be possible for architectural education to incorporate new bodies of research-based theory and technique while retaining the traditions of the studio as the heart of its curriculum'.

That goes near to identifying the problem of standards and criteria for architectural education. However much exact knowledge – in increasing but also increasingly inexact quantities – may be taught and examined, there always remains a significant area in which judgements are ultimately personal. But that area is at the heart of the discipline. In the end, the standards for a course are established by the community of teachers and taught, both internal and external, aware through publications and their own discussions and projects of the current state of the art and what might be expected of its future practitioners.

That is not as imprecise as it may at first sound, because there is today a growing awareness of modes of thinking and behaving not recognized in the narrow fields of inquiry of the traditional university. The entry of the polytechnics means that, provided they do not lose their nerve and bow to the limited discipline of traditional subjects, they have brought into higher education a wider understanding of human acts and aspirations that must be taught and examined in wider ways.

The manifesto of the group within the Royal Society of Arts described as 'Education for Capability' summarizes the position thus:

> There exists in its own right a culture which is concerned with doing, making and organising and the creative arts. This culture emphasises the day to day management of affairs, the formulation and solution of problems and the design, manufacture and marketing of goods and services.
>
> ...A well balanced education should, of course, embrace analysis and the acquisition of knowledge. But it must also include the exercise of creative skills, the competence to undertake and complete tasks and the ability to cope with everyday life; and also doing all these things in co-operation with others.
>
> ...Young people in secondary or higher education increasingly specialise, and do so too often in ways which mean that they are taught to practise only the skills of scholarship and science. They acquire knowledge of particular subjects, but are not equipped to use knowledge in ways which are relevant to the world outside the education system.

Architecture belongs precisely to that world. The resolution of its place and character in the education system may be of lasting importance in that system's future.

9

Inspecting Education

Alan Gibson

What follow are the personal views of the author. They are published here by his permission and that of the Inspectorate and the Centre for Educational Development and Training (FE/HE), Manchester Polytechnic. They were previously printed as part of the Proceedings of a Conference on Quality in Education held at Manchester Polytechnic on 30 October 1984, and appear here unchanged but for the exclusion of the formal opening paragraph. The editor wishes to record his gratitude for being allowed to include this chapter. (Ed.)

Her Majesty's Inspectors have a strong interest in quality. In every field of education we are continuously involved in the appraisal of quality through routine visits and by means of formal inspections which lead to published surveys and reports. In public sector higher education in particular, we published in 1983 a survey of 100 degrees: during the current academic year we shall inspect and report on a number of full-time vocational courses, including courses in the business studies and art and design fields, on a cross section of part-time advanced further education, and on some twenty-five degrees in the humanities and social sciences. In the teacher training field we are inspecting and reporting on all initial undergraduate and postgraduate courses over a period of four years including, by invitation, those in university departments of education as well as those in the public sector.

The appraisal of quality in higher education engages a good deal of attention and a great number of people. The greatest volume of appraisal activity in relation to any given course is surely carried out by the staff who are themselves teaching on it, as they conduct their own individual and collective evaluations as part of the normal process of course review and development. Their efforts are complemented and verified by the peer review of internal and external validation procedures, and for many courses a professional accreditation body provides a further specific appraisal. HMI offer a view from a very different perspective: the infrequency of our formal inspection and reporting reflect the scale of the system, but our appraisals, whether formal or informal, are based on the close observation of the wide variety of curriculum delivery which our widespread visiting makes possible.

Quality is notoriously elusive of prescription, and no easier even to describe and discuss than to deliver in practice. To try to capture some of its characteristics I shall talk first about quality in the purposes of higher education, then about quality in the content, procedures and processes, before saying something about HMI practices and concerns in appraising quality.

Quality in the Purpose

Everyone engaged in appraising quality will have implicit or explicit ideas about the purposes appropriate to high quality higher education. Most of them will probably acknowledge that we should expect to see the purposes exemplified throughout the course: if the purposes are the raison d'être of the experience, not simply a set of terminal competencies to be aimed at, then like the lettering in traditional seaside rock we should expect them to be discernible throughout.

Most appraisers would also probably agree that the purposes of higher education serve many ends and have many facets. Like a curriculum for any age or ability group, the succession of planned and sometimes unplanned learning experiences represents an attempt to develop a wide variety of aspects of personal ability.

Appraisers vary, naturally enough, in their formulation of this variety of purposes. Allowing for differences in emphasis and expression many of them might come close to asking the following questions: does the course provide a programme in which the daily and weekly curricular experiences:

a develop the students' intellectual and imaginative powers, for example:
  i inquiring, analytical and creative thinking,
  ii independent judgement and critical self-awareness,
  iii the habit of using critical apparatus for evaluating ideas and proposals, combining in that apparatus both conceptual and practical instruments and references;
b are useful to the students themselves and to society through the understandings and competencies developed, whether the study programmes are perceived as academic, vocational or a mixture;
c offer learning on at least two time-scales:
  i some learning which is of short-term, survival utility, for example in reliable execution of etablished processes of thought or action, and
  ii some learning which is of long-term utility, for example allowing for creative/constructive/adaptive engagement and a basis for continued learning growth and development;
d inculcate a capacity to see their subject/specialism in relation to:
  i other current and developing fields of knowledge and activity,
  ii social and economic changes, national and international, which may affect its nature and viability; and
e enhance ability to deliver their subsequent contribution as 'thinking graduates' in industry, commerce, the professions or elsewhere through:
  i an awareness of organizational and interpersonal processes, and
  ii a capacity for clear communication and logical argument.

Qualty and Content

Most appraisers will have a view about the content of a higher education curriculum. They will be concerned, like HMI, that it is unimpeachably 'higher'. In the academic disciplines on which it draws, and in any principles relating to the practice of a profession or occupation, they will expect it to be informed by contemporary scholarship, discovery and insight, and by the perspectives, hypotheses and interpretations which are broadly accepted in the chosen fields of study and/or practice. If the curriculum provides a fair understanding and appreciation of whatever stand as the currently accepted orthodoxies of the field, they will not expect it to shun – indeed they may think it has a duty to include – examination also of some contrasting and stimulating elements of the currently unorthodox, the schools of thought which challenge current consensus views.

Most appraisers of higher education are probably equally concerned, like HMI, with the processes and procedures which enable students to gain experiences of quality appropriate to the purposes suggested above. They will look at a great number of aspects of course delivery, and ask about their range, incidence and fitness to purpose: they will consider, for example:

a the management of an appropriate variety of teacher-led learning activities, lectures, demonstrations, teaching seminars;

b the sequence and structure in the material presented, including linkage and relationship; and the regulation of competing demands from different elements in the course so that students have a reasonable chance of managing a workload and of experiencing a real sense of progression and rigour;

c an emphasis on underlying principles, processes and concepts in the field under study, and a complementary avoidance of excessive content learning and routine exercise;

d planned diversity in the learning activities managed and conducted by the student, reading, writing, carrying out experiments, investigations and briefs, contributing to seminar work, all forms of student exercise, exploration, assimilation and ownership of learning;

e skilful and thorough use of student work, through marking and other feedback both to students and to course organizers, including the planning, supervision and systematic follow-up of placements and work experience where this is appropriate; and

f care in admission and induction, and in the monitoring of student progress, including the introduction of study skills where needed, especially guidance on independent or self-directed study.

The successful execution of such processes and procedures may be seen as the essential professionalism of higher education teachers, the very stuff of their occupational competence as people who not only have knowledge but introduce others to it. If such a competence were lacking, *some* students, perhaps the most successful, talented or fortunate students, might still derive experiences of quality from their higher education. The concern of teaching staff, in higher education as in many other parts of the education service, is to devise suitable procedures and processes so that *all* students are adequately challenged and that *most* are impelled into *many* experiences of quality. The procedures and processes will combine stimulus, expectation, reward and sanction so that there is a balance between:

a guidance or pressure to guarantee that essential experiences are undergone; and
b encouragement of students to develop increasing responsibility for their own learning.

HMI Practices and Concerns

HMI's distinctive contribution to the processes of appraisal derives from the privileges of access granted in consequence of the responsibilities of the Secretary of State. HMI are thus able to spend time in classes, laboratories and workshops, to have discussions with teachers and students, and to examine a wide range of documentation and student work. HMI appraisal is concerned to assess standards of learning and is based directly on judgements about:

a the teaching and learning observed and discussed, taken as illustrative examples of delivery strategies adopted in the course, and implicit in its design;
b student work, essays or practical, its qualities, its use in course monitoring and individual feedback;
c staff schemes of work (sampled or seen in their entirety);
d the course teams' plans or submissions, often supplemented by detailed proposals from specialist departments; and
e contextual and supporting matters:
   i   human resources: their allocation deployment and management,
   ii material resources: distribution and use,
   iii counselling and support of students,
   iv extra curricular activities, and
   v   quantitative data connected with the course.

We know of course that even this battery of evidence is not comprehensive, and that the resulting judgements are essentially subjective and essentially norm referenced. They are, however, reached by experienced observers who have taught in the field inspected, or in one closely analogous to it, and they are arrived at by a process which is interactive with the course team, and iterative over a period before, during and sometimes after formal visits: the process therefore includes professional dialogue and careful reflection.

It will be clear that HMI do not bring to the inspection of a course or a college any set of tightly defined, preordained prescriptions to which they hope the provision will conform: one fundamental reason for this is that our duties enable us to see the wide variety of working solutions, often very imaginative, to the multitude of problems and puzzles set by the differing combinations of curricular, institutional and resource factors.

If HMI have no tightly specified recipe for success in course provision, they do have some general predisposing assumptions accumulated over their collective experience. One of these is that high quality is not necessarily correlated with high spending on staff, facilities or equipment, though they recognize that there are certain levels below which quality is well nigh unattainable. If there is one common ingredient in courses of quality, it is probably the commitment, enthusiasm and delivered competence of the course staff. Some practical consequences of such qualities are frequently manifest in the efficient organization and management of a course, and in the generation of a sense of purpose, significance and mutual respect between staff and students. In the best cases, this leads to an unselfconscious observation by students of orderliness, application and engagement in the day to day conduct of their learning. This is not a plea for the higher education equivalent of 'good order and military discipline' for its own sake, but for the sake of the effective and economic execution of the various contracts implicit and explicit between the staff, the student and the wide society.

Any concerns which HMI have about higher education are usually expressed in relation to particular courses or institutions inspected, but the survey of 100 degrees published in 1983 made it possible to identify a number of operational deficiencies which occur more widely in the system than any of us here would regard as acceptable. There are four principal areas of concern: induction, lectures, seminars, and practical or project work:

a   in general, the students have adequate prior informtion about their courses, and most colleges provide an induction programme into life and work as a higher education student, including introduction to the library; in some courses attention is given to study skills BUT:

   i   some students, a significant minority, need more and early explanation of course structures, especially in complex modular courses with several options and option points; more care in matching qualifications and interest to study programmes would help to eliminate some wasted time, disappointment and under-achievement,

   ii   most induction programmes seem to have limited success because they are too hasty; introduction to the use of the library is often not reinforced in day to day teaching, and has to be repeated later, especially when students begin more independent study, and

   iii   many students need more help with the skills of independent study, for example in essay planning and in the gradual accentuation of analysis in their essays at the expense of description;

b   most lectures visited by HMI are carefully prepared and competently delivered BUT:

   i   some are not, and that seems professionally indefensible;

   ii   lectures are usually factual and descriptive, reviewing organized knowledge and including limited analysis; exciting lectures are rare; it appears unusual for lectures to expound and evaluate opposing viewpoints, and

   iii   lectures are accompanied by considerable and even continuous note-taking, including a fair amount of dictation and copying from the board; this habit is found in art subjects, but is prevalent in the technologies and in the sciences, to an extent incompatible with a 'higher' education experience;

c   HMI see many commendable seminars of various kinds; those in the humanities area are generally effective, and the best in other areas, for example in business studies and hotel and catering, reach very high standards indeed, BUT:

i many seminars are teacher-led extensions of a lecturing mode,

ii many seminars in which one or two students give prepared papers are ineffective at engaging other students because they have not prepared themselves or in some cases have not been given the opportunity to do so by prior notification, and

iii many seminars become dialogues between the tutor and just one or two students (even in humanities); and

d public sector higher education, in particular, places considerable and proper emphasis on practical and project work; staff in technology and science courses devote substantial efforts to planning and supervising laboratory work, which is rarely of a routine nature in science at least; other disciplines use practical and project work (for example, hotel and catering to encourage inquiry and the understanding of principles; business studies to stimulate the definition and analysis of business problems; and art and design to promote continuous self-and-peer-diagnosis); most student reports on practical and project work are marked regularly and returned quickly with helpful comments BUT:

i not all practical work is as well managed as it should be, given its prominence; in the technologies, design and quality are sometimes lacking; science projects do not receive proper discussion at the end of sessions; business studies projects sometimes omit appropriate analysis and some are too narrowly conceived,

ii not all student reports are well and quickly marked and returned, and tutors frequently fail to assess the quality of the practical work and the technical proficiency of its conduct,

iii marking schemes for practical work lack uniformity in some courses, and thereby confuse students,

iv in science and technology practicals, marks awarded tend to pick out the very good or very poor students and do not discriminate in the middle range; a serious defect where practical work carries a high proportion of the marks in assessment, and

v in some cases the learning gained from practical work is far from commensurate with the considerable time and effort put in by students, and in other cases staff have not thought seriously enough about the purposes of practical work.

Concerns about those four areas stand out disconcertingly from the HMI's extensive survey, and the attention given to them exemplifies very clearly the kinds of quality appraisal to which HMI are led by their privileged opportunities for observation of a system at work.

There are other concerns which HMI share with commentators and appraisers of the higher education service; they are not the subject of synoptic HMI reports or surveys because, rather than reflective appraisals of provision as it stands, they are deductions informed by those appraisals, and essentially contributions to debate about the future. It seems more appropriate therefore to put them in the form of questions:

a could we not provide better quality higher education more consistently through enriched staff development, giving emphasis to 'educational development' work on higher education curricula, and their design and delivery, alongside opportunities for consultancy, scholarly research and sustained links with practice in employment fields relevant to the courses taught?

b could some higher education curricula not be improved by discarding elements which may more accurately reflect the historical development of a subject than the needs of students or the modern state of a particular field and the cover of it which can be justified in the mid to late 1980s? Such pruning may entail some re-analysis of the understandings, skills, competencies and processes required;

c are narrowly specialized course designs, whether in academic or vocational courses, not a poor investment (from the viewpoint of both individuals and society) for a significant proportion of higher education students? Many degrees are valued for their capacity to develop generic skills, and recent DES-funded research by Brunel University suggests that employers continue to want the 'good all rounder' to meet a range of career demands at several levels, showing maturity and flexibility, including a reasonable proficiency in numeracy and writing skills commensurate with 16 years of full-time education;

d could a more positive place be found in academic high education courses for career education, a greater awareness of career possibilities, and perhaps more work-based learning in some courses? Just as vocationally related courses need breadth, context and eclecticism, more academic programmes are not the place for vocationalization of a narrow kind, but none can fairly adopt a cloistered aversion from the reality, which includes a clear expectation on the part of students that their studies will assist them in gaining and progressing in employment, contributing to their own and others' economic well-being;

e could more higher education courses be of greater benefit to both individuals and society if they made explicit the value frameworks of the contents and of the careers to which they may lead, and the relationship of these value frameworks to broader philosophies or systems of thought or to concepts such as that of an economically and ecologically 'interdependent world', or to other organizing and overarching ideas which enable students to locate their studies and possible future work against wider schemes. And should public exposition and comment on those value frameworks not be expected as much from those inside higher education as from those outside?

The theme of this book reflects the spate of current activity relating to appraisal in higher education. We can expect that the Lindop inquiry will open up the debate significantly. We are all aware that in the domain of the Council for National Academic Awards efforts towards 'partnership in validation' are helping to provide a better framework for correlation between internal and external validation. We have seen the efforts to establish a clear separation of powers between the plurality of bodies such as the National Advisory Board (NAB), the CNAA, the Council for the Accreditation of Teacher Education (CATE) and other professional accreditors, and the articulation of those various powers wth the responsibilities of others. For HMI, continuing to report 'as we find' to the Secretary of State presents excitement enough. The fact that all of the organizations I have mentioned (along with teachers, institutions and the general public) have access to our published reports is a stimulus, a safeguard and a sobering thought whenever we put our appraising pens to paper.

10

Research Funding

S.G. Owen

Edmund Halley is said to have been the first research worker in British history to have persuaded the government to part with money to finance the purchase of scientific apparatus. He had succeeded to the appointment of Astronomer Royal on the death in 1719 of his former mentor and later rival John Flamsteed, but the latter's widow had prevented him gaining access to Flamsteed's telescopes. Halley successfully appealed to the government of the day for funds to replace the equipment, thus establishing a principle which, though it took two hundred years to gain general acceptance, would not now be regarded as open to serious challenge in any developed country of the world, namely, that the support of research is a legitimate call on public funds and that a proportion of government expenditure should be devoted to this end. What proportion, and how it should be disbursed, are of course matters of perennial debate some aspects of which it is the purpose of the present chapter to ventilate.

In the United Kingdom, as in the United States and most other Western countries, there exist a number of 'private' bodies, such as charitable foundations and trusts, from which money can be obtained to support research projects carried out by university departments (mainly), or by other scientific or educational institutions, or which themselves directly conduct research by employing staff working in institutes which they own. Much research also takes place under the auspices of industry, by no means all of it directed towards obvious and immediate commercial objectives. Reviewing his own field, the medical and biological sciences, in which the drug industry has a large and competitive presence, the writer a few years ago estimated that about sixty per cent of all research was financed by commercial pharmaceutical interests as compared with about twenty-five per cent from government sources taken together (ie derived directly or indirectly from the University Grants Committee (UGC), the research councils and the in-house and out-house programmes of the health departments and other government agencies, excluding those related to defence); strictly private funds from charitable organizations accounted for a little over ten per cent. Other fields of scientific endeavour would doubtless yield quite different figures, but there can be no doubt that the publicly-supported component is essential to the maintenance of a significant, healthy and continuing base in science research, and that an adequate flow of public funds derived ultimately from the taxpayer will in the future be necessary for this purpose. In this context, and in the remarks which follow, the word science is used in its widest senses (*wissenschaft*), to include the humanities and the social disciplines as well as the traditional physical and natural sciences.

The basis for the public support of science in the UK is now and has for a number of years been the so-called 'Science Vote', a block of money allocated annually by central government to the Department of Education and Science (DES) which distributes it in turn to the Royal Society and the five research councils. The latter form the bedrock of the UK research support system: they are the Science and Engineering Research Council (SERC, until recently the Science Research Council); the Medical Research Council (MRC); the Agricultural and Food Research Council (AFRC, until recently the Agricultural Research Council); the National Environment Research Council (NERC); and the Economic and Social Research Council (ESRC, until recently the Social Science Research Council). (The reader will note that the fashion for name-changing is in the direction of presenting a more 'applied' image to the public and the councils' political paymasters. The pure-versus-applied dimension is a recurrent and disputatious theme whenever the use of taxpayers' money to enable scientists to pursue their preoccupations comes under discussion, particularly during periods of financial constraint – more of this below.)

The responsibility for advising the DES on how the global sum made available for science should be divided between the individual research councils and the other minor pensioners of the Science Budget lies with a committee known as the Advisory Board for the Research Councils (ABRC), a function carried out prior to 1972 by the now-disbanded Council for Scientific Policy. On this high-level body are represented the interests of industry and higher education as well as those of the major scientific fields. Meeting in the presence of DES civil servants, the ABRC attempts in the face of more or less limited resources (depending on the mood of the government at the time) to assess the competing claims of the individual rsearch councils as expressed in annual submissions to it by each council separately. Difficult choices are presented – by reference to what criteria can one compare the value of (say) leukaemia research with that of (say) a hydrological survey of the south Atlantic? – so that the tendency must inevitably be in the. direction of maintaining the historical status quo, tempered by marginal tinkering to satisfy the requirements of any 'policy' which the Board may have formulated. Moreover, other considerations than the purely scientific must enter the Board's deliberations: for example the political harmonics associated with continuance or otherwise of UK participation in expensive international organizations such as CERN (the European centre for nuclear physics research in Geneva, funded through the SERC) and EMBL (the European Molecular Biology Laboratory in Heidelberg, funded through the MRC); preservation (or not) of the traditional role played by some of the councils in postgraduate education; the extent to which the councils provide more general assistance to university departments through the 'dual-support system' rather than concentrating their resources on in-house research (such as that which takes place in MRC and AFRC establishments); the social and economic relevance of the programmes submitted; and so on. Perhaps the Board's most difficult problem is to decide what weight to give to these varied and possibly conflicting bases of judgement.

As has been said above, there has never existed a clear consensus about the extent to which research funding should be weighted in the direction of discernible relevance to socially desirable objectives (applied or directed research) rather than in that of allowing scientists to determine their own programmes of work and thus advance their subjects by a process of internal logic (pure or curiosity-orientated research). The dispute can be illustrated from the earliest days of systematic government assistance. The Medical Research Committee, the model for the research council system, was set up in 1913 with clear practical objectives. It owed its existence to the final report of the Royal Commission on Tuberculosis and to Lloyd George's National Insurance Act of 1911. Section 16 of the latter required the government annually to provide the equivalent of one penny for each insured person as a contribution to the expenses of sanatorium benefit. More significantly in the present context, the Act permitted the whole or part of that provision to be retained for 'the purposes of research'. The objective of this first national fund for research was thus quite clearly related to an area of applied science. On the other hand, the Council for Scientific and Industrial Research (the predecessor of the present Science and Engineering Research Council) was deliberately insulated from direct governmental pressures when it was founded, being set up under the control of a committee of the Privy Council. It thereby embodied the principle linked to the name of the then Lord Chancellor, Lord Haldane (one of its most vigorous protagonists), that research should not be subjected to the day-to-day pressures and needs of the executive departments of government. The Haldane principle also prevailed when, under the Ministry of Health Act 1919, the Medical Research Committee was later reconstituted as the Medical Research Council under the wing of a Privy Council committee and not of the new Ministry.

But the pure-versus-applied debate by no means ended there. Many readers will recall that it reached a new peak of intensity in the early 1970s as a result of the activities of another noble lord, Lord Rothschild, then head of the Government's Central Policy Review Staff. Rothschild proposed a reorganization of publicly-funded research along lines diametrically opposed to the Haldane principle. In a paper entitled 'The Organization of Government R & D', published in 1971 as part of the Green Paper (consultative document) *A Framework for Government Research and Development*, he recommended the application of his so-called customer-contractor principle to the funding of civil science. The recommendation was eventually accepted by the government (in a White Paper, Cmnd 5046, of the same title) despite the strongly expressed opposition of what seemed to be a large majority of the scientific community. The essence of the new arrangements was that a proportion of the annual financial allocation to each research council should be transferred to the control of the executive department or departments of Government whose interests were cognate to those of the Council. In the case of medical research, for example, one-quarter of the allocation to the MRC (the 'contractor') was passed over to the budgets of the Health Departments (the 'customers') who were then expected to employ the money in commissioning research from the Council in areas of specific interest to them (or, if the Council failed to give satisfaction, from other agencies). The departments themselves were to improve their scientific organization and each would appoint a Chief Scientist; they would thus be enabled to ask the right research questions. The change was intended to shift the balance of research expenditure in the direction of social need as reflected in the utilization of National Health Service resources. The reaction to these proposals of those actually engaged in research was generally unfavourable, ranging from scepticism to outright dismay. The history of science suggested that rarely if ever could genuine innovative progress, as opposed to technological development, be dictated by administrative targeting in the way that Rothschild seemed to be envisaging. On the contrary, the important advances tended to occur obliquely and to have applications that had not and could not have been foreseen. In the real world of science, the customer-contractor concept appeared simplistic and naïve, betraying an ignorance of the nature of the process by which new knowledge is acquired. Certainly in the case of biomedical research (the writer is not qualified to speak of other areas of inquiry), these fears proved to be only too well founded. No significant change in the pattern of research nor in its rate of progress could be demonstrated over the ensuing years, while cumbersome paperwork procedures for 'accounting' for the transferred funds placed a bureaucratic burden on customer and contractor alike. On the advice of the Public Accounts Committee, the Rothschild arrangements in respect of medical research were formally abandoned on 1 April 1981, when the transferred funds were returned from the Health Departments to the Council.

In the writer's view, the criticism of the research councils which underlay the Rothschild movement – namely that they are insufficiently responsive to social goals and public needs – has probably never had much justification. Those experienced in the administration of research funds know that it is only too easy to draw up a list of 'priority' areas, fields in which real progress would undoubtedly lead to predictable and even quantifiable social and economic benefits. But they also know that there is no simple equation between such progress and the crude expenditure of money without regard to scientific opportunity and scientific excellence; and that increasing a volume of already mediocre and unfruitful work may even be counter-productive. While it is perfectly legitimate for funding agencies (and of course particularly those independent bodies set up with terms of reference which dedicate them to specific ends) to draw up hierarchies of objectives against which their distribution of funds can be assessed, these should never be allowed to override the traditional research council criteria of 'timeliness and promise'. History provides innumerable examples of the value of encouraging fundamental research which is 'exciting', ie which is making progress, without having any immediately obvious application to the ills of mankind. The current explosion in applied biotechnology is a recent one; it could not and would not have happened had it not been for the ivory-tower (as many then judged it) research in molecular biology which took place (largely with UK research council support) during the 50s, 60s and 70s.

In discharging their responsibilities, research funding agencies in Britain, both public and private, have always been heavily dependent on the universities, where much of their work has been carried out. The essential requirement is a financially healthy and autonomous university system able and willing to generate a volume and quality of research proposals sufficient to allow the agencies, particularly the research councils, to select those which meet their criteria and are likely to further their scientific policies. In the past, reliance has been to a great extent on the traditional dual-support arrangements. The core-support of research was provided by university departments from their own (largely UGC-derived) resources. The core comprised such bricks-and-mortar as offices and laboratories, together with their maintenance, heating, lighting, cleaning and so on; the salaries of the senior staff, including senior technical staff involved in the work; and any back-up facilities necessary (secretarial, library, computer, etc.) other than those wholly and exclusively required for a particular research project. Expenses in respect of the latter would be met by a research grant made to the university by the funding agency, as would the salaries of the (usually) more junior, non-tenured scientific and technical staff employed whole-time on the project, and the costs of the equipment needed to carry it out. Administration of the grant was the responsibility of the university, which acted as the employer of the reimbursed staff, related administrative overheads being usually disallowed by the agency. In general the system worked well, and to the mutual benefit of the two parties to the contract; university scientists were provided with the staff and equipment to enable them to develop active research programmes, while research councils could deploy a substantial proportion of their resources in promoting the advancement of knowledge in those areas they wished to develop, while at the same time fulfilling their obligation to maintain an adequate infrastructure of research throughout the nation's institutes of higher learning (the latter a function as vital to the wellbeing of the research establishments of government and industry, and of the research councils themselves, as to that of the universities). It is a matter of great regret that the decline in university resources over recent years has perturbed these arrangements, making them difficult and in some cases impossible to operate by inhibiting institutions from entering into or from honouring the dual-support bargain. New employment legislation has presented obvious additional difficulties. The ability of funding agencies to be more flexible under such circumstances has, at the same time, particularly in the case of the research councils, been constrained by their own financial stringencies; and the latter have also resulted in a reduction in the overall number of grants available.

Alternative strategies to the short-term project grant are of course open to bodies with funds at their disposal for purposes of research. One such is to bypass existing institutions altogether in favour of creating one or more directly-financed research facilities. In this case the funding agency must rent, buy or build the space required and directly employ the staff to work in it, inevitably accepting career commitments to at least a proportion of these. Such direct support of research is therefore also long-term support and the resources devoted to it are unlikely to be redeployable for many years. It has nevertheless often been the preferred solution to research needs which were seen as requiring developments of such novelty or on such a scale or concentration of effort as to be beyond the scope of university departments which had other responsibilities and were committed to existing programmes. Many such establishments, ranging in size from small units employing a handful of workers to large institutes with a thousand or more, have been set up by the research councils: the AFRC and the MRC in particular devoting substantial proportions of their resourcses to their maintenance. A number also exist in the private and charitable sectors, particularly in the medical field – for example in cancer research and rheumatology. Circumstances may dictate that such institutions be free-standing; but more often, and with advantage, they are embedded in a university environment, when a state of valuable symbiosis usually prevails.

Arrangements intermediate between direct and indirect research funding are possible and may be particularly useful at a time, like the present, when departments are anxious to maintain active research programmes but find it difficult to do so because teaching and other commitments leave senior staff with little time to supervise research activity, much less to engage in it themselves. A guarantee of money to reimburse the salary and overheads of one or more senior academic appointments (either for a finite period say of five years, or until retirement age) may then be sought from outside sources, while financial support of the programmes themselves continues to depend on periodic competition in the indirect support market-place. The outside agency may be prepared to go a little further and directly employ the career scientist. The MRC for example, who have for many years employed a number of external scientific staff in universities and hospitals, have responded to the financial climate in universities by introducing (in 1978/9) four additional award schemes to provide personal support for individual research workers at a senior or intermediate level. The awards are linked with programme or project grants, an arrangement which allows the Council to exercise scientific oversight and a measure of control, and their titles are designed to reflect appropriately the academic status of the holders (eg Clinical Research Professorships, Research Fellowships for Academic Staff, Senior Fellowships (Non-Clinical, etc.). Other bodies – the British Heart Foundation and the Arthritis and Rheumatism Council are instances in the medical field – may be prepared to endow permanent university chairs in subjects in which they are particularly interested.

Other methods by which funding organizations seek to promote research include: block grants to assist with the core support of independent institutions; special equipment grants for the purchase of expensive apparatus; financial support of the various means of communiction exemplified by journals, societies, international conferences, etc.; training and travelling fellowships of various types; and research studentships (PhD awards, so-called partnership awards and advanced course studentships). PhD awards require special mention, because several of the research councils allocate a significant proportion of their budget to this heading and from the universities' point of view they constitute a major component of depart-mental activity and an important source of departmental finance. These research studentships, normally of three years' duration, are intended for recent graduates of special promise who have been selected to receive whole-time research training leading to a postgraduate degree (the PhD or equivalent) and who are expected ultimately to pursue an academic or research career. Though councils havè in the past sometimes made the awards directly to recipients, on the basis of their undergraduate record and the proposed programme of research training, it is now more usual for selection to be delegated to heads of department or institutions. The departments receive a numerical allocation of awards each year, sometimes with an intimation of the number to be expected in future years in order to assist departmental planning. Departmental competition for the awards, which carry with them a general subvention to cover research expenses, is often intense; in the writer's experience, the annual allocation exercise, involving as it must do a value judgement as to the research standing of individual departments as well as determining an important part of their income for the following three years, engenders more emotion and even hostility among disappointed members of the university community than any other research council activity. Any attempt by a council to operate, or even to adumbrate, a PhD policy (eg concentration in 'centres of excellence') seems to provoke alarm and dismay (from centres of mediocrity?). A topical instance is the outraged reaction to the recent (1985) proposal by the Economic and Social Research Council to withdraw PhD awards from universities whose research students consistently fail to complete their theses within the allotted three-year span. While in theory the councils can operate the system as a long-term regulator of the volume of research activity, moving allocations around between subjects as well as between departments in order to further the scientific policies of the moment, it is doubtful whether it can ever be an effective instrument for this purpose; data on the final career choices of PhD students are hard to come by, but there may be relatively little correlation with the subjects of their research degrees. Many would argue, moreover, that the educational component of the studentships is the important one and would question whether research agencies are the most appropriate channel for their public support.

Despite the difficulties already mentioned, the research grant (indirect support in research council terminology) is likely to remain a major mechanism by which research in institutions of higher education is financed in the future; and most academics would doubtless prefer it so. Most awards of this sort (project grants) are relatively short-term, given usually for a period of three years in relation to a finite piece of work which has a reasonable prospect of completion within that time. From the point of view of the research body, it is highly desirable that a significant proportion of the funds available to it be allocated to the project grant subhead, since one-third of such moneys falls in each year and becomes redeployable; only thus can the body remain flexible and responsive to changing needs. Some funding agencies will accept applications for longer-term support in relation to more ambitious programmes, requiring grants which extend over five years in the first instance and which may need to carry an implication of renewability for a further period if the work goes well; it should be noted however that the term 'programme grant' has no precise definition and in the writer's field at any rate varies in its terms between different awarding bodies. Whatever the duration and other conditions attaching to research grants – and as already stated a much greater degree of liberality may now be called for under the dual-support system than used to be the case – all agencies must employ some form of peer review to assess the scientific merit of the applications coming to them. This usually means consideration by a committee of individuals of similar academic or research status to the applicant (or his senior colleagues), one or more of whom may or may not have special knowledge of the subject matter of the application. Written opinions from independent referees, selected because they do have such knowledge, will be available to the committee, who will then make their judgement and attempt to relate it in terms of merit to other applications under consideration at the same awarding session or during a given accounting period (possibly by means of some semi-quantitative scoring or ranking method). A reference back to the applicant or the referees for clarification or further information may be necessary before an adequate judgement can be made. Where the committee, or its parent body, is attempting to implement a 'policy' – for example to promote certain areas of work, to encourage certain types of researcher, to develop certain departments, and so on – such considerations must be superimposed on the assessment of intrinsic merit before a final list is drawn up and matched against the funds available for award. Successful applications may be pruned, for example by reducing the sum of money requested for recurrent expenses or by declining items of equipment which should already be in the possession of a 'well-found' department or for which there are cheaper alternatives. Much less often, it may be considered that expenses have been underestimated in relation to the project proposed, and appropriate additions are made. The awarding body will usually require some formal reassurance from the host institution that the requisite facilities (laboratories, office space, animal accommodation, etc.) are to be made available for the work, and that the institution is prepared to administer the grant in accordance with the agency's terms and conditions. Many variations and refinements of this basic procedure are of course possible. It is not unusual, for example, for applicants to be interviewed by awarding bodies or, if committee time allows it, for a 'site visit' to be made so that the interview can take place in the host institution where the facilities can be directly inspected (a technique especially favoured in the USA).

All sorts of criticisms can be, and usually are, levelled at the methods by which decisions are reached by funding agencies, whatever procedures they adopt. The competitive allocation of a limited sum of money necessarily involves a 'cut-off point' which will appear (and be) arbitrary and unfair to those whose applications are ranked immediately below it (the face-saving transatlantic formula of 'approved but insufficient funds available' is sometimes employed as a palliative). Applicants often have difficulty in accepting as their peers (in the scientific sense) those charged with the responsibility of peer review. The more specialized the field of research, the more likely is it that the true independence of expert referees will be questioned. And so on. No system is perfect and some bad decisions are inevitable, not least because creativity and originality in science are not always accompanied by the patience, humility and literary skills required for the construction of persuasive grant applications. But the inbuilt plurality provided by the existence of multiple, even to some extent competing, sources of funds in many areas of inquiry provides some safeguard for the applicant with the virtue of persistence; it must be rarely that he cannot find a court of appeal.

Post-decision procedures, too, can arouse controversy, sometimes even bitterness. For example, does not justice as well as considerations of freedom of information require that unfavourable referees' reports be shown to unsuccessful applicants – should they not be allowed the opportunity to refute the criticisms or alternatively to accept them and subsequently to reshape and improve their proposals? The research administrator is likely to reply that the opinions were given in confidence and that had it not been so they would probably have been couched in terms so emasculated as to have had little value to the grants committee. This particular point of contention, like the many others which it would require another chapter to enumerate, will presumably never be resolved to everyone's satisfaction, but it is interesting to note that the latest (1984/5) Annual Report of the MRC announces at least a partial relaxation of the Council's past policy of witholding 'feedback' to applicants about the reasons for decisions.

It will be apparent from the foregoing that there can be an almost infinite number of methodological variations on the central theme of utilizing for its intended purpose money set aside for research. It follows that the administrative criteria adopted by the spending agencies will vary correspondingly, not only between agencies but from time to time in response to the changing situation in institutions of higher learning and in the state of their own finances. But whatever schemes are adopted to facilitate the conversion of the material resources into the acquisition of new knowledge, it will surely always be true that this process depends crucially on other considerations being subordinated to the two overriding criteria of scientific opportunity and scientific excellence – timeliness and promise.

This chapter has touched on some aspects of the methods by which academic research is financed in the United Kingdom. The situation has changed out of all recognition since Halley first pleaded with the government for his telescopes. But it is a matter of regret that an article written while Halley's comet is once again visible in the sky must conclude by recording that anxiety still prevails about the intentions of government towards the central support of scientific research. Present restrictions on the funds available to civil science, and to the institutions of higher learning on which scientific progress depends, must, if continued, raise the prospect of a serious and lasting impairment of the nation's research capacity.

11

View from Industry

Tom Cannon

During 1985 a series of events focused attention on the debate in higher education about direction and standards that had been growing in importance throughout the decade. Early in the year *Competence and Competition*, a report by the Manpower Services Commission (MSC) and the National Economic Development Office (NEDO 1983) acknowledged the increasing role played in international business competition by the skills and abilities developed through further and higher education. The government White Paper on education and training for young people (DES 1985a) restated the belief that:

> vocational education and training are not marginal activities, but are central to our economic growth and prosperity.

At about the same time the Green Paper on higher education into the 1990s (DES 1985b) and related statements indicated a steady reduction in numbers:

> The projections (for the period 1983-1999) suggest that demand for full-time courses is likely to stay fairly constant or increase up to 1990 and to fall after that by about 14 per cent by 1996.

Later in the year, the Confederation of British Industry (CBI) took 'Education' as the theme of its Annual Conference. The designation of 1986 as Industry Year was followed by a number of comments indicating that the main thrust of activities during this period would reflect the belief that:

> The most important area where a long term change in attitudes can be achieved is in education

These events illustrate the concern being expressed in many quarters about the role and function of higher education in a society such as Britain today. Much of this discussion has centred around the extent to which the goals of those formulating and executing policy within the institutions of higher education match the needs and expectations of different publics. Such goals shape direction and influence standards. The extent to which different expectations are met has a direct bearing on direction and standards.

The pace of the debate and the range of issues under discussion have both increased rapidly over the last decade, especially following the publication of the Leverhulme Report (1983). The priority given to the debate reflects a distinct change in perspective from that which was widely shared until fairly recently. Traditionally, many groups in British society appeared unconcerned about the degree to which the goals, structure and offerings of higher education met their needs. The Robbins Report paid far less attention to the responsibilities of universities to industry and the economy than to their own rights and those of their actual and potential students. Industry's views for much of the last hundred years, expressed through its leaders, were probably well summarized by Gowling (1976):

> The management of British Industry until after the Second World War... was nurtured in a tradition where such (scientific and technical) education counted for little.

In contrast to Britain's major industrial rivals there seems to have been no expectation that the objectives of education would reflect the needs of industry. This appears to be especially true of higher education. Specific initiatives, such as the creation of the engineering or technical institutions in the industrial centres in the late nineteenth centry, or the expansion of secondary technical education, foundered from a mixture of internal resistance and inertia and lack of sustained external effort. Many of the sentiments expressed today about the importance of industry/education links will find echoes in the Royal Commission on the 'Great Depression' of the 1880s.

In 1982 the then Director General of the NEDO, Sir Geoffrey Chandler, pointed out that:

> Comparisons with Germany indicate that from the 1850s onwards the UK educated a much smaller proportion of its population, particularly in scientific and technical subjects. Industry (in the UK) placed little faith in trained personnel by comparison with 'practical' men. At least four Royal Commissions in the second half of the nineteenth century identified this problem clearly and made strong recommendations for reform.

The persistence of this apparent gap between the alleged needs of an industrially developed society such as Britain for certain types of output from institutions of higher education and their supply has prompted many different explanations. Two are especially relevant to the present discussion. In many quarters it is suggested that resistance among educators to the changes, together with lack of responsiveness, provide the key:

> The whole intellectual establishment looks down on industry ('money making'), chooses other fields for its own careers, warns away its pupils and children, and consistently underrates the qualities necessary for success in it. (Nind 1980)

Elsewhere, it is suggested that the attitudes of industrialists to education have been a mixture of indifference and inconsistency.

Industrial inconsistency is seen to take a number of forms. In the past, forecasts of the types of skills likely to be required have been inexact and subject to considerable and fairly rapid changes, posing many problems for a system subject to the relatively long lead-times of universities and other institutions of higher education. The Finniston Report (1980) highlighted other inconsistencies. The statements of many industrialists that there were serious shortages of skilled engineers were linked to empty places in sciences and engineering in universities and colleges. However, it was noted that the relatively poor status, pay and conditions of qualified engineers suggested conditions more consistent with excess not shortage of supply over demand. Elsewhere the gap between stated needs and actual behaviour has been placed in a wider context.

Marsden (1982) notes that, on the one hand:

At meetings all over the country employers are telling teachers that there should be more emphasis on basic skills (eg communication and practical numeracy) and how to apply them in a number of situations, team-work, problem-solving....

While, on the other hand, largely contradictory messages seem to be communicated through the recruitment and selection procedures that firms follow:

...whatever employers say they want in recruits, the initial hurdle requires examination passes.

The same pattern can be seen across subject areas. Evidence by industrialists to the Select Committee on Higher Education emphasized the 'preference' for graduates with a general or broadly-based academic background of the type frequently associated with the humanities. But an examination of the employment pattern of recent graduates brings out the relatively high levels of unemployment among graduates in the humanities when compared with vocational subjects (Fig.1).

Subject	Unemployed plus temporarily employed as % labour market entrants
English	40
Sociology	36
History	32
French	28
Economics	21
Business Studies	13
Accountancy	5

Figure 1
Employment and unemployment of new graduates.

It is against this background that the following study of industry's view of standards and criteria in higher education was devised.

Investigating the Industrial View

The study was designed to explore a number of issues in a complex area. The primary task was to build up a picture of the prevailing attitudes towards present standards in higher education in the light of the issues raised both by the Green Paper and by parallel studies by the Reynolds and Lindop Committees. It was recognized that the definition of quality in education was:

> ...a subject extraordinarily difficult to come to grips with, and full of pitfalls. (Ball 1985)

However, it was thought important to pay considerable attention to: the views of different groups in the business community; and an examination of mechanisms for building a better interface between higher education and industry in this area.

The notion that 'industry' exists as a homogeneous grouping was questioned at an early stage. Much recently published work gives the impression that a single industrial view can or should be taken. But the very diversity of modern commercial activity reveals its fundamental heterogeneity. The heterogeneity can, for example, be illustrated by reference to the educational background of managers.

Fidler and others (Fig.2) demonstrate that on one dimension at least, and one relevant to this debate, a clear division exists in Britain: they show that about half of senior managers are not graduates.

Study	Sample	Graduates %
Copeman (1955)	Directors (1000 largest firms)	36
Guttsman (1963)	Officers of business organizations	46
Clarke (1966)	Directors (Northern Area)	37
Nichols (1969)	Directors (Northern City)	47
Hall and Amado-Fischgrund (1969)	120 CEOs	38
Heller (1973)	Directors (top 200 firms)	49
Fidler (1981)	90 CEOs	57

Figure 2
Percentage of senior executives who attended university.

An important partnership already exists between the institutions of higher education and the professions in setting standards and monitoring performance criteria. It is therefore possible that the views of industrialists with a background in a professional institute will differ from those held by their colleagues from other backgrounds.

Across the spectrum of business there exist other major differences. Sectoral variations, say between manufacturing and services, have been suggested by some commentators. There is some evidence (Watkins 1983) that the educational background and aspirations of those in small firms is different from that in larger companies. An important avenue of investigation in the present study was the impact of this heterogeneity on the approach of 'industry' to the idea of 'fitness for purpose', as Ball (1985) defines quality.

Turning now to research again, we find that industry has no single clear view. Although academics are increasingly being advised to turn to industry for research funding, this has to be seen against a background in which:

> Industry has very few mechanisms for finding out its needs. Few (trade or professional) associations ever discuss research or development and the NEDO sector committees rarely have 'research' on their agenda.

Apart from a small number of specific cases, the interface between the academic research policy makers and those in industry is poor. This seems to be especially true in terms of the mechanisms for setting overall priorities in the Research Councils and for selecting between research projects. The 'blind' peer-review system dominates selection and evaluation of proposals. The extent to which it is either understood or seen as relevant by industrialists was explored. Particular attention was paid to the role ascribed to academic research as well as the criteria used in selecting potential partners for future work.

In part, the concern for research reflected recognition that the discussion of 'quality' in education has many dimensions. Ball (1985) raises issues of plant, capital equipment and other physical resources besides exploring the broader matter of staff. Such matters were not raised directly in the initial study. They were mentioned spontaneously by a number of respondents.

The study consisted of three distinct parts: group discussions, in-depth interviews, and the comments of a further group of chief executives. Discussions were held with six groups of middle and senior executives from a number of industries. Three of the groups consisted of executives from differing backgrounds, industries and sizes of firm. Of the three others, one was made up solely of graduate managers, another of executives from manufacturers, and the third of executives from small companies. The primary purpose was to identify the major concerns of managers. The group discussions were also used to explore the opportunities for and constraints on greater industrial participation in setting and maintaining standards in institutions of higher education.

The groups were the basis for the second part of the study: the in-depth interviews. Unfortunately, as it turned out, the sample was confined to UK nationals. It was structured to include:

> Head office and divisional staff from large firms,
> Line and service functions,
> Graduates and non-graduates,
> Representatives of professional and representative bodies,
> Large and small firms, and
> Manufacturing and services.

Besides these representatives of the private sector, a small number of academics with recent industrial experience were also interviewed.

The results of the interviews were summarized and sent to the chief executives of a small number of large UK companies for comment. Their observations form the third significant element in the study.

The Managers Involved

The managers taking part in the study were asked to locate themselves in the management hierarchy of their firms. On this basis the majority saw themselves as middle and senior management. Apart from those belonging to identifiable professions, eg accountants, all did have job titles including the term 'manager', with the exception of a number of directors. The proportion with first degrees was slightly in excess of that expected, given earlier evidence. However, the inclusion of a specific sub-set of graduates among those taking part in the group discussions may account for this. A small number had postgraduate qualifications. These were either in business/vocational subjects or in engineering. Sixty per cent of the total sample (excluding the top managers who were asked for their comments on the findings) had first degrees while fifteen per cent held postgraduate awards.

The younger and more junior management groups were more likely to hold formal qualifications than the older and more senior groups. Exceptions to this were: members of the professions, especially those employed in the service industries; and directors of small, high technology firms. (The numbers in the latter group were so small that definite conclusions cannot properly be drawn about them as a distinct set.)

Their Contacts with Higher Education

In both the group discussions and the interviews a great deal of time was spent exploring the participants' experience and attitudes to higher education. It soon became clear that there was very little regular contact between these managers or their firms and universities or other institutions of higher education. This was not seen as a problem or a priority by any. Some belonged to firms with education/industry liaison officers. There was very little awareness of their activities among other managers. Where knowledge of their role existed it was centred on programmes in and with schools. As for research, they generally saw it as need-based: 'If I come across a problem that we cannot solve internally I might approach x University'.

Among graduates there was no differentiation between the institutions they had attended and other universities or colleges in terms of strength of connections. Responsibility for initiating and maintaining contacts was seen as the responsibility of those in higher education.

In some areas, notably training and consultancy, managers were aware of the services offered by higher education. But although they were welcomed, there was no evidence that the services provided by universities and colleges were held to be superior to those offered by other suppliers. A number of respondents commented on the contrast between their expectation of high quality provision and the poor presentation and inefficiency of the providers from higher education. The low quality of facilities in higher education was referred to on a number of occasions. It would seem that operating systems and plant were significantly more important to industry's perception of 'quality' than might be expected.

Similar comments were made specifically about research in the sciences and engineering. For example about:

— the quality of internal company facilities; and
— the impression that a marked deterioration had occurred in plant and equipment in science and engineering in universities and colleges.

Despite these comments, there was very little evidence of a belief that industrial concerns should play a larger part in providing improved resources. There were some indications that managers with experience of foreign owned (mainly US) companies held different views. They saw a much greater industrial role in providing material support to improve the quality of facilities. Even among these, there was a consensus that the quality and professionalism of initial approacher and follow-up needed to be far better if links were to improve. Most of the managers had apocryphal stories of promises unfulfilled and initiatives uncompleted by local colleges or universities.

Their Views on Recruitment

It became clear that most non-graduates in the groups did not know what to expect from higher education nor were they clear what expectations universities and colleges had of them. This was especially noticeable in discussions concerning the nature and level of undergraduate education and the quality of graduate entrants.

Contrary to what one had been led to expect, the non-graduate managers seemed to anticipate that graduates would hold relevant functional or technical skills. On a number of occasions it was suggested that the ability to apply their acquired knowledge was very important among new recruits, a sentiment especially strong among 'line management' and in smaller, manufacturing, enterprises. Such views were in contrast to those held by managers directly involved in personnel and related service functions. They also differed from those held by respondents from business associations and the professions. However, the number of non-graduates among these last groups was far smaller than the number in line management or small firms. Despite this, it would seem that important aspects of the inconsistency noted by commentators derive from the differences in opinion among key groups in industry. This was expressed forcibly by one respondent who pointed out: 'The graduate's salary comes off my establishment and out of my budget. I need to get immediate benefits'. An insight into the dilemma was given by one recent graduate manager: 'Most firms have either inflated or no expectations of their graduate entrants.'

Firms need more clearly defined policies about graduate entrants as well as better internal communication. The problems would seem to be greatest in smaller manufacturing enterprises and among science and engineering entrants. This may reflect a stronger sense that they 'ought' to have more immediately applicable skills.

Graduate managers held far more restricted views of the contribution that a new recruit from a university or college could make. The limited direct relevance of much academic study to industrial or commercial work was not held to be a significant problem. Some pointed out that holding a degree was an indicator of potential not achievement.

A great deal of discussion in the groups and in the interviews was centred on the apparent inconsistency between these findings and the graduate unemployment data referred to earlier. Among the explanations put forward were suggestions that:

The preference for students from vocational subjects was based on a belief that the choice of these subjects demonstrated the interest and positive attitudes (to industry) of candidates; and

The costs of graduate training for students from vocational subjects was expected to be lower than for other entrants. This was a common opinion among those working in personnel functions.

A number of the younger managers with vocational qualifications put forward a different explanation, namely that:

Comments about the value of broadly based 'arts' subjects reflect the views of older more senior managers, whereas recruitment was in the hands of younger more pragmatic managers.

There was no evidence that managers saw any difference in 'quality' between graduates in vocational or non-vocational subjects. There were some observations that interviewees from certain subjects appeared to have:

Undertaken some formal training in personal presentation or communication; or have

A better researched or more realistic knowledge of the firm undertaking the interview.

Although the bulk of the group discussions centred on undergraduate qualifications there was some comment on postgraduates. Virtually all respondents with experience of employing postgraduates spoke very highly of them. Their ability to apply their acquired knowledge was remarked upon. A number of respondents commented on their initial belief that postgraduates would be too specialized or inflexible. There was consensus that these fears had not been realized. On a personal level many made favourable observations about the maturity and team-working skills of postgraduate recruits. This may reflect the greater use of small groups and the integration of postgraduates into research teams in many universities and colleges. The data base was too small to permit any real differentiation to be made between masters and doctoral, taught-course and research students.

Their Views on Quality

In both the group discussions and the interviews it was generally believed that there was considerable scope for improving standards in higher education. However, there was considerable disagreement about the nature of the problems and their origins. These centred on: the relative importance of subject and 'life' skills; and whether responsibility for change lay with the students, academic staff or themselves. Many respondents expressed the belief that graduates seldom showed in-depth knowledge of their chosen areas of study. Perhaps inevitably, many of the comments on this topic centred on those entering industry with vocational qualifications. The view was that there were often major omissions from the knowledge base required in key areas of a given field. Some graduate managers suggested that there was a tendency to spend a great deal of time on degree programmes studying broadly based academic aspects of topics and too little on application areas.

These comments were closely related to a belief that students could be 'pushed harder' during their courses. There seemed to be two dimensions to this. A number of respondents believed that far more material could be communicated during a three- or four-year degree programme, and skills could be increased. None of the groups demurred. A number of executives compared university and college courses unfavourably in this respect with those run by internal training and management development programmes.

Some related the demands made on students by courses to wider issues of attitudes and values. Many of those interviewed, especially from smaller firms, felt that graduates lacked self discipline, motivation and drive. These personal qualities were seen as especially important in markets today. Graduate managers indicated that they felt that their student career had not prepared them for either the pace of work or the personal skills needed to succeed in business. There was a surprising degree of agreement on the need for more emphasis on 'life' skills in undergraduate studies.

The majority of respondents placed the primary responsibility for introducing changes on the institutions of higher education. Some felt that the students themselves should be more demanding. A number with US experience made unfavourable comparisons. However this was a very limited sample. Most indicated a belief that industry should be 'willing' to help but in limited and carefully husbanded ways.

Most respondents were highly critical of the standards of professionalism of the academics and of university and college administrators. Graduate managers noted the poor example given by many teaching staff in terms of pre-preparation, efficiency and overall standards. Again there were unfavourable comparisons with their internal training functions. These attitudes were expressed more vigorously by younger, more junior, less well qualified managers. They were far less widely held among members of the professions. It appeared that patterns of behaviour by academics in professional fields more closely mirrored those found among professionals everywhere.

A number of the managers had had dealings with universities and colleges in research and consultancy. They had very mixed views. A number were highly complementary. They outlined the very high standards achieved by university and college scientists and engineers in this respect. Others were more critical. They pointed to unreliability, delays, poor presentation and weak follow-up as common problems. All expressed disappointment at the lack of consistency and the inadequate 'quality controls' imposed by institutions on the work of their staff.

Throughout, there was a general view that responsibility for improving standards lay with the institutions themselves. Most believed that their firms lacked the time and resources to play a major part in influencing the process of change. This was most clearly stated by those in manufacturing, holding line or operational responsibilities. There was not a great difference between the opinions of small and large firms on this. Members of the professions and activists in associations were less likely to hold the view. The small number of well qualified, younger managers did indicate a wish to play a larger part in initiating change. Again this sub-sample was too small to draw firm conclusions.

An Alternative Point of View

During the period of this study, the author spent some time in the USA and elsewhere. This provided a brief opportunity to discuss both quality and the interface between higher education and industry from a different perspective. Although it would be wrong to imply that this limited access allowed any firm conclusions to be drawn, some relevant issues emerged from American experience. In the US it seemed that the individual and the corporation felt a far deeper sense of identification with and responsibility for specific universities.

Corporations appeared to become involved with specific institutions across a wide range of areas. They seemed to be more closely integrated in different areas. It was not unusual to find a number of managers from a specific firm working with the same university. In one case the chief executive was on the Board of Regents, two vice-presidents were on Faculty Advisory Boards and at least five other senior managers were working on joint projects. At the same time as many as three professors held non-executive posts in subsidiaries of the firm. A significant number of its senior managers were alumni. There was 'no sense of distance' between this firm and the university. It would be wrong to suggest that this is the norm but it reflects a pattern of close working relationships which is not as common in Britain. It would seem to preclude the indifference and lack of any true sense of involvement which seems to emerge from much UK evidence.

Alumni associations reinforce this involvement. This is partly in terms of the on-going programmes alluded to above. More generally, graduates appear to believe that the quality of their peers from the same college reflects on them. A deterioration in standards might reduce the 'marketability' of their qualifications. In an environment in which overall standards are seen to be more variable the issue is particularly potent. It was also suggested that the high cost of study in America added intensity to this jealous concern to maintain the reputation of a graduate's alma mater.

Two of the universities visited had very strong local roots, which appeared to stimulate widespread community interest in its work and standing. This was partly a function of scale. In both cases, student populations of over

35,000 existed in communities of about 100,000. The nature of the dependency relationship was very different from that in any UK town.

In general, it would seem that the extent of involvement and participation in the affairs of universities by industry in the US gives firms and individuals a direct interest in influencing and shaping standards at all levels. Many of the forces creating this pattern are related to specific environmental factors which do not exist in Britain. The transferability of this type of link, if seen as desirable, would require major changes in attitude and approach to working together on both sides.

Conclusion

In the first part of this chapter a number of issues relating to industry's view of the topic 'fitness for purpose' and its component elements 'standards' and 'criteria' were raised. The programme of research undertaken sought to explore these in ways which provided a different perspective from the conventional. Managers from a number of areas were given the opportunity to express their views in contexts which enabled group and individual perspectives to develop. The wealth of data which emerged will require further study before its full implications can be defined. However, a number of issues came to the fore.

It was clear that an understanding of the heterogeneity of commerce and industry needs to be more fully built into discussions about quality. There were marked and consistent differences between the stated needs and expectations of managers in small firms and large, or in manufacturing firms and services. Even within companies significant variations could be identified. This would seem to imply the need for much more wide-ranging and perhaps closer 'integration' between firms and institutions of higher education. It also suggests that large firms should develop and communicate policies to this end. The small sample of chief executive officers with whom this notion has been discussed appear sympathetic to the concept.

Despite this diversity there was a broad measure of agreement in certain key areas. Although most respondents would concur with Christopher Ball's proposition that quality in education is 'extraordinarily' difficult to define they do seem able to recognize poor quality at least. The managers in the study seemed to give far greater weight to operating systems than do most commentators. Inferior laboratory facilities were cited as a reason for not working more closely with science and engineering departments. Poorly maintained and serviced teaching facilities were given as reasons for not holding training and other programmes with academics. A great deal of criticism was made of the standards of professional practice. This ranged from slowness to respond, to inadequate 'quality controls'. There seemed to be many aspects of these operations where marked improvements in 'quality' could be achieved. It is worth noting that most interviewees felt that there had been 'marked improvements in standards' since 1981!

Attitudes to the graduates of institutions of higher education were diverse. It seemed that no great expectations were held, with the result that disappointment was limited. There was considerable debate concerning the balance of need for change. Some respondents felt that there was considerable scope for change in knowledge and skill levels. Others placed greater priority on improved 'life' skills. There was considerable criticism especially among recent graduates of the internal standards applied in higher education. Those managers with experience of both internal education and training processes and those provided by higher education tended to compare the latter unfavourably. Despite these views, there was general agreement that higher education was producing individuals of considerable potential. Especially favourable views were expressed about postgraduates. It would seem that restrictions on numbers in this area run counter to the high value industry places on them.

The study has highlighted a number of critical areas for policy and further research. It suggests that changes in approach within higher education are needed. Equally important, it indicates a worrying level of indifference and apathy among managers to the universities and colleges. Tackling this will be an important aspect of any attempt to ensure true 'fitness for purpose'.

References

Ball, C. (1985) *Fitness for Purpose. Essays in Higher Education* London: SRHE & NFER-NELSON

Clarke D.G. (1966) *The Industrial Manager* London: Business Publications

Copeman, G.H. (1955) *Leaders of British Industry* London: Gee

DES (1985a) *Education: education and training for young people* Cmnd 9482. London: HMSO

DES (1985b) *The Development of Higher Education into the 1990's* Cmnd 9524. London: HMSO

Fidler, J. (1981) *The British Business Elite* London: Routledge & Kegan Paul

Finniston, M. (1980) *Engineering our Future* Report of the Committee of Enquiry into the Engineering Profession. Cmnd 7794. London: HMSO

Gowling, M. (1976) Lost opportunities in an age of imperialism *Times Higher Education Supplement* November

Guttsman, W.L. (1963) *The British Political Elite* London: MacGibbon and Kee

Hall, D.J. & Amado-Fischgrund, G. (1969) The European business elite *European Business* 23

Heller, R. (1973) The state of British boardrooms *Management Today* May

The Leverhulme Report (1983) *Excellence in Diversity* Guildford: Society for Research into Higher Education

Marsden, D. (1982) *Workless* London: Croom Helm

National Economic Development Office (1983) *Competence and Competition* London: HMSO

Nichols, T. (1969) *Ownership, Control and Ideology* London: Allen & Unwin

Nind, P. (1980) Management and learning. In C.L. Cooper (Ed.) *Developing Managers for the 1980's* London

Watkins, D. (1983) Development, training and education for the small firm: a European perspective *European Small Business Journal* Spring

12

The All-Seeing Eye of the Prince in Western Europe

Guy Neave

In the course of the seventies, mass higher education became a reality in most Western European countries. By no means all, however, have reached the 'watershed' between élite and mass higher education, the point commonly held to be reached when 15 per cent or more of the relevant age group are enrolled. Switzerland is one exception, and some believe the United Kingdom is another (Neave 1985). And, despite dire prophecies to the contrary, quantitative growth has continued, so that by the mid-eighties France, the Federal Republic of Germany, Denmark and Italy anticipate participation rates of around 28-33 per cent (CRE 1984).

The type of relationship that exists between public authorities and higher education in its élite phase is very different from that which obtains when expansion is the order of the day. Governments are going to take a closer look at how universities operate the more the university budget grows. And so too, as the numbers of young people entering such establishments increase, do issues that hitherto remained largely internal to university administration come under closer scrutiny. Thus government intervention also increased in the seventies. In some cases – and France and Germany are perhaps illustrative here – government action was the price of restoring 'the social peace', either through redefining the powers and responsibilities of professors, junior staff and students in the area of internal governance or through changing the conditions of appointment (Neave and Rhoades, forthcoming). In others, spiralling costs plus the perceived need to encourage students to opt for courses deemed 'closer to the national interest' have brought about equally marked changes in the structure and duration of undergraduate education. Examples of this latter process are visible, for instance, in the Swedish 1977 university reform which replaced the traditional 'disciplinary structure' of undergraduate studies with five 'occupational sectors': technical professions; administrative, economic and social-work professions; health (medical and para-medical) professions; teaching professions; and information, communication and cultural professions (Ekholm 1985, p.110). Similar moves are visible in the French higher education Guideline Law of January 1984 (Neave 1985b).

Alongside such specific instances of intervention went another development which, no less important, also stood as testimony to the increasing complexity of higher education administration and the determination of the Prince to keep a watchful eye. This was the emergence of separate ministries with specific remits to deal with higher education. In the mid-sixties, the Office of the Chancellor of Swedish Universities began to assume that function, then with its transformation in 1976 into the National Board of Universities and Colleges, to assume planning and administrative oversight for the whole of higher education, university and non-university sectors alike. There were similar developments in the seventies in Spain, Portugal, Austria and France (though in France the Ministry of Higher Education has, since M. Mitterrand's party came to power in 1981, been restored to the National Ministry of Education).

This relocation of functions did not change the basic nature of the control exercised by administration over higher education, which tends not only to be financial but also extends to such areas as nomination into post at professorial level and the validation and recognition of degrees as well as the setting out of the formal conditions of access to higher education itself. There are, naturally, variations between countries as to the specific location of these responsibilities. In the Netherlands, for example, nomination into post at junior level may be made by the individual university, as is also the case in Sweden (Neave and Cerych 1982). In France and Belgium, by contrast, nomination to a full-time position requires the decision of the Ministry of Education. In short, the degree of formal control over areas which in the United Kingdom would fall under the responsibility of the academic staff of an individual university is far closer and tends to be more detailed. It follows from this that the twin functions of monitoring and validating the 'quality' of higher education, whether at the input or the output end, are located less inside what Clark has called the 'base decision-making units' of higher education – the Department, the *Unité de Formation et de Recherche* (Clark 1984) and more outside the university in various national committees in the appropriate ministries.

If we take as surrogates for 'quality monitoring' three elements that in essence are often held to be indicative of that idea – student access conditions, validation of degrees and courses in higher education, and nomination into post (which may be taken as a species of 'staff quality control'), we can explore some of the differences that exist between the United Kingdom and its European neighbours. (Other indices could be chosen, among them finance, but they would require book-length treatments.)

Monitoring: a Concept

Before going into the substantial part of this analysis, it is perhaps appropriate to give some thought to the two issues under discussion – monitoring and validation. Monitoring, at least as it may be presented, is that process of continued oversight and control exercised to ensure the achievement of a pre-specified end. It may be internal to the particular body in which the process takes place or it may be exercised by an outside agency with an official remit. Typical of the first variety in the university world is the selection of students for admission and their subsequent elimination if they fail to reach a particular level of achievement, which one finds in both British and American universities. Typical of the second would be, for instance, the part played by the Swedish Public Auditor's office and in France the *Cour des Comptes*, both of which make regular statements about the use – and sometimes the abuse – of financial resources and the allocation of teaching hours (the latter, in France, being a budgetary unit). There is, however, a third variety, in which members of a particular body carry out internal monitoring but have the authority delegated them from an outside source. This latter tends, on balance, to be the predominant form of monitoring found in most European universities, where the formal authority to assess 'quality' of achievement is delegated to academia from the state. It is to be found, for instance, in Belgium, where university examining boards are nominated by the (relevant) Ministry of Education and their composition laid down formally by law (*Lois coordinnées sur la collation des grades académiques et le programme des examens universitaires. Recueil des lois et des règlements* Bruxelles, janvier 1978, Ministère de l'Education Nationale et de la Culture Française, (¶40, §2,3, p.52).

One can argue that despite differences in the context and nature of the authority delegated, the function of monitoring remains similar. And that beneath the weight of legal detail that tends to prevail in French, Belgian and German Universities, the essential freedom to teach and to learn is preserved. This is true. But the fact remains that whilst universities in these countries have latitude in determining content and teaching methods, monitoring and validation are closely contained by an external legal framework which is determined at national level and not, as would be the case in Britain or America, by conventions, agreements and procedures formulated inside the individual establishment.

In addition, there are fundamental differences in the formal relationship between universities and the state in Western Europe which considerably affect the ability of higher education to control and monitor the quality of students applying for entry. Seen from a European perspective, the fact that the British government is taking an active interest – some might say an over-active interest – in defining 'quality', in terms of more graduate engineers and computer scientists, as well as in seeking the advice of industry in laying out higher education's priorities is neither radical nor startling. Indeed, their aim is very similar to one of those assigned to French higher education, namely to double the number of engineering graduates in the course of the next three years (Le Monde 1985). Indeed, it is possible to argue that by increasing the monitory oversight implicit, for instance, in additional funding recently given to engineering departments in the UK, Britain is moving towards a more 'European' mode of coordination, in which 'intermediary bodies' like the University Grants Committee or the National Advisory Body are, like the French *Conseil National de l'Enseignement Supérieur et de la Recherche*, expressions less of the ascending hierarchy of academia than of the descending hierarchy of national *règlement* and central government. Put another way, the strengthening of monitory and validatory functions, whether applied to student inflow or to staffing resources, constitutes a significant shift in system control in the United Kingdom. Paradoxically, there are signs at the present time, particularly in France and the Netherlands, of an equally significant shift in the location of system control, but in the opposite direction.

Monitoring Student Flows

From a Continental perspective, one of the more unusual features of British higher education has been its ability to control the quality of the students entering it. From this sprang a number of other elements which conferred upon academia the ability not only to monitor student inflow and to determine who was 'suitably qualified', but also to control the evolution of the academic profession itself. The Robbins covenant – that the government would ensure a place for every 'suitably qualified' applicant – was remarkable for several reasons. First, taken in conjunction with the UGC role as negotiating body on behalf of British universities, it virtually ensured that academia, by dint of its ability to select and admit candidates, indirectly also wrote its own budget. Second, control over student 'quality', and thus inflow, also determined staff appointments. Thus, at a time when in most other Western European countries, the expansion of the sixties was achieved at the cost of deteriorating staff/student ratios and the rise of a litigeous part-time 'academic proletariat' of 'Assistants', British academia grew in proportion to the student increase, and with relative stability (Neave and Rhoades, forthcoming). Third, the system of student grants further reinforced the power of British academia's ability to monitor and control its own house, since students failing en cours de route were highly unlikely to have their grant renewed or else found themselves, save in exceptional circumstances, obliged to repeat the year at their own expense.

Now none of this will appear exceptional to British readers. Such practices are part of a very particular 'British ideology' that governs the relationship between university and polity which, no less remarkably, continued throughout the period of the drive to mass higher education. Put succinctly, this 'ideology' was one that sought to minimize the intervention of the polity in the affairs of academe and, despite the fact that higher education was utterly dependent on the Prince for its finances, sought to maintain the historic fiction of universities acting as 'private corporations' (Eustace 1982). This 'ideology' had – and I use the past tense deliberately – direct consequences for the twin functions of monitoring and validating, and, although one can argue that the Council for National Academic Awards stands as an example of external validations in the public sector, the fact that it is not a direct emanation of central administration so much as an expression at national level of academia overseeing the house of others is a testimony to the continuing power of that ideology when the CNAA was first set up.

In Europe, as in Britain, the location of monitoring and validatory agencies is an expression of the historic place the university occupies in the polity. To put matters briefly, the predominant concept in such countries as France, Italy, Belgium, the Federal Republic of Germany and Sweden is that the university is most definitely within the public domain. The incorporation of that institution among government services began in the course of the eighteenth century in Sweden and Austria, and reached its clearest expression in the Humboldtian reforms of 1809 in Prussia and in the creation of the Imperial University in the French reforms of 1811 (Scotford Archer 1979; Clark 1977). It follows from this that the universities in particular, and higher education in general, are subject either to public or to administrative and constitutional law, in which academic autonomy is defined as a residual area wherein the state voluntarily restrains its right to act. There are, of course exceptions (Belgium and the Netherlands, for example) where religious establishments exist, and staff nominations, for example, are subject to the approval of the religious authorities rather than the ministry (Neave and Cerych 1981). By and large, the fact remains that the role of the state is to uphold a certain coordination and coherence in the conditions of access and in the types of courses leading to state recognized qualifications.

Central to any discussion on monitoring and validation is the question, 'Who or what determines whether an applicant is "qualified"?' And from this springs the subsidiary question, 'How far do individual establishments have the right to act in a monitory capacity over student inflow?' Historically, universities in Germany, France, Sweden and Italy have not had that right. The *academic* secondary school-leaving certificate – whether the *Baccalauréat*, the *Abitur* or the *Maturità* – conferred upon its holders the legal and constitutional right to a place in higher education. Such a function of certification lay in the hands of examiners nominated either by the Central Ministry of Education, working in conjunction with the National Inspectorate in France and Belgium (*Comités de Homologation*) or with the provincial Ministry of Education in the case of West Germany (*Kultusministerium*). In short, universities exercised neither a monitory or a validatory function at this level. They were, on the contrary, passive recipients of a 'quality control' exercised either federally or nationally that was located elsewhere in the education system. Nor, necessarily, were university departments able to control the type of studies their entrants might choose. In those countries which subscribed to what might be called a German model of university – the Netherlands, Denmark and Sweden being three examples – the *academic* school-leaving certificate was a general award – that is, it gave the right to follow any combination of courses that might take the individual's fancy. Furthermore, duration of studies was not subject to institutional control either. The freedom to learn (*Lernfreiheit*) was largely interpreted as the right of students to decide when they would present for final examination, with the result that, as the labour market deteriorated in the course of the seventies, so the time taken for individuals to graduate extended dramatically – 10 semesters being the average in 1981 in the Federal Republic and 13.6 in Denmark.

This lack of internal control, particularly in the German-speaking lands, has led many senior academics – the West German Rectors Conference and various spokesmen for its Austrian counterpart – to press for the introduction of 'an English style' degree structure, with a limited duration of studies, in which it is essentially the right of academics to control admission to certain courses and to determine the rhythm of examinations (Council of Europe 1983).

Pressure of student numbers, overcrowding and, more recently, growing employment difficulties for humanities and social science students, have forced government intervention. If, traditionally, and in certain instances constitutionally as well, entry to university has been 'open', the last fifteen years have seen a dramatic growth in what is usually termed the 'closed' sector of higher education. The characteristic of the 'numerus clausus' (limited intake) faculties is their selective nature, evinced either by a public competitive examination or by their reliance on high grade point averages in the school-leaving examination. In certain systems – the French and Belgian for instance – certain sectors or specialist institutions – the engineering schools in the case of the latter and the whole of the élite Grandes Ecoles sector in the case of the former – are subject to this stricture. Though an extra hurdle in the admissions procedure, such examinations are, once again, controlled by the ministry rather than by the individual institution.

The extension of the numerus clausus to engineering, medicine and pharmacy can be seen as an early example of 'capacity planning', the decision being taken at central government level in France, Sweden, the Federal Republic of Germany and the Netherlands. The reasons were several: to control costs in areas involving heavy equipment investment; to avoid an over-supply of highly qualified manpower at a time of incipient demographic downturn; and, last but not least, to introduce a certain measure of predictability in planning the future development of higher education (Lane 1979). At a high level of generalization, the effect of the West German *Hochschulrahmengesetz* (1976), of the Swedish higher education reforms of the following year, and of the introduction of a 'lottery system' for access to Dutch universities in 1978 was two-fold; they increased system control over student inflow through the setting up of national student allocation services; at the same time they strengthened institutional capacity to control student through-put, by laying down time limits for completion of degree courses (*Regelzeit*), by introducing in the case of the Dutch a so-called 'propadeutic' year, or by increasing the number of short courses available (Teichler and Sanyal 1982, p.68; Bladh 1982).

It is largely a matter of perception and personal opinion whether these same measures did not also reinforce what some have termed the bureaucratic as opposed to the professional control over higher education (Lane 1979). Much depends on whether the selection for 'closed access' faculties is carried out by central administration, as in Sweden (Premfors and Ostergrén 1978) and the Netherlands, by a national agency external to central government, as in the Federal Republic of Germany (SUNY 1979), or, as is the case unofficially in France, by faculties of law and business studies, which flunk large numbers of students at the end of the first year.

If, at first, the numerus clausus was seen to be a way of 'rationing' places at a time of high demand, there are now signs in certain countries, the Netherlands being one and Denmark another (Neave 1986), that this same instrument is beginning to serve other purposes: to 'profile' or to channel student demand away from areas of potentially high unemployment, a measure visible in Denmark; or to place restrictions on the number of diplomas a department may award, a matter which is currently under discussion in the Netherlands (Luttikholt 1986). In both cases, the numerus clausus mechanism is an instrument of forward policy planning rather than an essentially reactive response. Either way, restrictions on student numbers, whether at source or by dint of a more vigorous 'weeding out', which the Dutch proposals seem to suggest, show clearly that the price of an enhanced internal 'quality control system at the establishment level' is often an increase in the controlling power of the central administration, whether Ministry or Director of Higher Education.

Validating Degrees

One of the historic functions of universities in Western Europe has been the education and training of future members of government administration and school teachers who, in many instances, are regarded as state employees. This particular function has direct consequences for validation of degrees as well as for the mechanism for 'guaranteeing' their quality. In certain countries, amongst which are France, Belgium, Italy and the Federal Republic of Germany, there exists what might be termed a 'dual' system of awards and thus a dual system of validation. This duality emerges in the distinction made between university diplomas and national diplomas in France, between *les grades légaux* and *les grades universitaires* in Belgium, and between the various forms of *Staatsexamen* on the one hand and university awarded degrees (Magister, Doctorate) on the other that exist in the Federal Republic of Germany. The distinction between the two lies not merely in the fact that university awarded diplomas are internally validated, whereas the *grades légaux*, the French national diplomas and the *Staatsexamen* are validated by Equivalence Commissions (*Commissions de Homologation*) in Belgium, by the *Conseil National de l'Enseignement Supèrieur et de la Recherche* acting in the name of the Minister of Education in France, or by the provincial Ministry of Education in West Germany. The latter certificates are a conditio sine qua non to holding a post in public administration. In Belgium, legal diplomas are also a necessary prerequisite for qualification as a medical doctor, pharmacist or engineer. The legislation surrounding externally validated national diplomas is both considerable and detailed. The Belgian law of 27 July 1971 lays down the minimum number of subjects to be covered as well as specifying a minimum number of hours to be spent in lectures or practicals per year.

Similar detail is found in France where, for example, the recently restructured undergraduate diploma course (*Diplôme d'Etudes Universitaires Scientifiques et Techniques*) is held to consist of 1200 hours teaching over a two-year period, of which 25 per cent will consist of 'vocationally oriented' teaching. In Italy, state validation of university diplomas plays an equally important part. For although Italian universities, like those in France and Belgium, are free to develop courses and awards outwith the purlieu of central government, such awards carry very little weight in either public or professional employ and, indeed, may even penalize those who hold them.

In Germany, the *Staatsexamen* stands in a similar situation and is taken by candidates for the medical and legal professions, teachers, pharmacists and food chemists (SUNY 1979). In contrast to university diplomas, Magisters and doctoral degrees, which are administered and examined within individual universities, it comes under the validating oversight of the provincial Ministry of Education whose representatives sit on examining juries.

This 'dual validation' system is not only another example of the all-seeing eye of the Prince or his offical servants in the Ministry of Education. It is also, though by no means always, tied in with financial considerations. In France, for example, the resourcing of national diplomas is more favourable both as regards staff and finance than that of the internally validated and less reputable university diploma. In Belgium, the annual budgetary round involves individual universities sending in a list of their study programmes. These are examined by Ministry officials to ascertain whether they are in keeping with the legal framework, and whether they qualify for financial support. Such scrutiny is not intended to limit the right of the university to put on courses that are non-valid. But those deemed such are unlikely to be supported (Herlant).

A slightly different version of dual validation and financing is to be found in Sweden. Here the distinction lies not so much between externally validated national diplomas and internal institutional awards as between full degree 'long courses' and 'short courses'. Oversight and planning of the former rests with the National Board of Universities and Colleges and, more precisely, with the five planning commissions which correspond with the five occupational sectors mentioned earlier (Premfors and Ostergrén 1978, p.77; see supra p.157). For short course programmes validation and financing rests with the regional boards of higher education of which there are six (Lane and Frederickson 1983). The process of planning and thus of validation at both levels is thorough, to say the least, and includes statements as to the aim of the course, its structure and special admissions requirements, its main contents and the way it is to be assessed and marked (Premfors and Ostergrén 1978, p.117).

Given the status and importance accorded to state guaranteed diplomas, it is hardly surprising that the validatory mechanism seems to be assuming an increasingly central role: first in seeking to move student demand into areas reckoned important to the national economy and second in encouraging individual institutions to respond to the changed demands. To be sure, this can lead to spectacular abuses of administrative power, one of the most notorious of which was the sudden withdrawal of recognition from some 300 second-cycle courses (years 3 and 4 after the *Baccalauréat*) in 1979, during the 'reign' of Alice Saunier Seîté as French Minister of Higher Education. That many were subsequently restored in no way diminished the fact that the power does exist to act in this manner.

There are, however, two particularly interesting examples of the way validation and finance may be coupled together as instruments for encouraging universities to fall in with the will of Leviathan. The first is to be found in recent developments in France, the second in the Netherlands. Recent legislation in France provides for a new type of degree, the '*Magistère*'. The *Magistère* will be a three-year course at pre-doctoral level, of an élite type, with emphasis on student placement in industry and research laboratories (Le Monde de l'Education July-August 1985). The importance of this development does not lie in its apparent return to 'élitism' – it will be open only to a limited number of 'high fliers' – but rather in its explicit endorsement of 'quality based financing' or, to put it another way, extension of the principle of 'stratified' allocation already noted in conjunction with national and university diplomas. The *Magistère* will carry with it highly advantageous staffing ratios in addition to extra financing. It will, however, only be assigned to the most reputable universities with an outstanding record of performance. In short, it is seen as a means first of improving internal efficiency in the system as a whole and second of fostering a sense of competition between top level establishments. Finally, it goes without saying that the first *Magistères* created will be in the government's priority fields of engineering, computing and biology.

If the French strategy appears to be a positive incentive, current Dutch discussions seem to bear all the imprint of persuasion by threat of sanction. Government control over validation in the Netherlands is rather more indirect than in France. In essence, Dutch government strategy in the university sector has been, first, planned reduction in the university budget, second, the creation of national planning by sectors – that is by groups of disciplines across individual universities – and, third, obliging individual establishments to pay greater attention to student 'quality control'. In February 1985; the Minister of Education and Science laid a series of proposals before the States General. Though presented as a general plan for 'de-regulating' higher education (Luttikholt 1986) – a Dutch edition of 'rolling back the frontiers of the State' – the programme is very specifically geared towards forcing universities to exercise more rigour in student assessment and evaluation. First, universities will be required to submit an annual evaluation of their courses, the results of which will be compared with other establishments in the same 'sector'. And, then to give 'teeth' to this proposal, a series of 'Quality control commissions' will be set up. These will have visitatory and inspectorial powers and, although independent, will report back to the Ministry of Education and Science (NRC *Handelsblad* 26 February 1985; *ibid.*, 22 March 1985; *De Herkaveling van het universitaire onderwijs* 1985). The link between evaluation and finance is direct and is endowed with the apparent simplicity of folly. Sectors failing to maintain standards – and the folly consists in the ambiguity of the term – face the prospect of having their student places reduced or the relevant budget line cut.

These two examples are interesting to the extent that they reveal in clearer form than most what is, in effect, a rather more general tendency to shift quality control from the 'input' to the 'output' side of higher education, and more particularly, towards closer government control over the type of degrees produced and over entry to the research system (Neave 1984). In 'top down' higher education systems, which is essentially what we have been examining, validation and access constitute crucial instruments of national control. But, however crucial in 'driving' higher education as a vehicle of national manpower development, they stand as end products of a rather broader decision-making process which, in varying degrees of closeness and 'fit' links higher education with public authorities. Access and validation are important since their alteration and change can be used as correctives both in short- and long-term policy-making. This raises the question of the various bodies which, operating through the two 'monitory instruments', shape higher education policy in general.

Monitoring Bodies and Policy-Making

The trend towards more detailed government intervention, visible in the United Kingdom, is also noticeable elsewhere. But the nature of the linkage, like the location of other 'monitory bodies' feeding into higher education policy-making, displays considerable variation. Some countries – and Sweden is a particular case in point – have direct linkage and control exercised through Parliament (Ekholm 1985, p.110). Others link through the national ministry of education, and in a third model – found in the Federal Republic of Germany – some have a two-tier Federal system of negotiated agreement between provincial ministries of education, a Standing Conference of Ministers of Education, the Federal Ministry of Education and Science, and national university bodies such as the Academic Council (*Wissenschaftsrat*) which act in an advisory capacity (Teichler and Sanyal 1982, p.62).

One of the clearest examples of the strengthening of the long-term 'guidance capacity' of government over higher education is to be seen in the recently emerging French reforms from the new Higher Education Guideline Law of January 1984 and its aftermath. Three reforms are of particular interest: the *Commission interministérielle de prospective et d'orientation*, the *Conseil National de l'Enseignement Supérieur et de la Recherche* and the *Comité National d'Evaluation de l'Enseignement Supérieur*. The first, as its name implies – acts as liaison between the Ministry of Education and the main national planning agencies, of which the *Commissariat Général du Plan* and the *Centre National de la Recherche Scientifique* are the most significant. The first is responsible for drawing up the national 4-year plans, the second controls the national research system. The main purpose of the *Commission interministérielle* is to advise on the skill and qualification implications of medium-term economic change. It is, in short, engaged in monitoring economic trends with a view to recommending subsequent adjustment in higher education. The second stands as the highest discussion forum between universities and administration. Its powers extend to validation, the accreditation of establishments to teach *national* diplomas, and oversight of such matters as the framework conditions for accreditation in general. It acts as a recommendatory body to the Minister for Education, who chairs it. If comparable in many ways with the CNAA, the *Conseil National de l'Enseignement Supérieur* has one additional function. It reviews individual appointments into post (Neave 1985c). The *Comité National de l'Evaluation* is a more recent addition to intelligence-gathering in French higher education. Its remit is to assess and evaluate the performance of individual establishments, and it has the power to make recommendations for improved efficiency in such areas as research, student guidance and access procedures ('Décret No. 85-258 du 21 février 1985 relatif à l'organisation et du fonctionnement du Comité National d'évaluation des établissements publics à caractère scientifique, culturel et professionnel', *Journal Officiel* No. 46,23 février 1985). In addition, it will draw up once a year an interim statement on the condition of higher education, based on the reports that individual universities are now required to make of their activities and achievements. A more definitive analysis will be made every four years. Both statements are to be addressed to the President of the French Republic (§3). The committee also has the power to require individual universities to present data of a qualitative and quantitative nature when requested (§6).

To some, these measures might appear to be simply an extension of the well-established 'top down' model of policy formulation and control seen elsewhere in Western Europe. But from a French standpoint, the Evaluation Committee is necessary for ensuring strategic coordination at a time when universities are being encouraged to be more enterprising in developing new courses and being more responsive to the regional rather than the national labour market.

Reinforcement of public accountability and of central government monitoring capacity in higher education is equally visible in Sweden, following the 1977 reforms. Long-term monitoring capacity, which in France is firmly located within central administration, in Sweden tends to penetrate more deeply into individual universities. This 'locational stratification' can be seen in the three research bureaux set up to integrate quantitative and qualitative planning. They are respectively Long Range Planning, Follow up Studies and the Research into Higher Education Programme. The first two are located inside the National Board of Universities and Colleges, the former being responsible for prospective research on qualifications and likely economic trends, the latter for monitoring the effects of higher education reform in terms of student flow characteristics and changes in demand. One of the latter's major areas of investigation has been the assessment of the so-called 25/4 scheme which sought to increase adult access to university (Kim 1981). The Research into Higher Education Programme, however, is of a more independent nature and seeks to develop the capacity of higher education to evaluate and assess long-term changes and their consequences both in terms of the policy-making mechanism itself and of the types of relationship between higher education and the polity. In effect, central administration seeks both to sponsor and to draw in academic research on the university in order to assess the efficacy of the policy-making process as well as institutional performance. The latter, significantly, is structurally and budgetarily separate and concentrates on what is otherwise known as 'institutional research' – student-flows into working life, teaching techniques, etc.

An additional feature of policy development in Swedish higher education has been the extensive use made of Royal Commissions in monitoring, assessing and proposing change (Premfors 1984). The part played by these bodies is considerable, as is their role in policy-making generally (Kogan and Husén 1984). Amongst their various functions they bring together experts and participants from various constituencies in higher education and elsewhere, principally the main 'social partners' – government, industry and trades unions – to address specific topics. Effectively, they can perhaps best be seen as a mechanism for extending the 'monitoring function' beyond the usual limits of experts and bureaucrats, thereby affording some recognition of the public interest in this domain.

In the Federal Republic of Germany the main responsibility for planning the development of higher education comes under joint state and federal control, with individual universities under the supervision of state ministries of education (*Kultusministerium*) in such matters as finance and personnel (SUNY 1979). The Federal Ministry of Education and Science, which replaced the Ministry for Scientific Research in 1969, is responsible for the allocation of building finance – a crucial point since it affects intake capacity. Planning proposals which require agreement between the *Länder* are worked out in a joint Federal-State committee for higher education and research (*Bund-Länder Kommission für Bildungs-planung und -forschung*). This body, however, has less the function of 'monitoring' and 'validating' (since this touches upon the twin principles of freedom to teach and to learn and because validation, as was pointed out earlier, is a matter for individual universities save in the fields governed by the *Staatsexamen* (Kunzel 1982)) and more that of forum for negotiation and legislative drafting of national frame-work plans (Teichler and Sanyal 1982, p.65).

In the seventies, a crucial role was played by the National Academic Council (*Wissenschaftsrat*). Strictly speaking, this federal body acts in an advisory capacity, and though its recommendations carry weight, they are non-binding (*Stiftungverband für die deutsche Wissenschaft*, 1957). It acts as a platform for discussing structural and curricular change as well as capacity planning for higher education. It brings together representatives of both Federal and *Länder* ministries, as well as those from the German Research Association, the *Max Planck Gesellschaft*, which maintains a network of university-based research institutes and laboratories, and members of the West German Rectors' Conference – the counterpart of the Committee of Vice-Chancellors and Principals. It is probably more correct to regard this agency as an observatory of developments in higher education than as one possessed of a statutory oversight.

The differences which characterize those agencies between university and local and federal administration in West Germany and their apparently indirect role in the decision-making process, spring from the twin limitations of the Federal constitution itself on the one hand and the time-honoured concept of *Lehr und Lern-Freiheit* on the other. Since the individual state ministry has oversight of higher education, agreements at federal level are subject to negotiation between the two. The power of federal bodies directly to influence policy in areas deemed of provincial interest is thus circumscribed and recommendatory, as we have suggested, while in areas of 'academic standards' stricto sensu, their upkeep and maintenance is a matter for individual universities and departments and thus of the academic profession. The coordinating framework may be laid down at federal level, but the decision to implement or to act rests with the individual university. Thus, in contrast to France and to the Netherlands, though West Germany's provincial and federal governments may constrain universities through expenditure limitations, the joining together of finance and validatory procedures as a means of ensuring compliance is not an option that may realistically be entertained.

Conclusion

Concern over the 'quality' of higher education's output is not limited to the United Kingdom. On the contrary, it is widely shared amongst other Western European countries at the present time. It is a preoccupation that springs, in the main, from three developments: the needs first to limit social expenditure; second, to guide student demand away from fields held to have a high risk of unemployment; and third, to develop that type of 'qualification output' perceived as necessary for the transition to a high technology-based economy. Though strategies vary, some concentrating on regulating access, others on influencing 'output', evidence from Western Europe suggests a substantial increase in the type of control governments are now prepared to exercise in this field. The use of both monitory and validatory instruments to guide institutional response into those paths the Prince deems imperative, are clear in the case of the Netherlands and France. Similar mechanisms of control are well established in Sweden: whilst the extension of limited entry faculties in Denmark points to a similar displacement of power from the base to central administration, or – and this may be seen as a more nuanced statement – its relocation in national agencies or bodies which, if not strictly situated in the corridors of power, are most definitely not placed in the groves of academe.

The significance of developments such as these does not, ultimately, reside in where such agencies lurk and have their being. In any debate about the 'upkeep' of 'standards' or 'quality' – which are two aspects of monitoring and validation and thus by no means exhaustive – the prime question must, surely, be 'Standards for whom to do what?' Are the 'standards' that are being developed – some might argue, enforced – to do with the cultivation of the well-rounded individual and the well-educated society, or simply to do with induction into the various techniques and manipulative skills that would create upon this earth the Heavenly city of the solid-state physicist or a latter day edition of Saint Simonism's Parliament of the Engineers? No sane man would, I think, deny the importance of providing those skills necessary for the upkeep of the Commonweal and the opportunities they create for its citizens to participate in, and contribute to, the collectivity. Bearing this in mind, one should resist stoutly the temptation, first, to confuse the issue of organizational arrangements with the substantive changes such organizational shifts entail in the type of knowledge deemed 'relevant'; and second, to fall into the Manichean error of defending a cultural vision of the university simply because at the present time a more utilitarian definition of 'standards' happens to find favour on high. A balanced system of higher education must have place for both and that, perhaps, is the major task that monitoring and validation may uphold.

References

Bladh, Agneta (1982) *The Trend Towards Vocationalism in Swedish Higher Education* Report No.16. Stockholm: Group for the Study of Higher Education and Research Policy.

Clark, Burton R. (1977) *Academic Power in Italy* Chicago: University Press

Clark, Burton R. (1983) *The Higher Education System: academic organization in international perspective* Berkeley: University of California Press

CRE (1984) Le moins est-il corrollaire du pire? *VIIè Assemblée Générale de la Conférence des Recteurs Européens* Athènes: CRE

Ekholm, Lars (1985) Sweden. In Burton R. Clark (Ed.) *The School and the University* Berkeley: University of California Press

Eustace, Rowland (1982) Higher education and the state in Britain *European Journal of Education* 17(3)

Council of Europe (1983) Federal Republic of Germany: Higher education policy in the 1990s *Council of Europe Newsletter* 5(83)pp.18-21

Herlant, Claude (personal communication from), Ministère de l'Education Nationale et de la Culture Française, Bruxelles

Journal Officiel (1985) Décret No. 85-258 du 21 février 1985 relatif à l'organisation et du fonctionnement du Comité National d'évaluation des établoissements public à caractère scientifique, culturel et professionnel No.46, le 23 février 1985. Paris

Kim, Lillemor (1983) *Widened Access to Higher Education: the 25/4 scheme* Stockholm: Almqvist & Wiksell

Künzel, Klaus (1982) Higher education and the state: the Federal Republic of Germany *European Journal of Education* 17(3)

Lane, Jan-Erik (1979) The budgetary process in Sweden. In Lyman A. Glenny (Ed.) *Funding Higher Education: a six nation analysis* New York: Praeger

Lane, Jan-Erik and Frederiksson, Bert (1983) *Higher Education and Public Administration* Stockholm: Almqvist & Wiksell

Lois (1978) *Lois coordonnées sur la collation des grades académiques et le programme des examens universitaires: Recueil des lois et des règlements* Bruxelles: Ministère de l'Education Nationale et de la Culture Française

Luttikholt, Harry (1986) The Netherlands: reform and de-regulation in higher education *European Journal of Education* 21(1)

Monde, Le (1985) La rentrée universitaire á l'heure de la nouvelle loi. Le 19 novembre 1985

Monde de l'Education, le (1985) July-August

Neave, Guy (1985) Strategic planning, reform and governance in French higher education *Studies in Higher Education* 10(1)

Neave, Guy & Cerych, Ladislav (1981) *The Structure of the Academic Profession: United Kingdom, France, the Netherlands and the USA: memorandum to the Stiftung Volkwagenwerk* Paris: Institut Européen d'Education et de Politique Sociale

Neave, Guy & Rhoades, Gary (forthcoming) The academic profession in Western Europe: divided albeit national. In Burton R Clark (Ed.) *The Academic Profession: an international perspective* Berkeley: University of California Press

NRC Handelsblad (1985) Commissie voor visitatie: Kamer stemt in mit inspectie van universiteit, February 25th

NRC Handelsblad (1985) Deetman steelt voor alle studentenstops af te schaffen. March 22nd

Peeters, H.F.M. (1985) *Herkaveling van het Universitaire Feld: een historische beshowing* Tillberg: André Volten

Premfors, Ruen & Ostergrén, Bertil (1978) *Systems of Higher Education: Sweden* New York: International Council for Educational Development

Scotford Archer, Margaret (1979) *Social Origins of Education Systems* London: Sage

Suny (1979) *The Education System in the Federal Republic of Germany* New York: College Board

Teichler, Ulrich & Sanyal, Bikas (1982) *Higher Education and the Labour Market in the Federal Republic of Germany* Paris: UNESCO

The Society for Research into Higher Education

The Society for Research into Higher Education exists both to encourage and co-ordinate research and development in all aspects of higher education, including future policy, and to provide a forum for debate on issues in this field. Through its activities, it draws attention to the significance of research and development and to the needs of those engaged in this work. (It is not concerned with research generally, except, for instance, as a subject of study or in its relation to teaching.)

The Society's income is derived from subscriptions, book sales, conferences and specific grants. It is wholly independent. Its corporate members are universities, polytechnics, institutes of higher education, research institutions and professional and governmental bodies. Its individual members include teachers and researchers, administrators and students. Members are found in all parts of the world and the Society regards its international work as amongst its most important activities.

The Society discusses and comments on policy, organizes conferences and encourages research. Under the imprint SRHE & NFER-NELSON it is a specialist publisher, having some 30 titles in print. It also publishes Studies in Higher Education (three times a year), Higher Education Abstracts (three times a year), International Newsletter (twice a year), a Bulletin (six times a year), and jointly with the Committee for Research into Teacher Education (CRITE) Evaluation Newsletter (twice a year).

The Society's committees, study groups and local branches are run by members (with limited help from the small secretariat at Guildford), and aim to provide a forum for discussion. Some of the groups, at present the Teacher Education Study Group, the Staff Development Group and the Women in Higher Education Group, have their own subscriptions and organization and publications; so too do some Regional Branches. The Governing Council, elected by members, comments on current issues and discusses polices with leading figures in politics and education. The Society organizes seminars on current research for officials of DES and other ministries, and is in touch with official bodies in Britain such as the NAB, CVCP, UGC, CNAA and the Britsh Council and with sister-bodies here and overseas. Its current research projects include one on the relationship between entry qualifications and degree results, directed by Prof. W. D. Furneaux (Brunel) and one on Questions of Quality directed by Prof. G. C. Moodie (York).

The Society's annual conferences take up central themes, 'Continuing Education' (1985, with Goldsmiths' College and the Open University and advice from the DES and CBI), 'Standards and Criteria in Higher Education' (1986), 'Re-structuring' (1987). Joint conferences are held, viz. on Information Technology (1986, with the Council for Educational Technology, the Computer Board and the Universities of Glasgow and Strathclyde) and on the Freshman Year (1986, with the University of South Carolina and Newcastle Polytechnic). for some of the Society's conferences, special studies are commissioned in advance.

Members receive free of charge the Society's Abstracts, annual conference papers, the Bulletin and International Newsletter, and may buy SRHE & NFER-NELSON books at trade price. Corporate members also receive the Society's journal Studies in Higher Education free (individual members at a heavy discount). They may also obtain Evaluation Newsletter and certain other journals at a discount, including the NFER Register of Educational Research. There is a substantial discount to members, and to staff of corporate members, on annual and some other conference fees.

Further information from SRHE At the University, Guildford GU2 5XH UK. Telephone 0483 39003
Book catalogue from SRHE & NFER-Nelson, 2 Oxford Road East, Windsor SL4 1DF, UK. Telephone Windsor 858961.